POLITICS, ECONOMICS, AND WELFARE REFORM

The Failure of the
Negative Income Tax
in Britain and the
United States

Leslie Lenkowsky

UNIVERSITY
PRESS OF
AMERICA

LANHAM • NEW YORK • LONDON

AMERICAN ENTERPRISE INSTITUTE
FOR PUBLIC POLICY RESEARCH

Copyright © 1986 by

American Enterprise Institute for Public Policy Research
University Press of America,® Inc.

4720 Boston Way
Lanham, MD 20706

3 Henrietta Street
London WC2E 8LU England

Co-published by arrangement with the
American Enterprise Institute for Public Policy Research

Library of Congress Cataloging in Publication Data

Lenkowsky, Leslie, 1946-
  Politics, economics, and welfare reform.

  Bibliography: p.
  1. Negative income tax—Great Britain.   2. Guaranteed
annual income—Great Britain.   3. Negative income tax—
United States.   4. Guaranteed annual income—United
States.   I. Title.
HC260.I5L46   1986   362.5'82   85-29456
ISBN 0-8191-5215-3 (alk. paper)
ISBN 0-8191-5216-1 (pbk. : alk. paper)

All University Press of America books are produced on acid-free
paper which exceeds the minimum standards set by the National
Historical Publications and Records Commission.

For Kate

Acknowledgments

This book was originally written to fulfill the requirements for the degree of Doctor of Philosophy in Education from Harvard University. During its long journey to completion, many people provided valuable assistance.

I am especially grateful to the participants in the events described herein for giving so generously of their time to enlighten a curious graduate student. I also wish to thank the Trustees of Harvard University for awarding me a Frank Knox Fellowship that enabled me to spend a year in Great Britain and Richard Rose, University of Strathclyde, for helping make my stay there so productive and enjoyable.

My adviser, Nathan Glazer, was patient and encouraging beyond the call of duty, for which I am most grateful. Special thanks are also due to Neal Kozodoy, whose critical eye helped me avoid too many confusions of thought and style.

To my former colleagues at the Smith Richardson Foundation and most of its grantees and applicants, who kindly put up with my paying less than complete attention to their ideas and needs while I was preoccupied with my own project, I also give thanks. To my current home, the American Enterprise Institute for Public Policy Research, this is meant as a partial repayment not just of a small grant (which was intended to produce something else) but also for inviting me to join its distinguished group of scholars at a time when such encouragement was most welcome.

Senator Daniel Patrick Moynihan first aroused my interest in the subject of welfare reform, was the initial adviser for this dissertation, and gave much more help than the many cartons of his papers in my study began to indicate. That this work was at last finished was undoubtedly the only surprise he had in his re-election year.

Finally, my greatest debt of gratitude is to my wife, Kathleen, and my children, Adam and Matthew, for their willingness to let me spend so many summer evenings and weekends with my typewriter, instead of them.

Contents

1   A CONVERGENCE OF POLICY   1

2   THE WELFARE STATE AND ITS DISCONTENTS   11

3   THE RISE OF THE INCENTIVE THEORY   35

4   THE PROPOSAL OF FAP AND FIS   55

5   INCENTIVES AND DISINCENTIVES   83

6   THE DEFEAT OF THE NEGATIVE INCOME TAX   116

7   AFTERMATH OF AN IDEA   143

8   THE POLITICS OF CONVERGENCE   169

APPENDIX   192

BIBLIOGRAPHY   195

1

A Convergence of Policy

*In attempting to explain economic policy decisions we may well be
dealing with actions which because of the limited number of observa-
tions and participants and because of the importance of personalities
do not lend themselves to any generalization or to any testing of
hypotheses. Yet why not try if the subject is sufficiently important?*
— ALBERT O. HIRSCHMAN, Journeys Towards Progress[1]

In August 1969, President Richard M. Nixon proposed, as his major
item of domestic legislation, a bill to transform the American public
welfare system. Entitled the Family Assistance Plan (FAP), the legislation would have replaced the existing program of Aid to Families with
Dependent Children (AFDC) with one providing cash benefits to *all*
low-income families. For the first time, virtually every American
would be eligible for an income supplement in time of need.[2] Until his
diplomatic initiatives in the People's Republic of China and the Soviet
Union in 1972, hardly any of the President's other actions—and none
of his other domestic proposals—received as much acclaim. *The Economist* of London called the proposal "historic" and asserted it "may
rank in importance with President Roosevelt's first proposal for a social security system in the mid-1930s . . ." while even a less-than-satis-
fied John V. Lindsay, then mayor of New York City, conceded that FAP
was "the most important step forward by the Federal Government in
this field in a generation."[3]

In October 1970, Anthony Barber, Chancellor of the Exchequer in
Britain's newly-elected Conservative Government, announced plans
for an "interim" program to supplement the earnings of low-income
families. This addition to the British system of public assistance was
named the Family Income Supplement (FIS) and was also, like the
Nixon Administration's Family Assistance Plan, a landmark proposal;
for the first time in more than a century, all British families would be
eligible for cash benefits based simply on their financial needs.[4] By
the time the program began to operate in August 1971, the Chancellor's special adviser on taxation had already outlined the next step, a
scheme integrating FIS and certain other benefits with a revised income tax. In a Green Paper a year later, the Government described its

1

"tax-credit" plan as "a radical new approach—in which this country is leading the world."[5] Whether a family would pay taxes or receive public assistance would depend upon a single, simple accounting of income.[6] Professor Richard M. Titmuss of the London School of Economics welcomed the proposals as laying "the foundations for further progress towards the alleviation of hardship," while Samuel Brittan, the distinguished correspondent of *The Financial Times*, hailed them as the most important for social policy since the wartime report of Sir William Beveridge.[7]

These strikingly similar developments in the United States and Great Britain addressed what had once been the central issue of social policy: the treatment of the able-bodied worker. To provide help for the needy without inducing dependency was the foremost concern of the "Poor Law" guardians as well as of would-be reformers. Modern social policy did not so much resolve this issue as by-pass it. In both the United States and Britain, welfare benefits were given mostly to those deemed incapable of self-support; eligibility depended not on financial need but on experience of a hazard—such as old age, disability, or unemployment—which would normally reduce income. For those who did not suffer one of these misfortunes, such assistance as was available subsidized socially approved expenditures, such as, in Britain, the costs of raising children and in the United States, the costs of buying a home. Frequently, it was given in kind, not in cash. Otherwise, a combination of relatively full employment, adequate wages, and investment in community services, such as hospitals and schools, was expected to allow anyone able to work to earn a decent living, if he so desired.

For the most part, the arrangement succeeded, although for sizable numbers of families in each country, it proved unable to eliminate poverty. For those eligible, flaws in the coverage and benefits of the assistance programs were to blame. But for a large proportion of employable people, neither a buoyant economy nor such social benefits as were available fully succeeded in aiding them.[8] Moreover, as income support programs were improved to relieve hardship among the unemployable, their benefits became increasingly competitive with the amount that could be earned by a full-time worker. This situation created what is known as a "moral hazard"; because eligibility depended upon conditions over which an individual could conceivably exercise some control (such as unemployment), a generous welfare policy had the potential of expanding the population in seeming distress.[9] Although the United States and Britain relied on administrative controls to forestall this eventuality, so long as able-bodied workers remained needy, modern social policy rested on an unsteady foundation.

FAP, FIS, and the tax-credit scheme proposed to deal with this problem by simply supplementing the incomes of people who worked. This was by no means a new idea in either country. Indeed, the provision of aid solely according to need was the essence of the older "Poor Law" tradition which both nations shared. Such help, however, had been judged to have created a sense of shame and failure among employable recipients, while stigmatizing them within their communities. Lacking adequate controls or penalties, it seemed to foster dependency, reduce the desire to earn and to save, and produce a pauperized class that was a growing economic and social burden. But proper supervision proved to be difficult and almost inherently inequitable; an intrusive bureaucracy, monitoring needs and determining benefits, had nearly as little appeal as the punitive measures (like the "workhouse") it had to employ. For these reasons, the "Poor Law" was abandoned and eligibility for public assistance was restricted to those whose plight was apparently not of their own making.

The new wage supplements relied on a new theory for avoiding dependency among employable recipients. "Poor Law" relief, like most existing public assistance programs, reduced benefits by an amount equal to any earnings or other kinds of income. By contrast, demogrants, such as the British program of family allowances, were unaffected by changes in income. FAP, FIS, and the tax-credit plan offered a third approach; each would have reduced benefits by less than the full amount of new earnings. One version of the Family Assistance Plan, for example, would have withdrawn approximately one dollar in aid for every two dollars in wages. This was the theory of the "negative" (or "reverse") income tax. So long as the able-bodied worker also had a financial incentive to remain employed and earn money, it was safe to supplement his income.[10]

To account for this apparent convergence of policy in the United States and Britain is one aim of this study. Similar instances in this and other areas of policy are not uncommon. Indeed, in the five years following the proposal of FAP, not just Britain but ten other major countries—Canada, New Zealand, the Netherlands, Denmark, Norway, France, Australia, West Germany, Japan, and even the U.S.S.R.—seriously considered adopting one or another version of the negative income tax.[11] Most explanations of such convergence emphasize the similarities in social and economic circumstances that lead decision-makers in one country to become interested in the programs developed by their counterparts elsewhere.[12] Particular proposals are like books in a library, there to be borrowed when conditions are ripe, with the more progressive nations going first.

The proposal of FAP, FIS, and the tax-credit plan seems to challenge this understanding. In the first place, the United States and Britain differed considerably in the social and economic conditions most relevant to welfare policy. In the former, business was booming, and poverty, while greater than in Britain, was declining, especially among families headed by a person with a job. In the latter, the economy was in the midst of a period of slow growth and the number of poor was going up. The condition of blacks and other minorities, an issue of the utmost importance in the United States and one that would give an air of great urgency to proposals for reforming public assistance, was still inconsequential in Britain. By contrast, rising concern over the role and power of British trade unions, a matter that could not help but be affected by a scheme for wage supplementation, had no real American equivalent.

Moreover, Britain already had embraced a more expansive view of government, one which even made a difference to the able-bodied worker. While relying, like the Americans, on rising wages to aid those who could work, the British had been less reluctant to add subsidies for housing, clothing, and other major expenses. Since 1945, a cash benefit—family allowances—had been provided to all families with two or more children in order to assist the working parent with his financial obligations. No similar program existed in the United States, although under certain circumstances an employed person could obtain help (such as surplus food or emergency relief) that was often small and sometimes of dubious respectability. Though the Truman Administration had sought to provide public assistance "for any needy person," this aid would not have gone to the working poor. In fact, the more memorable proposal was a "full employment" bill, and even it ultimately foundered on the issue of public responsibility.[13] Thus, there was little in the values and practice of American welfare policy to suggest agreement with the British on the need to guarantee income to people who were fully capable of earning their own.

Nor was there any reason to expect that the United States would be among the leaders in proposing such an idea. Despite prominence in other areas and a reputation as a progressive society, it had never been among the innovating nations in social policy; more often, it had lagged far behind.[14] Not until the Great Depression did the United States adopt measures that had been in use elsewhere for a generation or more; even afterwards, it remained something of an exception to

4

the tendency of industrialized nations to pursue similar social policies. Britain, on the other hand, was one of the pioneers of the modern welfare state. Yet with the proposal of FAP in 1969, the United States found itself at the head of the parade, with the British and the rest of the world following.

What explains this surprising convergence? Had the United States suddenly become more like the rest of the world in matters relevant to social policy? Or had social and economic conditions elsewhere caused other countries to act more like the United States? Or does the conventional explanation of why nations adopt similar policies need revision? As we will show, the last is more nearly the case.

The proposal of FAP, FIS, and the tax-credit plan was only part of the story. In neither the United States nor Britain were these efforts to aid the poor and rationalize social policy fully successful. Only FIS, the most modest of the three proposals, was eventually enacted, and even it became embroiled in controversy. Although twice close to becoming law, FAP was never enacted; after lingering for more than a decade, it was finally laid to rest by the election of Ronald Reagan. The tax-credit plan, despite endorsement by a bi-partisan Select Committee of the House of Commons, was shelved when the Conservative Government left office in March 1974; the successor Government proceeded to enact only part of the scheme, a "child benefit," which was little more than an expansion of family allowances. Both countries continued to tinker with their traditional forms of income support and for some of those eligible, the amount of aid grew steadily. But for those who were employed, such help as was provided came increasingly through in-kind programs, especially for food and medical care.

Though official studies of low wages and income maintenance policies were undertaken by both governments, the "historic" proposals for change thus largely resulted in a reaffirmation of the *status quo*, broader and more complicated, but fundamentally unchanged in the treatment of the able-bodied worker. Neither the United States nor Britain appeared willing to reform its social policies by guaranteeing a sufficient income simply on the basis of need.

To account for this apparent failure in policy-making is another aim of this study. Examples of the inability of governments to adopt supposedly rational solutions for complex problems are not hard to find. Still, the history of the negative income tax seems to offer a particularly dramatic instance. It was the quintessence of "the professionalization of reform," an idea developed largely in the academy and championed by ostensibly disinterested experts within and outside

5

government. It claimed to offer a new technique for alleviating poverty while avoiding dependency. In some versions, it would even have been virtually self-implementing. Nonetheless, in the United States, Britain, and wherever it was proposed, the negative income tax was, for the most part, unsuccessful.[15]

The most common explanation of such failures is that the pluralism of democratic government makes rational policy-making difficult, if not impossible. The ability of many different groups, with many different goals, to influence the political process at many different points, it is argued, prevents the logical solution of public problems.

Comparing the fate of FAP in the United States with FIS and the tax-credit scheme in Britain should provide a good test of this argument. Although British government is by no means closed, its political parties are more cohesive, its civil service more careerist, and its institutions more centralized than their American counterparts. These features offer a potential for decisive action unlike that in the United States, where authority is shared not only among the institutions of the national government, but—in the case of welfare and other domestic policies—those of the states, counties, and cities as well. No observer of the American cabinet could write, as Samuel Beer has of the British, that its members, "while exercising the whole panoply of executive powers, also in effect command the legislative power, including that crucial power of any polity, the power to tax and spend."[16]

To this cohesion of formal powers, Britain also adds a greater harmony of interest. Social policy is basically about social class, and for more than a century, no characteristic of British life has been more dominant than social class.[17] It has been central to political activity, with one major party explicitly championing the interests of the working class and the other drawing enough support from it to be especially solicitous. Despite postwar affluence, few other interests can compete with the class interest. By contrast, in the United States, social class has been only one among many cleavages in the population; while important in some periods, it has as often been overshadowed by ethnic, geographical, religious, or other loyalties. A class-based politics has rarely thrived in the United States, and as for its labor unions, they have been notably reluctant to become a "movement." For some observers, these divisions of power and interest are enough to explain why America has lagged in adopting programs to assist the poor.[18]

Why in this case was Britain no more able than the United States to provide income support to the able-bodied worker? Had British government succumbed to the same sort of disjointed politics that has seemingly made incremental change the rule in the United States? Or did the prospect of redistributing income to the poor have no more political appeal in Britain than it did in the United States? Or are the real reasons for the failure of the negative income tax to be found elsewhere, perhaps in the idea itself? Although there is some truth to each of these, as we will show, the last is again the most correct.

Of course, a case study of three proposals cannot be the basis for sweeping generalizations about American and British government. Indeed, no claim is made here that FAP, FIS, and the tax-credit plan are even typical examples of decision-making in either country. To the contrary, cases to be studied in this sort of research are more often chosen because they are *not* typical, or at least are sufficiently distinctive to catch the eye of the researcher. In this instance, the apparent similarity of objectives in the proposal of FAP and FIS was the initial ground of their attractiveness. When this study was begun, the outcomes were still unclear; though in trouble, FAP still had a chance of enactment, FIS had just started to pay benefits, and the tax-credit plan had not even been proposed. Thus, this was an open-ended inquiry into how two countries which supposedly differed in important ways dealt with one significant issue. At the very least, the results should shed light on the dynamics of social policy in the United States and Britain. Whether or not they will do more either for other types of policy or for other countries, only additional research can show.

The methods used in preparing this account are the familiar ones of the case study and are subject to the familiar limitations. The primary source of information has been the public record, supplemented by more than one hundred unstructured interviews with most of the key participants in each country.[19] Relying on such materials is necessarily risky. Not everything in a political process becomes public, and that which does may be partial, in both meanings of that word. Even though the interviewing was completed within no more than two years of the events, participants might still have suffered from deliberate or involuntary lapses of memory, or indeed, may not even have known the real reasons for their actions. Short of waiting a generation or so for Cabinet minutes, internal memoranda, or personal diaries to become available, anyone interested in contemporary events has no alternative but to exercise the utmost care, to check and re-check information, and to accept the inevitability of error.[20]

Even so, one should not minimize what can be learned from studying public documents and interviewing key participants in two places as voluble as Washington and London. Like anyone else, politicians are interested in having their work appreciated, especially, as was true in these cases, if it carried more than a routine importance to them. Moreover, contrary to some opinion, a researcher studying the government of a foreign country may have a special advantage. Access to participants was *easier* in London than in Washington, perhaps because Britons believe an American student is either less threatening or more greatly in need of enlightenment.

Comparative analysis also confers another benefit on this kind of research. In examining the histories of FAP, FIS, and the tax-credit plan, it is less important to know, for example, that an American president was willing to trade a certain public works project for a favorable vote in the Senate than to recognize that this sort of bargaining occurred in one country and did or did not take place in the other. Comparison allows the researcher to skim fine details in order to perceive more general patterns of behavior. If the facts are not entirely complete, interpretations should nonetheless be comprehensive. The sources for this work could no doubt have been improved, but as with any study, the reader must ultimately judge for himself whether or not the available ones have led to an accurate account.

Apart from its methodological advantages, one might ask why one should compare policy-making at all. What can be learned from a comparative study that could not be gleaned from looking at each case singly? One response is to recall Samuel Beer's observation that comparison is the social scientist's equivalent of the natural scientist's laboratory and furnishes a means of discovering whether patterns of behavior in one context are also found in other settings.[21] Does a "welfare state" like Britain act differently in making social policy than a "liberal state" like the United States? Or are the sources of change and continuity in public policy alike in each? However inexact its methods, comparison offers the prospect of new insights into familiar ideas about government.

But it also has a less theoretical use. Odin Anderson has noted that the question "How does it work elsewhere?" is the basic sign of curiosity about the social policies of other nations.[22] In the cases at hand, a more appropriate query might be "Why does it *not* work anywhere?" The persistence of poverty, if neither as widespread nor as desperate as in times past, seems to be an enduring feature in countries of such great wealth that one would have expected them to have little difficulty in eliminating it. In the United States and Britain, the proposal of FAP, FIS, and the tax-credit plan might be seen as a kind of "critical test" of anti-poverty policy, since each was a measure that would have simply increased the incomes of those in need. Judged in this light, neither Britain nor the United States deserves high marks. Only the most limited of the three measures was actually enacted; the pattern continued of indirect (though sometimes generous) aid, through family allowances or food and housing subsidies.

What happened? The answer has much to do with the nature not just of politics but also of poverty—and both the United States and Britain spent a good part of the 1970s finding out. By comparing their experiences, we can learn much about what social policy can do—and what it cannot.

Notes

1. Albert O. Hirschman, *Journeys Toward Progress* (1965), p. 20.

2. The main exceptions were single individuals and childless couples. For a description of the Family Assistance Plan, see, Daniel P. Moynihan, *The Politics of a Guaranteed Income* (1973), pp. 229–35.

3. Ibid., pp. 253 and 367.

4. This reversed the position taken by the Royal Commission on the Poor Laws, 1834, whose recommendations, it should be noted, were not uniformly implemented. See, *The Poor Law Report of 1834*, ed. S. G. and E. O. A. Checkland (1974), pp. 33–39, 42–47. For a description of the Family Income Supplement, see, e.g., David Bull (ed.), *Family Poverty* (1971), pp. 70–82.

5. Great Britain, Chancellor of the Exchequer and the Secretary of State for Social Services, *Proposals for a Tax-Credit System*, Cmnd. 5116, October 1972, p. iii. This document also provides a description of the plan.

6. The main exceptions were families and individuals with very low incomes.

7. Richard M. Titmuss, Letter to the Editor, *The Times* (London), October 14, 1972, p. 17; Samuel Brittan, "Economic Viewpoint: The Tax-Credit Scheme," *The Financial Times* (London), October 11, 1972, p. 18.

8. Robert J. Lampman, *Ends and Means of Reducing Income Poverty* (1971), pp. 67–132; A. B. Atkinson, *Poverty in Britain and the Reform of Social Security* (1969), pp. 29–43.

9. This phenomenon was noted by Alexis deTocqueville in his nineteenth-century tours through Britain and Portugal; see, "Memoir on Pauperism," *Tocqueville and Beaumont on Social Reform*, ed. Seymour Drescher (1968), pp. 1–27.

10. Christopher Green, *Negative Taxes and the Poverty Problem* (1967), pp. 51–67; Anthony Christopher et al., *Policy for Poverty* (1970), pp. 33–50.

11. The O.E.C.D. also established a working party to share information among its member countries. On Canada, see Christopher Leman, *The Collapse of Welfare Reform* (1980).

12. Harold L. Wilensky, *The Welfare State and Equality* (1975), pp. 50–59; Ramesh Mishra, "Convergence in Welfare Programs," *Sociological Review* (November 1973), pp. 535–60.

13. Stephen Kemp Bailey, *Congress Makes a Law* (1950), pp. 3–12.

14. Hugh Heclo, *Modern Social Politics in Britain and Sweden* (1974), pp. 10–12; David Collier and Richard E. Messick, "Functional Prerequisites *Versus* Diffu-

sion: Testing Alternative Explanations of Social Security Adoption" (unpublished paper delivered at the 1973 Annual Meeting of the Midwest Political Science Association, Chicago), pp. 4–9; Otto Eckstein, ed., *Studies in the Economics of Income Maintenance* (1961), pp. 13–48.

15. In Canada, a "Family Income Security Program" (FISP) was withdrawn by the Trudeau government after meeting serious opposition. Instead, family allowances were raised and corresponding adjustments were made in children's tax allowances. West Germany also eventually adopted a unified child benefit, while the U.S.S.R. added a new allowance for low-income families.

16. Samual H. Beer et al., *Patterns of Government: The Major Political Systems of Europe* (2d ed. rev.; 1973), p. 143.

17. Nathan Glazer, "The Limits of Social Policy," *Commentary* (September 1971), p. 51; T. H. Marshall, *Social Policy in the Twentieth Century* (3d ed. rev.; 1970), chap. ii.

18. Andrew Martin, "The Politics of Economic Policy in the United States: A Tentative View from a Comparative Perspective," *Sage Professional Papers: Comparative Politics Series* 4 (1973); Arnold Heidenheimer, "The Politics of Public Education, Health, and Welfare in the USA and Western Europe: How Growth and Reform Potentials Have Differed," *British Journal of Political Science* (July 1973), pp. 315–40.

19. A complete list will be found in the Appendix.

20. The author had access to the papers of one key participant, Senator Daniel P. Moynihan, then domestic affairs adviser to President Richard M. Nixon. The author also served as an adviser to Senator Moynihan during the debates over the Carter Administration's welfare reform plan.

21. Samuel H. Beer, "The Comparative Method and the Study of British Politics," *Comparative Politics* (October 1968), p. 19.

22. Odin W. Anderson, *Health Care: Can There Be Equity?* (1972), p. 3.

2

The Welfare State and Its Discontents

In a real sense, the "welfare state" is a British invention. Although social insurance originated in Imperial Germany, the purposes and techniques adopted elsewhere were more likely to be those of Edwardian England. If to Lord Bryce, New Zealand had once seemed "the social laboratory of the world," the research and writings of British political economists and social reformers enjoyed a far wider influence. While the Scandinavian nations proved more adept at fashioning durable social reforms out of the economic slump of the 1920s and 1930s, the plan that captured the imagination of the world was the one put forth in the 1940s by Sir William Beveridge. Indeed, the term "welfare state" came into widespread usage primarily to denote the postwar programs for social insurance and health care established by Britain's Labour Government.

In contrast, few major countries had been so reluctant to employ government to assist the needy as had the United States. It was the "land of opportunity," where poverty, as Robert Bremner has argued, was not considered inevitable (as in other nations) but abnormal, a failure of man and, more importantly, of the national ideal.[1] "From involuntary idleness, servile dependence, penury, and useless labor," Crèvecoeur wrote of the new American settler, "he has passed to toils of a very different nature, rewarded by ample subsistence."[2] The United States did not lack welfare programs. From colonial times, public provision for the poor had been a responsibility of local government, and throughout the nineteenth and twentieth centuries, it gradually became more extensive and centralized. But all this occurred within a tradition that emphasized opportunity and self-help. Even Franklin D. Roosevelt, who signed the legislation laying the cornerstone of current welfare policy, the Social Security Act of 1935, confided to an aide: "I cannot say so out loud yet but I hope to be able to substitute work for relief."[3]

Despite these seemingly vast differences, in the 1960s, discussions of welfare policy in Britain and the United States sounded remarkably alike. In both countries, there was concern that the existing

11

programs left too many people in poverty. At the same time, the cost and the economic impact of these programs were also troubling. Moreover, in each nation, the problems of welfare policy took on especially grave significance. In the United States, they raised doubts about the value of opportunity and self-help for newer minority groups. In Britain, they called into question the social and economic course the country had been following since the end of the Second World War. In short, in both places, welfare policy seemed to typify all that had gone wrong by the 1960s. How this came about is the subject of this chapter.

Welfare Policy in Britain

Drawing on the lessons of the 1930s, the plan offered by Sir William Beveridge was based on the belief that poverty in Britain resulted either from "interruption or loss of earning power" (the main cause) or from "failure to relate income during earning to the size of the family."[4] Accordingly, in addition to full employment, two steps were necessary: improved social insurance programs and some form of children's allowances. Although such aid could have been given only to those who needed it, with remarkably little discussion of the matter Beveridge proposed universal coverage. Both the administrative failures of earlier welfare programs based on need (or a "means-test") and the experience of wartime solidarity had persuaded him that this was the only feasible form a new welfare policy could take. Everyone was to pay the same contribution and, in turn, would be entitled to receive the same pension or unemployment benefit; everyone who had children would be given a family allowance; everyone who was sick would get medical treatment. Although he allowed for a means-tested program of national assistance for those with special needs, Beveridge insisted that only by guaranteeing "the same basic provision for all" (as one of his associates put it) could freedom from want truly be attained.[5]

Despite the precarious economic climate of postwar Britain, this plan for social security was put into effect. A series of White Papers led to the creation in 1946 of social insurance programs for the elderly, disabled, and unemployed, as well as a national health service, much as Beveridge had recommended. For those whose needs were not met through these programs, local relief was transformed into National Assistance, a country-wide, means-tested program that provided income to those who could not support themselves. Perhaps the most significant departure from previous policy was the enactment of the Family Allowances Act in the last weeks of the Coalition Government.

Backed by a diverse alliance (including many who hoped it would increase the British birth-rate), the new program breached the established principle of not paying welfare benefits to full-time workers by providing a weekly grant to every family with two or more children.

But in one key respect, the Beveridge recommendations were not followed. Neither the Churchill coalition nor the subsequent Labour Government felt able to provide universal benefits at the level deemed necessary to abolish want. Beveridge had gone to great lengths to show that available resources would be sufficient to eliminate poverty by paying benefits at the rates he proposed.[6] However, the 1944 White Paper on Social Insurance noted:

> Benefits must be paid for, and a high level of benefit must mean a high level of contribution. The Government therefore conclude that the right objective is a rate of benefit which provides a reasonable insurance against want and at the same time takes account of the maximum contribution which the great body of contributors can properly be asked to bear.[7]

What this meant in practice was left to the Labour Government's Minister of National Insurance, James Griffiths, to spell out: a "broad subsistence basis" for benefits, using 1938 standards of need adjusted for rises in the cost of living, and subject to regular review. To Beveridge, now in the House of Lords, this was not satisfactory; either the Government should raise the benefits of social insurance or declare that it had abandoned the aim of "security against want without a means test."[8] In this case, he did not prevail; from the start, the amount of aid available from the needs-based National Assistance exceeded that provided through the contributory programs.

Nonetheless, the new "welfare state" proved to be a politically attractive creation. Churchill, although initially cautious because of its cost and the possibility it would distract attention from the war effort, declared in a radio broadcast a few months after publication of the Beveridge plan that he and his colleagues were "strong partisans of national compulsory insurance for all classes for all purposes from cradle to grave."[9] The Conservative Party had not been reluctant to use government for welfare purposes. It viewed social policy as providing, in Churchill's words, "a ladder up which all may climb" and "a net below which none can fall."[10] For this, Beveridge's proposals were nearly ideal. As he repeatedly pointed out, benefits by contribution, rather than a test of means, encourage thrift; aid provided at a standard minimal level, rather than varied by circumstances, offers an incentive for individuals to make their own provision as well. The main worry of the Conservatives was that the

13

Beveridge plan would be so costly as to hinder postwar economic recovery, but this ultimately led them to oppose only the establishment of the National Health Service with any vigor.

It was Labour, the party of British socialism, that initially had more trouble with Beveridge's design. As a program for social reconstruction, it fell far short of what the party wished to see. As Ernest Bevin told the Scottish Trades Union Congress, the Beveridge report offered a "social ambulance scheme, . . . a coordination of the whole of the nation's ambulance services on a more scientific and proper footing."[11] As early as 1911, the principle of contributory social insurance had split the Labour Party, and Beveridge's version—the same payment by all workers regardless of income—amounted, in Labour eyes, to a regressive tax. Nor did Labour have any illusions about *whose* thrift was to be encouraged by a uniform benefit. To a large segment of the party, the real lesson of the 1930s was that poverty was endemic to capitalism. True social security required major changes in wealth and ownership, such as a program of nationalizing key industries.

Yet in the end Labour came around and its Government, under the leadership of Clement Attlee, proceeded to translate the Beveridge plan into legislation. On balance, social insurance seemed preferable to the despised "dole" (local relief) of the inter-war period. Moreover, the regressivity of uniform contributions could be offset by other taxes and economic policies Labour intended to propose. For a party of great historical sensitivity, it was also important that "universal enforcement of the national minimum" had been one of the four pillars of the "new social order" Labour was to construct after the *First World War*. With its carefully-reasoned, statistically-supported argument that a state-mandated, common level of provision could abolish want entirely, the Beveridge report seemed to vindicate much of what Britain's socialists had maintained for decades.

However, ideology may have had less to do with the political acceptability of the "welfare state" than the simple fact that it seemed to be both effective and popular. Two years after the first benefits were paid, Seebohm Rowntree returned to York, the site of his pioneering survey in 1899, and discovered that poverty—as he had scientifically defined it—was well on its way toward being eliminated. Only 1.7 percent of the population appeared to be needy in 1950, compared with 18 percent in his last survey in 1936.[12] One reason was that unemployment had reached an unexpectedly low level. The Beveridge plan had been predicated on a jobless rate of 8 percent, but by 1950 it had fallen to 2 percent and would rise higher only occasionally during the next fifteen years. Social insurance was also doing its part. The purchasing power of pensioners had increased by half since the last year before the war and Rowntree concluded that the remaining poverty could be substantially diminished by further increases in benefits.

Not surprisingly, these accomplishments proved to be quite popular in Britain. Runciman's 1962 survey found that only 6 percent of his sample did *not* approve of the "welfare state" in principle; even among non-manual workers who supported the Conservative Party, only 13 percent registered an unfavorable opinion.[13] In 1963, the open-ended questions put by Butler and Stokes revealed a "one-sided" preference for increasing government expenditures on social services (with two-thirds of the respondents perceiving the Labour Party as more likely to do so).[14] With the partial exception of family allowances, support for particular programs was also strong; in one survey, an extraordinary 92 percent of those polled said that the National Health Service had been of "great help," and 82 percent that it had been of more help than any other program.[15] Even a survey undertaken by the Institute of Economic Affairs, an organization devoted to reducing the role of government in British life, wound up finding sizable majorities for continuing public provision of welfare services.[16]

In this climate, British politicians vied to win votes by promising to improve or expand the "welfare state." Upon taking office in 1951 amidst Labour warnings of the imminent demise of the new social policy, Churchill and his colleagues pursued a course not much different from the previous Government's. A decade later, Conservative leaders, like Sir Edward Boyle, Financial Secretary to the Treasury, were eager to claim that "we have a better and fairer distribution of incomes today than we had ten or eleven years ago," and that they could provide a better deal for the working class than their opponents could.[17] Labour spokesmen such as C. A. R. Crosland did not so much deny these accomplishments as urge new tasks. ". . . Social distress and need today," Crosland wrote in 1956, "are a product not solely of primary poverty or an absolute lack of means, but also, and indeed increasingly, of other more varied and subtle causes, which operate far above a subsistence level of income."[18] Around this time, the Labour Party started work on a series of post-Beveridge reforms, including an earnings-related pension scheme that aimed not just at preventing poverty but also at preserving pre-retirement standards of living.

As the 1960s began, approximately one in six Britons received help either from the social insurance programs or from National Assistance. More than three million families, including nearly ten million children, obtained family allowances.[19] Yet, there was little controversy about so large a commitment. As the dean of social policy experts, Richard Titmuss, told a Fabian Society audience in 1959:

> . . . It is coming to be assumed that there is little to divide the nation on home affairs except the dreary *minutiae* of social reform, the patronage of the arts, the parking of cars, and the effectiveness of corporal punishment.[20]

For all practical purposes, the "welfare state" seemed above politics.

Welfare Policy in the United States

In the United States, although the level of commitment was lower than in Britain, much the same situation prevailed. The Roosevelt Administration's Social Security Act seemed to be both effective and popular. Except in certain localities and occasionally in Congress, welfare was not a political issue at the beginning of the 1960s.

Like the Beveridge plan, the Social Security Act relied on a combination of social insurance and means-tested assistance to help the needy. The contributory programs were to provide benefits to the elderly and unemployed when their earnings were interrupted, while the others were to aid those who were not covered. Chief among the latter were expected to be mothers with young children, whose husbands were dead, divorced, or otherwise unable to support their families, but who were not eligible for one of the social insurance plans. Almost every state had been giving them some form of "mother's pension." Although it was not a major item, the Social Security Act created a new federally-financed program, Aid to Families with Dependent Children, to look after their needs.[21]

These New Deal programs were efforts to assist the dependent, those who were not and perhaps, in some cases, should not be employed. The Social Security Act did not contain anything to help the family whose head was working but earning an insufficient income. Indeed, even the breadwinner who was unemployed, unless also a mother, could not normally apply for support from one of the means-tested schemes. For such people, the New Deal offered a different solution; economic recovery, coupled with regional development, job training, minimum wage laws, and the like would put the country back to work and free the worker and his dependents from want. Public aid, either through insurance or relief, would go only to those who could not support themselves.

Another difference between the British and American approaches to welfare policy was that the Social Security Act did not even pretend to put benefits at a level sufficient to abolish poverty. The amounts provided by the insurance programs were not set at a standard rate, but varied according to the previous income of the recipient. As for the means-tested programs, for both political and constitutional reasons they were to be controlled by state governments, with Washington doing no more than establishing administrative guidelines and paying part of the bill. Instead of a nationwide standard of need, there would be as many standards as there were states.

This 1930s design proved to be an enduring one. In part, this was because it ingeniously managed to reconcile the conflicting imperatives of encouraging self-help and aiding the needy. Through work, Americans would be able not only to support themselves but also to build up eligibility for social insurance benefits that could be drawn when earnings stopped. For those who had not worked long enough to qualify or whose incomes had been low, locally-run (that is, closely-supervised) public assistance would be available. As the economy revived and wages rose, the contributory programs would become more generous and extensive, while the means-tested programs were expected to become less important—if not, as some experts hinted, to wither away altogether. Ultimately, the opportunities of the land could provide not just toil but relief.

In addition, as Martha Derthick has shown, the success of the Social Security Act depended on efforts by politically astute experts to put its main provisions above the political fray.[22] By calling attention to its contributory financing, its precisely forecasted benefits, its high standards of administration, and so on, they established the idea that social insurance, especially for the elderly, was unlike other government programs and virtually sacrosanct. The Democrats, as the original proponents, were delighted to partake of this myth, while the Republicans did so out of necessity and the lack of a viable alternative. The last Republican presidential candidate to call for the abolition of social security was Alf Landon in 1936, and even when it controlled both the White House and Congress in 1953, the G.O.P. failed to enact any far-reaching changes. While other countries have shaped and reshaped their welfare policies since the 1930s, Americans have largely been content with "tireless tinkering."[23] Coverage has grown, benefit-levels increased, administration improved, but apart from a campaign to add health insurance, the basic approach of the New Deal went unchallenged into the 1960s.

The main exception to the pattern was Aid to Families with Dependent Children (AFDC). Despite the growth of the social insurance programs, the number of fatherless families receiving assistance increased, reaching 800,000 by 1960. (In contrast, the number of aged, blind, or disabled people helped by means-tested programs declined, as expected.) Moreover, AFDC, being state-run, had never acquired the political insulation that surrounded the other parts of the Social Security Act. As costs mounted, local officials began to suspect abuse, especially with regard to the availability of paternal support. Drastic remedies were proposed, most notably in Newburgh, New York, where in 1961, the city manager issued a thirteen-point code which among other things would have limited the duration a family could go on receiving assistance. At the Federal level, other rules were passed or investigations launched.[24]

However, for the most part these were isolated episodes. In most of the country, AFDC, although not a favorite program, was not an object of great controversy. Even in Washington, the major change made in the Social Security Act was to declare that "rehabilitation," not punishment, was to be the objective in dealing with AFDC mothers. "While suspicious of the effect of the 'dole' on work incentive and while almost eager to suspect the relief recipient of 'cheating,' " the average American, Michael E. Schiltz has written, "is at the same time willing to support cash transfer programs for those who need assistance."[25] Among those interested in welfare matters, the greater problem was not that AFDC was under attack, but that it was too often ignored and begrudged by policy-makers.

Despite its acceptability, the Social Security Act was not fully successful in achieving freedom from want. According to a 1961 Bureau of Labor Statistics survey, approximately 16 percent of American families remained impoverished.[26] Although this proportion would have been half again as large without the Social Security Act, the Act could not have done much better without radical alteration. By design, the largest share of payments went to pensioners on the basis of their lifetime earnings, not their current needs. Moreover, since state governments set benefit-levels in the means-tested programs, the amount of aid available to families with similar needs varied greatly around the country. No help at all was generally given to poverty-stricken families headed by a father who was working or able to work. Changing any of these elements would have raised difficult questions about the philosophy upon which the American version of the "welfare state" was based.

In any case, the postwar years were not a time for such changes. Although spending on income support programs nearly tripled during the 1950s, poverty was not a major political preoccupation. Indeed, as John Kenneth Galbraith observed, the poor had become so localized they were hard to notice. "In the contemporary United

States," he wrote, poverty "is not annoying but it is a disgrace."[27] He urged "the affluent society" to rediscover and assist the needy.

In the 1960s, that is precisely what Britain and the United States proceeded to do.

The Rediscovery of Poverty

Following in the footsteps of Charles Booth and Robert Hunter, social scientists launched the initial attack on welfare policies in Britain and the United States. In both countries, they compiled evidence purporting to show that poverty was extensive, more so than even Galbraith had imagined. They also designed and advocated measures for reducing it, which differed sharply from traditional ways of helping the needy. By the middle of the 1960s, poverty had again become a major issue in two of the wealthiest nations in the world, but the prospects for dealing successfully with it seemed remote.

In Britain, the rediscovery of poverty was led by a group of Fabian academics at the London School of Economics: Brian Abel-Smith, Peter Townsend, and Richard M. Titmuss. As early as 1952, Townsend had questioned the optimistic reports of Rowntree and others on methodological grounds, arguing that they employed a standard of poverty which implied that "poor working-class people should and could live as social scientists and administrators think they should live."[28] By the end of the decade, the group's preliminary investigations had led them to conclude that poverty in Britain was far more widespread than official sources indicated. According to their figures, five years after the "welfare state" had been established, one in ten households still lived on inadequate incomes; by 1960, the proportion had *increased* to nearly 18 percent. During a generally prosperous time for the nation as a whole, the number of poor had risen from four million to seven and one-half million.[29]

Even more surprising were their findings about who was impoverished. Not unexpectedly, poverty turned out to be especially common among the elderly, sick, disabled, and others who could not support themselves. But in addition, one in three households with low incomes was headed by a person who worked full-time. In these homes were some two and one-quarter million children. Although average earnings had increased by 50 percent during the 1950s, the combination of rising wages and family allowances inexplicably seemed to be insufficient for many people.[30]

Like Booth before them, Titmuss, Abel-Smith, and Townsend painted a gloomier picture of poverty in Britain than was probably warranted. (A Cambridge economist, A. B. Atkinson, later estimated that the frequency of poverty was really in the range of 4 to 9 percent.)[31] However, the aim of this group was not simply disinterested research, but rather a restructuring of the "welfare state." Since no statutory provision had been made for adjusting social insurance benefits to reflect changes in the cost of living, the growing inadequacy of the Beveridge pensions was apparent without a detailed survey. Indeed, in 1959, nearly two million people relied on the more generous National Assistance to meet their minimal needs, and an equal number was thought to be eligible but, because of the means-test, unwilling to submit a claim. Family allowances had lagged even more than pensions, having last been increased in 1956, and full-time workers were not allowed to obtain a supplement from National Assistance.

A straightforward, though costly, solution to the problem of poverty would have been to raise all benefits to the levels recommended initially by Beveridge. But this was not what Titmuss and his colleagues wanted. Their idea of poverty was not the subsistence concept favored by Beveridge, but a relative one. The persistence of poverty in Britain, they argued, reflected the tendency of official definitions of basic needs to fall behind what the community regarded as necessary to live on. (Abel-Smith and Townsend justified their choice of a poverty-line greater than the amount National Assistance would provide to someone with no other income by noting, ". . . we found that there were many households receiving National Assistance whose level of living was forty percent or more above the basic rates.")[32] Establishing a national minimum—if it could be done at all— would not be enough. The aim of the "welfare state" should be to make sure that the normal events of a lifetime, such as retirement, sickness, and creating a family, did not produce a precipitous decline in a person's standard of living.

The implications of this goal were more ambitious for those outside the labor force than for the low-paid worker. As early as 1955, the Titmuss group had been co-opted by the Labour Party to design a pension policy that would provide "half-pay" on retirement to the average worker. As Richard Crossman later observed such a plan would have provided all employees with the kind of insurance available to the more privileged:

> In the philosophy of Titmuss . . . I found my ideal of socialism: the transformation of economic privileges into citizens' rights. Wherever you find something really good which a small group of citizens have, you don't feel envious and take it away from them. You make sure that everybody can have it too.[33]

In truth, this scheme would not have been so painless. Unlike the Beveridge plan, where everyone made the same contribution and received the same pension, in the Labour Party's plan, both payments and benefits would depend on earnings. In order to give proportionately more money than they put in to people with low wages during their working lives, the pretence that this was insurance would have to be abandoned.

While similar arrangements were envisioned for the unemployed, sick, and disabled, the restructuring of the "welfare state" proposed by Titmuss and his colleagues did not entail such a policy shift for the lately-rediscovered poor families. Increasing family allowances still seemed to be the sensible strategy. However, they also noted that more than two-thirds of the public help for the family was in the form of children's tax deductions, which were more valuable to upper-income families (who paid higher rates of tax) than to lower-income ones. This seemed unfair. In order to give a better deal to the large family, "the commonest cause of relative poverty" next to old age, Titmuss called for shifting the balance between the two types of aid.[34] More clearly than the earnings-related pension plan, this recommendation displayed the essence of the proposed new approach to welfare policy. If Beveridge was concerned to achieve security against want, Titmuss and his colleagues sought to redistribute income.

In Washington, critics of the American version of the "welfare state" were reaching a similar conclusion. Guided by writers like Michael Harrington and economists like the University of Wisconsin's Robert J. Lampman, the United States also rediscovered poverty at the beginning of the 1960s. And the amount of it was substantial: nearly thirty-three million people—approximately 18 percent of the population—lived in households with incomes below the accepted poverty-line (which was based on a subsistence budget). Although one-third were headed by an elderly person, half of the low-income families were supported by someone who was employed. Some eleven million children lived in poverty.[35] As in Britain, these figures may have been exaggerated. (Using different data on incomes, Morton Paglin suggests the estimates of the poverty population in the early 1960s may have been as much as 25 percent too high.)[36] But they were taken quite seriously at that time and, with little other prodding, led to a major presidential initiative.

In his first State of the Union message in 1964, Lyndon B. Johnson declared an unconditional "war on poverty" and pledged the United States to its eradication.[37] But if, as he claimed, this was an historic commitment for American government, the tactics were mostly conventional, relying on education, manpower training, regional development, and economic growth. Even the most innovative feature, a "community action program," was meant, Johnson said, ". . . to help individuals, families, and communities to help themselves."[38] Not by accident was the agency with overall responsibility for the campaign called the Office of Economic Opportunity.

At least initially, the traditional formula for aiding the needy seemed likely to work. Congress approved the major items of the Johnson Administration's program, including a measure for federal aid to education which had been stalled for two decades and a plan of medical insurance for the poor and elderly which had been blocked even longer. Community action agencies sprang up rapidly, (though not without difficulty in several places). The stimulative tax cut of 1964 and the deepening American involvement in Vietnam fueled an economic expansion that had begun toward the end of the Kennedy Administration. Within three years after its start, the "war on poverty" had registered a decline of eight million people in its "target" population, with most of the improvement occurring in families headed by a full-time worker.[39] One in eight Americans remained poor and in some parts of the country, such as the Southern states, the proportion was considerably higher. Nonetheless, the first results gave little reason to think that the engine of opportunity had lost much steam.

In the newly-established planning staffs of the Federal bureaucracies concerned with social policy, the view was not so sanguine. The efficiency experts and social scientists who manned these staffs, some of whom had been instrumental in the rediscovery of the poor, believed that too much emphasis was being placed on social services, education, and the like, and not enough on the creation of jobs and the support of the dependent. Some troubling evidence had begun to appear suggesting that the Johnson Administration's main programs might not bear much more fruit.[40] Insofar as they did succeed, an increasing proportion of those who remained poor would be people incapable of self-support and assisted by (or else eligible for) the programs of the Social Security Act. Yet, because this Act countenanced low benefits and uneven coverage, the Federal government would be at least partly to blame for the persistence of poverty.

Before the end of 1965, the planning group at the Office of Economic Opportunity sought to remedy these weaknesses by proposing a new five-year plan for the abolition of poverty. Community action and social services remained in it, and a public employment program was added, but the most important innovation was a proposal to provide income on the basis of need to all the poor, including those who were not currently eligible for welfare—the "working poor." With an eye toward traditional views, the planners claimed such a scheme would not just help people unable to support themselves, but also strengthen the other efforts of the "war on poverty." As Robert A. Levine, the director of the planning unit, would later tell a Congressional committee, income maintenance ". . . is a program of opportunity for the next generation":

> It is a program which supports other programs such as Headstart, such as Neighborhood Youth Corps, supports them because a child in a family which is stable and which has a stable, albeit low level of living is, we believe, far more likely to succeed in these other opportunity programs.[41]

With a suitably designed plan and the willingness to commit the necessary resources, a 1966 memorandum predicted, poverty could be eliminated within a decade. This was to be known as the "income strategy."

The idea of guaranteeing a minimum income to all Americans was not a new one. Arthur J. Altmeyer, the first director of the social security system, later recalled that the failure to have done so in 1935 was a "cardinal mistake."[42] Since then, a variety of proposals had been made, usually connected with efforts to reform public assistance. None had succeeded. Nor had the United States chosen to join the rest of the industrialized world in adopting a program of family allowances, despite the urging of Catholic welfare specialists and the arguments of the Labor Department's planning unit, under the direction of Daniel P. Moynihan, during the Kennedy years. All of these had seemed too costly or too likely to encourage fecklessness of one sort or another. The social scientists at the Office of Economic Opportunity did not expect their plan to have a more favorable reception. Despite their bows toward "opportunity programs," they knew that what they were really proposing was not a scheme for increasing self-reliance, but for redistributing income.

The Costs of Welfare

Not least among the problems facing such egalitarian measures was that in both Britain and the United States, many people felt that too much income redistribution was already occurring. What bothered them was not the theorizing of influential social scientists so much as the increasing costs of those welfare programs that were already operating. Although there can be some question about whether or not the "welfare state" was really out of control, there is no doubt that by the middle of the 1960s, its growth had become a major political issue.

This was true even in the country that invented the "welfare state." Indeed, even before the Beveridge proposals had been enacted, concern was expressed about their cost and the burden they would place on middle-income taxpayers. In 1949, a Tory leader, R. A. Butler, wrote, "It is on the weight of taxation that the clash between Conservative and Socialist policies is the sharpest."[43] Although the Conservative Party's 1950 election manifesto promised to reduce expenditures drastically, nothing so dramatic occurred in office; in its first budget, the Churchill Government did little more than eliminate some general subsidies (as for food), while providing a modicum of income tax relief. The pattern of the Tory years was to be one of sizable growth in public spending, coupled with a modest decline in taxes. By 1959, spending on welfare by central and local governments had doubled, and in the next five years, it increased again by one-third.[44] Yet the burden of the "welfare state" hardly increased at all. As a proportion of Gross Domestic Product, expenditures on social services (excluding housing and education) rose by little more than 1 percent during the thirteen years of Conservative government.[45] The weight of taxation was actually reduced during this period from 37.4 percent of national product to 33.2 percent.[46]

This was still quite high, as a number of Conservatives (and Liberals) contended. In 1961, a young Tory, Geoffrey Howe, wrote that ". . . redistribution may be pushed to a point where it produces economic evils which will outweigh any possible advantages in the field of welfare."[47] In the same year, a respected expert on public finance, Alan Peacock, outlined ways to "dismantle certain parts of the welfare edifice gradually" in order to promote a "more responsible attitude to public services."[48] Other economists joined in this criticism. Just when social scientists of the "Left" were rediscovering poverty, their counterparts on the "Right" (and the younger politicians they influenced) began to argue that the "welfare state" was wasteful and counter-productive.

Like the Titmuss group, these critics held a view of welfare policy that was quite different from the Beveridge version. Within Conservative circles, the deficiencies of the social insurance schemes had long been recognized. But drawing an analogy between the universal pensions of Beveridge and the public utilities of Disraeli, spokemen for traditional Toryism, such as J. Enoch Powell, defended the existing programs as necessary forms of state intervention and argued that they could be improved by adhering more closely to the original design. With regard to costs, Powell and others like him noted only that since the level of public spending and taxing also affected social welfare, government should rely on means-tests, fees, and other ways of providing a national minimum more efficiently.[49]

The younger Tories, particularly those associated with the "progressive" Bow Group, had more radical ideas. About Powell's acceptance of universality in the social services, Howe wrote:

> This is a long way from the doctrine on which Conservatives of my generation were nurtured. "Our civilization," we were told, "is built up on private property." It was our objective to "restore the freedom of each individual to spend his income as he thinks best or to save it in order to create more wealth or to provide for some future emergency." Has all this been swept away?[50]

These younger Tories, who were businessmen and professionals, and who had been influenced at university by liberal economists such as F. A. Hayek and Walter Hagenbuch, believed that the Beveridge programs might have been appropriate for a working-class Britain still recovering from war, but in the more prosperous circumstances of the early 1960s people could—and wanted to—help themselves. Government had an obligation to see that no one starved, but, as Howe wrote:

> It is . . . supremely important in this context to ensure that our benevolent concern for those who will not make provision for themselves does not become oppressive to those who would gladly stand upon their own feet.[51]

Even if the Beveridge programs could be made sounder, the burden of the "welfare state" would still be excessive so long as a large proportion of the public was capable of taking care of itself.

This conception of social policy envisioned a greater role for the private sector in providing welfare services. Schemes for de-nationalizing the health service or giving vouchers to enable children to attend private schools were discussed (often in the publications of the Institute of Economic Affairs, which had been created in 1957). However, as with the Titmuss group, the most distinctive proposal concerned pensions. In 1961, responding to the Labour Party's pledge of "half-pay on retirement," the Macmillan Government abandoned Beveridge's flat-rate pensions in favor of one which offered additional benefits above the basic level according to the pre-retirement earnings of the recipient. At this, Howe queried:

> Is there any reason why the State should begin to insist upon the provision of a scale of benefit beyond that which would suffice to keep people alive until they can fend for themselves?[52]

As an alternative, he urged the Macmillan Government to encourage, by tax concessions and in other ways, expansion of the private insurance industry so that it could both replace earnings and, crucially,

25

maintain a minimum standard of living. A state-run program would be required only for those people who could obtain no other pension.

Neither this nor other Tory ideas for reshaping the "welfare state" produced any immediate results. The Macmillan Government generally remained committed to preserving and expanding it as resources allowed. In 1958, Powell, then Financial Secretary, and two colleagues in the Treasury were forced to resign when the Prime Minister rejected an anti-inflationary budget, sharply curtailing public spending. On the other side of the aisle, defenders of the "welfare state" treated its critics with scorn and one social policy expert accused them of wanting to return not just to the pre-Beveridge days, but to arrangements antedating Lloyd George.[53] Nonetheless, the papers and speeches emanating from Conservative Party groups and sympathetic think-tanks had managed to turn the cost of Britain's welfare programs into a matter for serious debate.

A parallel development occurred in the United States as public assistance rolls, instead of disappearing, continued to grow. To the 800,000 families receiving AFDC in 1960 were added another 250,000 within five years, and from all indications more were still to come. Despite nearly complete coverage by social insurance and a prosperous economy, more than $5 billion would be spent on public assistance in 1965.[54] This was not how the Social Security Act was supposed to work.

This growth also had certain characteristics that heightened its political importance. For one, it was not evenly distributed around the nation. Because control over the public assistance programs resided chiefly in state governments, some—the more generous ones—were facing especially rapid increases in caseloads and costs. In New York City, for example, the number of AFDC recipients grew by 10 percent between October 1964, and March 1965; new applications were still coming in at a rate of thirteen thousand per month. During 1964, spending for welfare in New York State went up 14 percent, causing Governor Nelson Rockefeller to call such payments—when employment and national income were at an all-time high—"the most serious economic paradox of our times."[55] He, and other, primarily large-state, governors who were similarly affected lost little time in trying to call national attention to what was going on.

In addition, the composition of the welfare rolls had changed in a way not likely to generate sympathy for the recipients. In 1935, the typical beneficiary of AFDC was expected to be someone like a coal miner's widow and family, who had not yet qualified for survivor's insurance payments. Even at that, it was not a popular program; grants for mothers with children were set at a level below those for the elderly, and the disparity was never overcome. By 1965, however, AFDC had become a program supporting women and their children whose husbands had left home, often through divorce or desertion but also, in nearly one-quarter of the cases, because the couple had not been married at all. Only one of twenty families was on relief because of the death of the father. Such a shift invited suspicion.

There was also a pronounced change in the racial composition of the welfare rolls. In 1961, 44 percent of the families receiving AFDC were Negro and three-fifths of the increase since 1948 could be accounted for by Negro enrollment.[57] This was not entirely unexpected; in 1939, the sociologist, E. Franklin Frazier, had predicted that the migration of Negroes from the agricultural South to the industrial North would expand their reliance on welfare. However, the early 1960s also saw the flowering of the civil rights movement. Its call for ending legal restraints and improving economic conditions for Negroes stood in troubling contrast to their increasing dependency on public assistance, and added another reason for concern about AFDC.

Among welfare policy experts, the reaction to these trends was divided. Some had always regarded the hope that public assistance might "wither away" as fanciful and viewed such assistance as an integral part of the nation's income maintenance system. They considered the real issues to be raising benefits, extending Federal control over state and local governments, and erasing any "Poor Law" stigma that still adhered to the program. Insofar as it meant more aid for the needy, these experts welcomed the growth of the welfare rolls and favored further expansion. In 1961, they helped persuade the Kennedy Administration to extend AFDC to cover families headed by employable but jobless fathers who lacked other forms of help. This was as close as the United States had come to providing a minimum income on the basis of need to people who were normally expected to take care of themselves.

Other experts viewed the rise in welfare dependency with greater concern. They attributed it to social and personal problems such as illegitimacy, family stability, racial discrimination, and urban rootlessness. In their judgment, families on relief were families that needed help in becoming self-sufficient. As the privately-run Ad Hoc Committee on Public Welfare reported in 1961:

> Financial assistance to meet people's basic needs for food, shelter, and clothing is essential, but alone is not enough. Expenditures for assistance not accompanied by rehabilitative services may actually increase dependency and eventual costs to the community.[58]

27

By adding programs to deal with the underlying causes of the growth in AFDC caseloads (and which would require the services of more experts), the Social Security Act could be made to work as intended.

Although some Federal and state politicians wanted to take the more direct approach of tightening administration and prosecuting cheaters, the main line of government policy reflected the influence of the Ad Hoc Committee. In 1962, the Kennedy Administration proposed an expanded program of social services for welfare recipients. "The byword of our new program," declared Abraham Ribicoff, the Secretary of Health, Education, and Welfare, "is prevention—and where it is too late—rehabilitation, a fresh start."[59]

As Gilbert Y. Steiner later observed, the 1962 amendments to the Social Security Act fed expectations that were as illusory as the idea that public assistance would "wither away." The chief proponents did not really know how to reduce the growth of AFDC, he judged, "nor did they really mean to let the impression get abroad that this was to be expected."[60] That they nonetheless did so testifies to how important (or politically useful) it had become to control the costs of welfare.

A Welfare Nation?

Before long, it was to become even more important. Events in both Britain and the United States suggested that the problems of social policy, bad as they were when looked at discretely, were also intertwined with more serious and far-reaching issues. By 1965, the question of "What to do about the 'welfare state'?" had been transformed into "What kind of nation have we become?" and the answers added great urgency to reforming programs for the needy.

In Britain, the dominant concern was the condition of the nation's economy. Since 1950, national income had risen by less than 3 percent annually, the lowest rate of increase among the industrialized countries.[61] The pattern was one of "stop" and "go," rather than steady expansion, and while Harold Macmillan might have thought Britons never "had it so good," the cold winter of 1962–63 demonstrated that high unemployment was not just a memory of the past. Though sometimes hesitantly, both major political parties were responding by endorsing greater planning and management of the economy, and this had implications for welfare policy.

On the Conservative side, the problem of economic growth gave greater credibility to those who felt the "welfare state" was too big a burden. "No programme worthy of this country can be cheap," the

Tory election manifesto for 1964 asserted. "But it must be kept within bounds, and related to the growth of the national income."[62] Moreover, if Britain was not really a prosperous country, it made sense to encourage individuals to earn, save, and look after their own needs. The Conservatives, especially those who had served in government, were not unmindful of the political value of pensions, unemployment benefits, and other social programs in winning the support of the trade unions for their economic policies, but getting the economy right was increasingly likely to come first.

Although not so ready to blame Britain's problems on the "welfare state," the Labour Party's leaders were also urging a measure of restraint in social policy. Crosland, for one, contended that the most difficult problem facing British socialism would not be the achievement of greater social equality, but rather finding ways to reward "extra responsibility and exceptional talent."[63] And in its 1964 manifesto, the Labour Party made its priorities clear:

> Two giant tasks now await the nation: *first*, we must energise and modernise our industries—including their methods of promotion and training—to achieve the sustained economic expansion we need; second, we must ensure that a sufficient part of the new wealth created goes to meet urgent and now neglected human needs.[64]

To be sure, the party also promised a variety of social reforms, including the Titmuss group's new pension scheme, but the primary theme of the campaign was Harold Wilson's Kennedyesque pledge to get Britain moving again.

The guiding idea behind the creation of the "welfare state" had been that a worker who felt more protected from the major risks of life would be more productive. By the middle of the 1960s, British leaders were no longer certain this assumption was true and some were convinced it was harmful. In this emerging consensus, the low-paid worker and his family were less a problem for welfare policy than a symbol of the errors of Britain's postwar social and economic strategy. No domestic issue was more important than changing that course.

Likewise, in the United States at this time, no domestic problem was more significant or troubling than the social and economic status of the Negro. Bringing this group, with its unique and often tragic history, into the mainstream of American life had virtually become a test of the justness and utility of the nation's political and economic traditions. The early results were not auspicious. Despite the elimination of many legal barriers, Negroes remained disproportionately poor and disadvantaged compared to whites in education, health care, and numerous other ways. Crime and rioting in the large cities of the North and West, where many had settled after migrating from the South, added especially ominous overtones to their plight.

In 1964, Daniel P. Moynihan of the Labor Department finished a study linking welfare policy to the social and economic status of Negroes. Although in the past, new enrollment in AFDC had paralleled changes in the unemployment rate of Negro men, he reported that since 1962 the latter had dropped while the former continued to rise. These and other data, he argued, were "a measure of the steady disintegration of the Negro family structure over the past generation in the United States."[65] Some of the reasons were rooted in the special history of American Negroes, but more immediate causes were unemployment, low income, and the rules governing public assistance. The underemployment of the Negro father, he wrote, has led to the breakup of the Negro family; this, in turn, was responsible for the increase in welfare dependency. AFDC caseloads were rising because Negro men were unable to earn enough to support their families and so left home in order that their wives and children might obtain relief.[66]

Moynihan's thesis was a controversial one. Indeed, many Negro leaders and their white allies denounced his report, charging it was an effort to blame poverty and dependency on the cultural patterns of Negroes themselves. Although it inspired a major address by President Johnson and a subsequent White House conference, it produced no substantive changes in welfare policy. Moynihan himself pressed for a large public employment effort and cash benefits for men at work (i.e., family allowances), but got neither and left government in 1965. While endorsing the need to improve the economic status of Negroes, the White House conference adopted the traditional formula of jobs for those who could work and "improved public assistance" for those who could not.[67]

Nonetheless, the slow pace of upward mobility within the Negro population had already raised the question of whether or not opportunity and self-help would be enough. The Moynihan report, together with the growth of Negro dependency on AFDC, required that an examination of American welfare policy be part of any answer. By the summer of 1965, after the Johnson Administration had used Moynihan's thesis to explain rioting by Negro men in the Watts area of Los Angeles, a closer look at public assistance became even more imperative. The failings of the American "welfare state" had become inextricably tied to the apparent failure of the nation's most visible minority to realize the promise of American life.

Conclusion

In a few years, welfare policies in Britain and the United States had gone from being the objects of general support and even admiration to being matters of contention and growing controversy. To some extent, of course, what happened at the start of the 1960s was a reprise of earlier disputes over the "welfare state." But there were new factors at work. By the 1960s, welfare policies in the two countries had matured. Their costs were becoming clearer, as were their social consequences. Features that initially seemed less important had begun to loom larger, and standards of acceptability had changed. Britons and Americans were looking not at shiny new designs for post-Depression or postwar security but at real programs, run by generally uninspired bureaucrats and subject to worldly strains. Under these circumstances, only a program blessed by politically gifted leadership (such as the old-age insurance plan of the Social Security Act) could avoid criticism for long.

Something else had happened as well. The late 1950s and early 1960s saw the emergence of groups and individuals who sought political influence by analyzing and promoting new social ideas. Their motives varied: ideological, partisan, professional, and personal. Their ideas were not beyond dispute. But through argument and persuasion, a relatively small number of people in Britain and the United States managed to bring poverty and welfare issues to the fore and set the stage for a decade of policy-making in which they themselves would play important roles.

The "welfare state" may be especially susceptible to this form of influence. In the most general sense, its aim is to assure public happiness and security through government action. This is, however, an impossible task. One man's safety net is apt to be another's smothering blanket; one man's plan to encourage self-help may be another's reckless disregard of basic needs. As the goals of government become so ambitious, the opportunities for criticism grow legion. Thus, whatever it may do to promote happiness and security, the "welfare state" will inevitably produce much discontent.

Notes

1. Robert H. Bremner, *From the Depths: The Discovery of Poverty in the United States* (1956), p. xi.

2. J. Hector St. John de Crèvecoeur, *Letters from an American Farmer* (Dutton paperback ed.; 1957), p. 40.

3. Daniel Patrick Moynihan, *The Politics of a Guaranteed Income* (1973), p. 131.

4. Great Britain, *Social Insurance and Allied Services,* A Report to Parliament by Sir William Beveridge (1942, Reprinted 1968), p. 7.

5. Sir John Walley, *Social Security: Another British Failure?* (1972), p. 74.

6. Beveridge, *Social Insurance and Allied Services,* pp. 165–70.

7. Maurice Bruce, *The Coming of the Welfare State* (1961), p. 313.

8. T. H. Marshall, *Social Policy in the Twentieth Century* (3d ed. rev.; 1970), p. 81.

9. Bruce, p. 311.

10. Ben Patterson, *The Character of Conservatism* (1973), p. 41.

11. Bruce, p. 309.

12. B. S. Rowntree and G. R. Lavers, *Poverty and the Welfare State* (1951), p. 30.

13. W. G. Runciman, *Relative Deprivation and Social Justice* (1972), p. 263.

14. David Butler and Donald Stokes, *Political Change in Britain* (1969), pp. 343–46.

15. T. H. Marshall, *Class, Citizenship, and Social Development* (1965), p. 320.

16. Ralph Harris and Arthur Seldon, *Choice in Welfare 1970* (1971), p. 33.

17. Richard M. Titmuss, *Income Distribution and Social Change* (1962), p. 19.

18. C. A. R. Crosland, *The Future of Socialism* (2d ed.; 1964), p. 89.

19. Great Britain, Central Statistical Office, *Social Trends,* No. 4 (1973), Tables 49, 50 and 53, pp. 107–109.

20. Richard M. Titmuss, *Essays on the Welfare State* (2d ed. rev.; 1969), p. 219.

21. Prior to 1950, when an allowance for the caretaker of the children was added, the program had been called Aid to Dependent Children.

22. Martha Derthick, *Policymaking for Social Security* (1979), pp. 206–10.

23. Gilbert Y. Steiner, *The State of Welfare* (1971), pp. 31–74.

24. Gilbert Y. Steiner, *Social Insecurity: The Politics of Welfare* (1966), pp. 108–40.

25. U.S., Department of Health, Education, and Welfare, Social Security Administration, *Public Attitudes Toward Social Security 1935–65,* Research Report No. 33 by Michael E. Schiltz (1970), p. 174.

26. Robert J. Lampman, "How Much Does the American System of Transfers Benefit the Poor?" *Economic Progress and Social Welfare,* ed. Leonard H. Goodman (1966), pp. 137–39.

27. John Kenneth Galbraith, *The Affluent Society* (1958), p. 258.

28. David Bull, ed., *Family Poverty: Programme for the Seventies* (1971), p. 14.

29. Brian Abel-Smith and Peter Townsend, *The Poor and the Poorest* (1965), pp. 52–58.

30. Ibid., pp. 65–66.

31. A. B. Atkinson, *Poverty in Britain and the Reform of Social Security* (1969), p. 38.

32. Abel-Smith and Townsend, p. 18.

33. Richard Crossman, *The Politics of Pensions,* "Eleanor Rathbone Memorial Lecture" (1972), p. 10.

34. Richard M. Titmuss, *Commitment to Welfare* (1968), chap. xiv.

35. Robert J. Lampman, "Population Change and Poverty Reduction, 1947–75," *Poverty amid Affluence*, ed. Leo Fishman (1966), Table 2.1, p. 21 and Table 2.6, p. 29.

36. Morton Paglin, *Poverty and Transfers In-Kind* (1980), Table 8, p. 61.

37. Daniel P. Moynihan, *Maximum Feasible Misunderstanding: Community Action in the War on Poverty* (1969), pp. 3–4. Planning of the war on poverty had begun under President John F. Kennedy.

38. James L. Sundquist, ed., *On Fighting Poverty* (1969), p. 23.

39. U.S., Office of Economic Opportunity, *The Poor in 1970: A Chartbook* (1972), p. 66.

40. The "Coleman Report," for example, raised questions about the value of additional spending on education; see, U.S., Department of Health, Education, and Welfare, *Equality of Educational Opportunity* (1966).

41. U.S., Congress, Joint Economic Committee, *Hearings: Income Maintenance Programs*, 1 (1968):159.

42. Arthur J. Altmeyer, *The Formative Years of Social Security* (1966), p. 260.

43. Samuel H. Beer, *British Politics in the Collectivist Age* (1969), p. 304.

44. Samuel H. Beer et al., *Patterns of Government: The Major Political Systems of Europe* (3d ed. rev.; 1973), p. 281; Brian Abel-Smith et al., *Socialism and Affluence: Four Fabian Essays* (1970), pp. 10–11.

45. Richard E. Caves et al., *Britain's Economic Prospects* (1968), p. 34.

46. Beer et al., *Patterns of Government*, p. 293.

47. David Howell and Timothy Raison, eds., *Principles in Practice: A Series of Bow Group Essays for the 1960's* (1961), pp. 58–59.

48. Alan Peacock. *The Welfare Society*, "Unservile State Papers," No. 2 (1961), pp. 12–13.

49. Iain Macleod and J. Enoch Powell, *The Social Services: Needs and Means* (2d ed. rev.; 1954), p. 40; J. Enoch Powell, "A Policy of Savage," *The Future of the Welfare State*, Conservative Political Centre (1958), pp. 38–47.

50. Howell and Raison, eds., p. 60.

51. Ibid., p. 62.

52. Ibid., p. 66.

53. Marshall, *Social Policy*, p. 93.

54. U.S., Bureau of the Census, *Statistical Abstract of the United States* (93d ed.; 1972), p. 299.

55. Steiner, *Social Insecurity*, pp. 6–7.

56. Steiner, *The State of Welfare*, p. 69.

57. Daniel P. Moynihan, "The Crises in Welfare," *The Public Interest* (Winter 1968), p. 13.

58. Steiner, *Social Insecurity*, p. 38.

59. Ibid., pp. 39–47.

60. Ibid., p. 47.

61. Caves et al., p. 232.

62. F. W. S. Craig, ed., *British Election Manifestos, 1918–66* (1970), pp. 221–22.

63. Crosland, p. 149.

64. Craig, ed.,, p. 232. Emphasis added.

65. U.S., Department of Labor, *The Negro Family: The Case for National Action*

(1965), p. 14.

66. Daniel P. Moynihan, "Employment, Income, and the Ordeal of the Negro Family," *The Negro American*, ed. Talcott Parsons and Kenneth B. Clark (1967), pp. 134–59.

67. Lee Rainwater and William L. Yancey, *The Moynihan Report and the Politics of Controversy* (1967), pp. 284–85.

3

The Rise of the Incentive Theory

In 1909, when the Old Age Pensions Act of 1908 started paying benefits, no sector of Britain seemed as eager for them as Ireland. This bill—one of the first steps toward the creation of the British "welfare state"—authorized weekly payments of five shillings to any low-income person over the age of seventy. In short order, according to Bentley B. Gilbert, a "remarkable number" of Irishmen were claiming their pensions. The reason the number was so "remarkable" had less to do with the impoverished state of the island than with the difficulty of determining the correct age of would-be recipients. Although the Church of England kept fairly complete birth records, official registration did not come to Ireland until 1865 and in the Roman Catholic churches, which most inhabitants attended, baptismal and confirmation data were sketchy. Consequently, many elderly Irishmen professed ignorance as to when exactly they were born, except to recall their parents' telling them it was in the year of "the big wind," which, conveniently, was 1839. By March 1911, with the census taken that year estimating the population over seventy at 191,720, there were 201,783 recipients in Ireland. Partly because of the unexpectedly high costs of these pensions, the next major step—the National Insurance Act of 1911, which created unemployment and health insurance—made eligibility conditional upon a record of contributions.[1]

This is just one example of the importance incentives have always had for welfare policy. The way recipients (or potential recipients) have responded to particular programs has often been more significant than what the program is actually designed to achieve. In the past, people have been thought to move from county to county, to quit their jobs, and to abandon their families in order to obtain higher benefits. In the Irish case, the availability of pensions even caused a portion of the population to "become" older.

Welfare policy-makers have tried a variety of techniques to prevent such behavior. Residency requirements, "relative responsibility" rules, work tests, and other administrative measures have been employed. Eligibility for assistance has been defined in terms of conditions which most people cannot or will not wish to affect (such as, today, age). As the British discovered, a record of contributions can serve not just to pay for benefits but also to establish entitlement. In each case, the aim of these devices has been to make welfare programs less attractive or accessible to those for whom they are *not* meant.

None has been foolproof. Administrative controls have generally been the easiest to circumvent, either through loopholes or because of bureaucratic laxness. Although age is now a relatively objective way of determining eligibility, other commonly used conditions, like disability and involuntary unemployment, have not been so immutable. Even the requirement of a certain number of contributions has not prevented some people from figuring out how to obtain high benefits with minimal payments. Furthermore, the attractiveness of welfare programs has increased with their generosity. Without ways of confining assistance to the "truly needy," help becomes available to those who do not deserve it and the costs of welfare policy are apt to become excessive.

In the 1960s, a new idea for controlling eligibility captivated policy-makers in Britain and the United States. It held that rather than making welfare benefits harder to obtain, policy should aim at making it more appealing to give them up. Programs should be designed so that recipients would always have a financial incentive to rely on something other than welfare benefits. Moreover, this should be done not by lowering benefits themselves (which would have been unfair to the "truly needy"), but preferably by reducing them by less than the full amount of any additional earnings or other income a recipient might have. For every extra dollar or pound gained, the public support a person had been drawing would be reduced by, say, half as much, leaving him better off in total than before. Past a certain point, he would no longer be eligible for any assistance at all and instead would start paying taxes, ideally at the same rate by which his benefits had been lowered. This idea was most widely known as the negative income tax; if it was applied properly, its proponents argued, only those who were really unable to support themselves would remain on relief.

Aspects of the negative income tax did become part of British and American welfare policy during the 1960s. However, despite its seeming virtues, in neither country did it come close to being embraced fully. How this idea originated and why its initial reception was so guarded are the subjects of this chapter.

The Negative Income Tax and the Great Society

In the United States, the idea of the negative income tax first appeared in 1946, when an economist, George J. Stigler, in a scholarly article about the detrimental effects of minimum wage laws on employment, suggested an alternative way of reducing poverty: supplementing earnings via the tax system.[2] In this, Stigler drew upon discussions with Milton Friedman and other economists who had served in the Treasury Department during the Second World War. Friedman later developed the idea in a widely-read book, *Capitalism and Freedom*.[3] An income transfer scheme incorporating financial incentives to work, he argued, would not only be an efficient way of helping the poor, but also a means of replacing many existing welfare programs.

Friedman and Stigler were regarded as conservatives, but the idea also appealed to liberal economists, such as Robert J. Lampman and James Tobin. Unlike Friedman, they viewed the negative income tax as one of several complementary ways to help the poor, though they shared his appreciation of its efficiency. By using the principles— if not the actual machinery—of the tax system, benefits could be paid to those who needed them and withdrawn by less than the full amount of any increased income. Just as only a portion of earnings are paid in taxes, only part of the supplement would be reduced—thus presumably preserving an incentive to work. By 1966, several versions of this idea had been developed, and it had won the wide public support of economists whose influence in general had risen during the Kennedy and Johnson Administrations.[4]

One version formed the core of the proposal by the planning staff of the Office of Economic Opportunity to end poverty within a decade. Although the main thrust of the Great Society consisted of social services and education, in one or another way income support already accounted for more than half of all federal aid to the poor.[5] The planners sought to replace most of this with a single scheme to be operated by the Treasury Department. For an expenditure of $2.9 billion in 1968, benefits of $450 for a single person and $1,500 for a family of four could be provided; if the program were gradually improved, the same family by 1977 could have been assured a poverty-level income ($3,500), even if it lacked other sources of support. The total cost of such a plan would then have been $17 billion and approximately fifty-nine million people would have been covered.[6]

Though bold, the proposal was not outlandish. Spending requests for all federal programs to aid the poor approached $30 billion for the 1967 fiscal year; the Office of Economic Opportunity itself had asked for $3.5 billion and was allocated half of it.[7] Economic growth continued to generate increased revenues, and some analysts foresaw a "fiscal dividend" that could be used for social programs when the war in Vietnam ended. In any case, the costs of the plan would not necessarily remain high, since many of those covered would already be working and others would have a strong reason to become employed. For a slight increase in expenditures, or a rearrangement of the existing programs, this "Graduated Work Incentive Program" could achieve President Johnson's goal of eradicating poverty.

To an increasingly embattled administration, this idea should have been appealing, and in certain quarters it was. Both the top officials of the Office of Economic Opportunity and staffers in the White House and the Bureau of the Budget showed interest. A 1965 task force of the Council of Economic Advisers, set up under Gardner Ackley, concluded that a "strong case can be made for a negative income tax."[8] Studies undertaken in subsequent years confirmed this assessment.

Yet little of substance resulted. In part, this was because neither the reports of the Council of Economic Advisers nor the planning memoranda from the Office of Economic Opportunity were documents that required action. Instead, they were devoted to analysis or advocacy, they were often kept confidential, and they did not necessarily flow into the main channels of decision-making—which, for domestic policy, emanated mostly from the office of presidential assistant, Joseph A. Califano, Jr. "The economists in the program analysis office," Franklin D. Raines has written, "formed a small and insignificant minority voice" in the debate over anti-poverty strategy.[9] In contrast, proponents of education and social services were more numerous and better-placed, since their programs were constantly being scrutinized in connection with budget reviews, Congressional hearings, presidential messages, and the like.

A larger reason had to do with the importance of mission and territory in government. Income maintenance was not one of the tasks assigned to the Office of Economic Opportunity, but was instead the responsibility of the Department of Health, Education, and Welfare. There, it was in the near-personal charge of the Undersecretary, Wilbur J. Cohen, who had come to Washington to work on the staff which had drafted the Social Security Act and had been a dominant figure in welfare policy ever since. The policy planners in his department (who, by training and approach, were nearly interchangeable with those in the Office of Economic Opportunity) had concluded that a negative income tax offered the best way of providing assistance to the poor. Cohen did not so much disagree with them as judge that such a step was not politically feasible. Fresh from a difficult struggle with Congress over the 1967 amendments to the Social Security Act, he foresaw a long period of education before an American public, and pressure groups such as the labor unions, would accept a "guaranteed income." (Public opinion polls consistently showed that two out of three people opposed the idea.)[10] In the meantime, there were other changes, such as national standards in benefits and administration, which he believed could be achieved and which had the further advantage of keeping welfare policy in his department, rather than moving it to Treasury or some new agency. Although several versions of the negative income tax were presented to him, Cohen offered little encouragement, and the White House deferred to his view.

Cohen's success in blocking the new strategy for dealing with poverty reflected not just his personal influence over welfare policy but also an astute sense of the President's interests. When the notion of a negative income tax began to be considered seriously in 1965, Charles L. Schultze, then director of the Bureau of the Budget, doubted that a program of cash assistance to " 'able-bodied employable males' " could be enacted.[11] This involved a judgment less about Congress (which had recently enacted much major social legislation and was at its most pliant) than about Lyndon B. Johnson. A plan which, in effect, divided all citizens into one group that paid taxes and another that received benefits may have been attractive to economists, but Lyndon B. Johnson's "war on poverty" was one of self-help and self-improvement, and its goal was to make "tax payers" out of "tax eaters."[12] Despite the sophisticated talk about incentives, to a Southwestern politician who had been nurtured in the New Deal the negative income tax was too reminiscent of relief.

The idea was kept alive within the Washington bureaucracies as well as at universities and research institutes. Different versions were discussed and numerous technical details explored. In June 1967, with no legislation in prospect, the Office of Economic Opportunity began an experiment in New Jersey to test the effects of income supplements on work incentives; results were not expected for at least five years. The Internal Revenue Service also examined the issue and concluded it could operate a negative income tax—a decision not unrelated, Robert A. Levine has suggested, to the fact that Bertrand Harding, then director of the Office of Economic Opportunity, had been a senior official with the tax agency.[13] Other ways of assisting the able-bodied poor, like food stamps, were reviewed, but Congressional opposition kept these in-kind programs from being expanded or converted into a simpler system of cash assistance.

The likelihood that anything more would happen seemed slim, since the last days of the Johnson Administration, unlike its beginnings, were not a propitious time for new social reforms. The war in Vietnam had induced caution in proposing costly domestic outlays, while the Great Society had virtually exhausted liberalism's legislative agenda. Even as the lame-duck Administration prepared to leave office in 1968, the package of ideas prepared for the President's final

State of the Union message ruled out a commitment to income maintenance and instead endorsed a series of modest changes in the existing welfare programs. By that time, the continuation of the "war on poverty" was in doubt, since its "victories" in community organization had hurt its political support, just as disillusionment had accompanied its inability to achieve a swift triumph.[14] Under the circumstances, guaranteeing an income to those who could already earn one was not a matter of great moment.

Incentives and the Welfare Crisis

This disposition was reinforced by the outcry over the continued growth of the public assistance rolls. Between 1965 and 1967, another one-quarter million families began to receive AFDC, and in just another year an equal number was added, bringing the total to more than one and one-half million families, containing six million people. Not knowing what else to do, the Johnson Administration intensified its efforts to treat the various problems supposedly facing welfare mothers. In May 1967, a task force on "Services for Self-Support of AFDC Recipients" was set up within Health, Education, and Welfare. At the same time, the Department reorganized its public assistance operations into a new bureau, the Social and Rehabilitation Service. Its 1967 legislative proposals asked for an extension of the Community Work and Training program, which aimed to give job experience to "employable" recipients (as defined administratively). However, to the normally cautious fiscal committees of Congress, who were presiding over this seemingly uncontrollable eruption in welfare spending, these measures were losing their appeal. Judging from the uneven results of the existing social services programs, they began to suspect that some state and local officials—and, perhaps, federal ones as well—did not share their own enthusiasm for limiting costs and turning those on relief toward self-support.

The Moynihan report had suggested another way of dealing with the problem of dependency. It argued that the cause of rising caseloads was to be found not just in the characteristics of recipients, but in the rules of the program, which encouraged husbands to leave their wives in order to increase the family's total income. Additional research seemed to confirm this theme. The geographical variations in welfare growth, some experts maintained, were due to the six-fold differences in benefit-levels around the nation, which induced potential recipients to move to the most generous states. Others pointed out that except for an allowance for work expenses, every dollar earned by a welfare mother resulted in the loss of a dollar in public assistance, leaving her no better off than before. In short, for low-income people, obtaining relief seemed more rational at times than efforts at self-support. According to this view of the problem, dependency could be reduced only by first removing the incentives to use AFDC.

With little prodding from the Johnson Administration, Congress took up this new approach. When finally enacted, the 1967 amendments to the Social Security Act created a new "work incentive" program that was to be mandatory in every state. All welfare mothers, even those with young children at home, would be required to look for a job or participate in a training program. No longer would the fact of being the female head of a household assure eligibility for relief. At the same time, those recipients who did work would not find the entire amount of their earnings offset by a reduction in public assistance. Instead, work and child-care expenses, the first $30 of monthly wages, and one-third of the remainder would be disregarded in computing AFDC benefits, thus providing a financial incentive to become employed. In these ways, the 1967 amendments sought to make dependency less appealing than self-sufficiency, at least for those families who were already eligible for assistance.

For others, Congress added a provision, over the opposition of the Johnson Administration and despite a threatened filibuster by Senate liberals, limiting the federal share of spending for new AFDC cases caused by desertion or illegitimacy. If neither social services nor altering incentives succeeded and welfare rolls continued to grow, their costs would have to be met by the state and local governments that ran the program. For the first time since the New Deal, Washington was threatening to stop paying for assistance to the poor. "No congressional welfare action since adoption of the Social Security Act," Gilbert Y. Steiner has written, "has been attacked more vigorously than this so-called welfare freeze."[15] So distasteful was it, even to some of its supporters, that it was never implemented and was eventually repealed. However, the provision was an indicator of the urgency which Congress attached to ending the welfare crisis.

In signing the 1967 amendments, Lyndon B. Johnson voiced the now prevailing judgment of AFDC:

> The welfare system today pleases no one. It is criticized by the poor and the wealthy, by social workers and politicians, by whites and by Negroes, in every area of the nation. . . .
> The welfare system in America is outmoded and in need of a major change.[16]

Since his advisers were without useful notions of what to do, the President appointed a Commission on Income Maintenance Programs, a body originally proposed by his Council of Economic Advisers to consider alternative ways of aiding the poor. The occasion for its creation now was the need to stem the growth of dependency. Although the technical features of using a negative income tax to end poverty were beginning to be well-known, few agreed that such an approach should be taken. Almost the opposite was true for public assistance. Few disagreed that some change had to be made, but the details of an alternative to AFDC were hardly evident. As he approved the new amendments to the Social Security Act, Johnson charged the Commission to "examine any and every plan, however unconventional."[17] But after the presidential election of 1968, the future of its recommendations was left in doubt, since the victors were not the heirs of the New Deal and the Great Society but rather their Republican opponents.

The Negative Income Tax and Selectivity

Just as the Commission on Income Maintenance Programs was beginning its work, the British were in the midst of their own reassessment of how best to aid the poor. In the 1964 elections, this had not been a major issue between the parties. Although the Conservatives had pledged to concentrate help "first and foremost on those whose needs are greatest," they vigorously denied they planned a return to means-testing for all benefits.[18] The Labour manifesto described "drastic reforms" for the social services, including Labour's new retirement scheme, but added the proviso that the "new wage-related benefits must be self-supporting" and financed primarily by employer and employee contributions.[19] The plight of the unemployed, sick, disabled, and especially the elderly attracted virtually all the attention of the parties; the low-income family, none. When in his final election broadcast, Harold Wilson promised a "minimum income guarantee," it was to be for pensioners; when his party declared a "war on want," the target was not to be the poverty rediscovered by the Titmuss group but rather the "gross inequalities of circumstances between the rich and poor nations."[20] Far from disavowing the "welfare state," the Conservatives proclaimed that they had increased social security benefits faster than both prices and earnings, while their leader, the former 14th Earl of Home, committed himself to using national prosperity for expanding them further.

The results of the elections indicated that the technological dynamism espoused by Wilson seemed more promising to the public than the aristocratic manner of Sir Alec Douglas-Home. Yet, the Labour Government, more faithful to past traditions than to current realities, proceeded to raise most welfare benefits within a month of entering office, thus setting off a sterling crisis which seriously undermined its plans to increase the rate of economic growth. These first actions, Samuel Brittan has written, fostered "a generalized resentment that, after having shouted from the rooftops about the mess they inherited, the new ministers were showing they still put welfare benefits above economic recovery."[21] In an effort to restore confidence, the Chancellor of the Exchequer, James Callaghan, introduced a series of deflationary measures; and the Government's 1965 "national plan" forecast a growth rate for spending on public services and housing through 1970 that was *lower* than what the Conservatives had achieved in the six years prior to 1964. Nonetheless, the cold economic climate produced by this episode virtually guaranteed that the Wilson Government would have little leeway for expanding welfare programs.

In this context, the prospect of merging social benefits and the tax system began to seem appealing. This was, in fact, an old idea. In 1942, a well-known social reformer, Juliet, Lady Rhys Williams, had advanced such a scheme, which came to be known as the "social dividend" plan. She was fearful that the Beveridge proposals constituted a "serious attack upon the will to work":

> Not only will the idle get as much from the State as will the industrious workers, they will get a great deal more. Indeed the whole basis of the Scheme rests upon the conception that those who serve the community by working and producing wealth must not on any account receive any State assistance or reward, but must be heavily taxed instead.[22]

Her solution was to provide everyone with the same basic benefit at all times and to tax all earnings at the same rate:

> To every individual his basic needs; from every individual the same percentage of his income varied only in accordance with the prosperity of the whole community.[23]

Other social benefits and tax allowances would have been abolished; a work-test and even a signed contract between each individual and the government would prevent any decline in effort. For those with low incomes, the new grant would serve as a cash supplement; for those with earnings above the standard of need, the grant would be less than all or part of their tax liability. No new means-test would be required; the administrative savings, she estimated, would be "enormous."

The "social dividend" idea proved no match for the popularity of the Beveridge plan and remained little more than a curiosity. The Liberal Party did adopt a version of it in the late 1940s, and along with Lady Rhys Williams testified in favor of it to the Royal Commission on the Taxation of Profits and Income in 1951. But, the Commission rejected the proposal because it seemed too costly, would have resulted in higher taxes for many low-income payers, and violated the "generally accepted" principles of not giving money (except family allowances) to people at work and of taxing different individuals at rates reflecting their capacities to pay.[24] Despite this setback, the "social dividend" continued to be discussed and modified, chiefly by economists, such as Cambridge University's J. E. Meade.

However, as concern about the costs of the "welfare state" mounted, a different rationale was put forth for linking taxes and social benefits. In this view, the problem of the existing arrangements was that they gave too much help to people who did not really need it. Yet a test of means might have discouraged the incentive to work, or caused some potential recipients to avoid seeking assistance. On the other hand, the income tax system seemed like a fair and efficient device for cutting back. To Conservatives like Sir Geoffrey Howe and the members of the Bow Group, this meant, for example, withdrawing family allowances from upper-income households while permitting them to retain children's tax deductions. (To the rest would have gone larger benefits, perhaps through the tax system as well.) On the "Left," the Titmuss group favored the opposite approach; it called for removing tax deductions from the well-to-do, while raising family allowances at the same time. Where Beveridge sought to provide the "same basic provision" for all, these proposals tried to make the "welfare state" more selective.

Considering the economic situation, the Labour Government was inevitably drawn toward these ideas, but little that was new resulted. Having to shelve its grand plans for providing "half-pay on retirement," Labour turned to a supposedly interim measure, the "minimum income guarantee," which was to use the income tax mechanism to assist the elderly with pensions below the poverty-line. The cost of this was not the major problem; the workload of the Inland Revenue Service was. Callaghan had introduced both corporation and capital gains taxes during 1965, leaving the civil servants little time (or so they claimed) to face the seemingly major problems of converting a "pay-as-you-earn" system into a "receive-as-you-need" one.[25] The proposal was abandoned; on the eve of the 1966 elections, the Government announced plans to convert National Assistance into "Supplementary Benefits." By renaming it, publicizing it, improving its administration, and proclaiming entitlement by right, Labour hoped to dispel the stigma of means-tested aid as a way of supplementing the pensions of the aged and other dependent groups. At least initially, selectivity meant yet another effort to transform the "dole."

For the low-paid worker and his family, even less happened. A proposal to increase family allowances did come before the Cabinet, but was far too costly to be considered seriously. As an alternative, Callaghan suggested paying benefits only to low-income families: a means-tested allowance. Although this would have been far less expensive, it aroused fears of lowered work effort and interference in collective bargaining, a matter of no small concern to Labour's trade unionists. Titmuss and other social policy experts advising the Government also pointed out a number of technical problems, including the likely difficulty of finding and persuading those eligible to submit claims. Without ever being presented to the Cabinet, Callaghan's plan, together with other ideas like using the income tax mechanism, was sent back to the bureaucracies for further study. As the Labour Government ended its first term, its main response to the discovery of family poverty had been to initiate a survey to determine its true extent.

Next to the sterling crisis, the most important event for welfare policy during Labour's first term was probably one which occurred outside the Government. In March 1965, Brian Abel-Smith previewed the findings of his research on poverty at a meeting of the Society of Friends. Out of that came the formation of "a pressure group for the poor," ultimately to be called the Child Poverty Action Group (CPAG).[26] Never a large group, it consisted primarily of intellectuals and community organizers, including many of the most competent and respected students of British social policy, like Titmuss and his colleagues. Its tactics were neither mass protest nor drawing-room conversation; rather, CPAG sought to "create opinion about public opinion."[27] The Parliamentary question and the newspaper story were its main weapons, its reputation for having the "best information" its main asset.

Not unimportant either was the fact that its natural loyalties were to the Wilson Government. Several of its founding members had been Labour advisers and its first secretary, Tony Lynes, had been given an unusual appointment (for British government) as a temporary civil servant in the Ministry of Pensions when the party took office in 1964. When Abel-Smith and Townsend's findings were finally published during the Christmas season of 1965, a CPAG memorandum and delegation went to the Prime Minister, urging prompt action in behalf of the poor. Wilson's response was suitably non-committal:

> I thanked the Group for the work it was doing and told it that its memorandum would be taken fully into account in the review of the social services now being undertaken.[28]

In fact, the condition of the low-income worker and his children could no longer be treated as a routine matter. With the formation of CPAG and the criticisms of Labour's own supporters, it had become a serious political problem for the party.

During 1966, pressures to act continued to build. Although, as in 1964, welfare policy was not a major issue in the national elections, both parties made reference to family poverty. The Conservatives pledged to "give more generous help to children in families where the income is below minimum need," while Labour promised to create a new Ministry of Social Security which would "head a drive to seek out, and alleviate, poverty whether among children or old people."[29] The Tories did not offer specific proposals. Labour hinted at plans for integrating tax allowances and social benefits, as well as for improving low wages.

After the Wilson Government regained office with a larger majority, Conservative members of the House of Commons seized any opportunity to chide it for its inaction on family poverty. More dismaying, however, was continued criticism from Labour's own ranks. At the end of 1966, a backbencher, David Owen, led an adjournment debate on poverty by noting that the nation was approaching its third Christmas under a Labour Government without any action on family allowances. The previous autumn, a speaker at the annual party conference had even urged abolition of the traditional rule forbidding payment of public assistance to people in full-time employment.

The Wilson Government tried to plead for more time. It could not do everything at once, Margaret Herbison, the minister responsible for social security, explained:

> The very serious problem of the low-wage earner has been with us for a very long time, and I assure the House that the Labour Government have no intention of shelving it.[30]

Its survey of family incomes had been made during the summer of 1966 and was being analyzed; a proposal was promised afterwards. But by this time, Britain was in the midst of another economic crisis, which had forced the lowering of even the cautious forecasts for public spending in the 1965 national plan.

Selectivity thus seemed essential, but the Cabinet had still not decided on how it was to be achieved. Without expressing a preference, CPAG had proposed two options: the use of the income tax "in reverse" to pay social benefits, or the withdrawal of children's tax deductions in order to increase family allowances. The first, however, required the certainly lengthy and perhaps impossible feat—nine years in the estimate of one junior minister—of converting a collection system into a dispensing one, while the second involved the distasteful prospect of taking from some families in order to give to others. (Because British family allowances are paid directly to mothers, while tax deductions are normally credited against a father's earnings, the latter plan also redistributed income within households.) In addition, neither the Treasury nor the Inland Revenue had much enthusiasm for linking taxation to social security. Callaghan, in particular, was fearful such arrangements would encroach upon the powers of the Chancellor to adjust tax rates as needed for economic policy. He insisted that more help for the poor could be given by modifying the existing welfare programs.

Nonetheless, as Harold Wilson later recalled, "poverty could not wait."[31] By early 1967, the Government's survey of family incomes was completed. It showed that while the number of poor was not as large as Abel-Smith and Townsend had claimed, the true figure—1.1 million children in 345,000 families, nearly half of which were headed by a full-time worker—was too great to ignore.[32] Moreover, Labour's economists had concluded that the time had come to reflate and were urging an increase in public spending. Because of the indecision over what to do, Wilson took the uncommon step of putting the issue to a show of hands; in June 1967, the Cabinet voted by a narrow margin to increase family allowances for everyone by seven shillings. The debate over selectivity had resulted in an across-the-board raise in this feature of the British "welfare state," its first in eleven years.

The Adoption of "Clawback"

The Labour Government managed to receive but little political credit for this action. Margaret Herbison resigned the day after the increase in family allowances was announced. Although her resignation apparently had more to do with pension than with family policy, it inevitably fed speculation that she was disappointed with the size of the raise. CPAG made no effort to conceal its displeasure; the proposed hike, it declared, was "ludicrously small."[33] This was hardly the view of the Treasury, which calculated the net cost of the increase at £83 million. Yet spread among all families with two or more children, that amount would bring less than half of the working poor above the poverty-line. This was, said Conservative spokesmen in the House of Commons, "only a thin, inadequate smear of help," and some Labour backbenchers agreed.[34]

Even before the family allowances bill was enacted, the Government devalued the pound. In his speech announcing this long-postponed action, Wilson promised to protect the neediest from the higher prices that would result. In Parliament, his new Minister for Social Security, Judith Hart, hinted that the following year's budget would contain additional help for the poor. No sooner had the Cabinet made a decision about family poverty than the debate was re-opened.

This time, however, a resolution occurred swiftly. Devaluation also brought a new Chancellor, Roy Jenkins, a sophisticated and ambitious man, known to be willing to espouse unorthodox ideas. Influenced by the arguments of his special adviser on taxation, Nicholas Kaldor, a Cambridge University economist, he endorsed the plan for reducing the cost of family allowances by lowering tax deductions. Capitalizing on the traditional dominance of the Chancellor over budgetary matters, Jenkins overcame the objections of the Inland Revenue as well as lingering doubts in the Cabinet and unveiled the scheme (together with a further three-shilling increase in family allowances) in a January 1968 message on post-devaluation spending cuts. Only the relatively small number of families in the surtax bracket were to pay more because of smaller deductions than they were to receive from larger benefits. Low-income families would reap the full amount of the higher family allowances, while anyone who paid income taxes at the standard rate—then 41.25 percent at approximately the average wage and above—would break even on the transaction. The net cost to the Treasury was estimated at £30 million. First called "give and take," the idea was later renamed "clawback." It was, Jenkins told the House of Commons, "selectivity in a civilised and acceptable form."[35]

For all its ingenuity, the Wilson Government's new device proved neither as popular nor as effective as its advocates had hoped. Since the maximum benefit any family could receive would be ten shillings per child, one-quarter million children would still be living in low-income households. In light of the effects of devaluation, Lord Balniel, the Conservative "shadow" minister, criticized it as a "rather sad little bill."[36] Labour stalwarts had little defense, except to say they had created a method which would permit paying larger allowances to the low-income family.

Whether it would do so remained in doubt. When clawback was introduced, Douglas Houghton, who had headed the Wilson Government's review of social security, defended its feasibility in comparison with benefits provided through the tax system:

> There is no nightmare; it works like a charm. . . . If the husband pays a little more in tax and the wife gets still more in extra family allowance, what is there to grumble about.[37]

A great deal, as it turned out. Within months, a Labour Party guide for speakers was warning:

> It must be admitted that the decision to "claw-back" the increases in family allowances from tax-payers has provoked a

hostile reaction. Inland Revenue staff have been overworked in answering complaints from angry husbands who did not know that their wives were receiving an increased family allowance. Others have found the administration of the system very difficult to understand.[38]

Part of the problem was that family allowances were the least popular of "welfare state" benefits. Many people still thought they encouraged poor families to have more children, and those dependent on other forms of assistance, especially pensioners, felt they were a needless extravagance at a time when public spending was being curtailed.

Compounding this was the manner in which the new arrangements were implemented. For administrative reasons, the rise in benefits could not be synchronized with the lowering of deductions. Over an eighteen-month period, the average household first paid more tax than it obtained in increased aid; then, it received a larger grant; and finally, six months afterwards, its tax bill rose again.[39] When combined with normal delays in altering withholding tax tables and also with the shifts within households, the fact that the average family was coming out even was almost certain to be obscured. Among Labour Party supporters, the major accomplishment of clawback was widely held to be the loss of a by-election at Dudley, where the Government's new approach to family poverty had been an issue.

Apart from the confusion, a more serious problem was discovered which seemed to preclude further use of the technique. Each lowering of tax deductions had the consequence of reducing the level of gross income at which tax liability would commence. The January 1968 measures, for example, added an estimated 350,000 new taxpayers, many of whom would otherwise have been excluded because the size of their families, together with larger deductions, left their net incomes below the tax threshold. As a result of rising wages and other changes in the tax structure, it turned out that another round of increased family allowances with offsetting revenue adjustments would have taken benefits away from many families who needed them. By effectively raising taxes on many low-income families, clawback assured that they would be no better off if government tried to provide more help.

Labour and the Poor

Once again, the task of finding an alternative was given to interdepartmental committees of civil servants and junior ministers. Kaldor had suggested creating a uniform tax credit for children, which would be paid as a benefit to low-income families and subtracted from tax liability for others. This and other negative income tax plans were referred to a Treasury committee chaired by Jack Diamond, the Financial Secretary, which had performed a similar function in connection with the proposed "minimum income guarantee." Just as then, it found a number of practical problems with these ideas: income for tax purposes was usually at least twelve months out-of-date and did not include such items as assets; many of the poor were self-employed and thus more difficult to monitor than the average worker; sizable amounts of new information about family arrangements and similarly sensitive topics might have to be supplied to Inland Revenue or employers. At least for the foreseeable future, the Treasury group concluded that using the income tax machinery to pay social benefits was not possible at an acceptable cost.

A social security policy group under the chairmanship of R. H. S. Crossman, then Secretary of State for Social Services, had no more success. It too rejected the negative income tax, as well as a plan to extend Supplementary Benefits to full-time workers. But its preferred approach, clawback, had by 1969 already lost the support of Chancellor Jenkins, for reasons both political and financial. The only viable option seemed to be a straightforward increase in family allowances. However, this was still too costly for a cautious pre-election budget and evidenced the lack of alternatives—the "sterility," in Crossman's later judgment—of Labour's policy for family poverty as the party neared the end of six years in office.[40]

Indeed, by its earlier increases in social insurance and Supplementary Benefits, the Government had already produced a backlash of sorts among the working-class supporters of the Labour Party. The more generous level of assistance available to the unemployed gave rise to complaints of "malingering" and "scrounging." In July 1968, Judith Hart announced a series of measures to deal with the "work-shy." After receiving aid for four weeks, men under the age of forty-five must either have found a job, be "genuinely seeking work," or else lose their benefits. This was the first such condition imposed, CPAG noted, since the pre-"welfare state" days of the 1930s. That it was accompanied by an insistence on entitlement to Supplementary Benefits and by campaigns to urge those eligible to claim them was little consolation.

As Labour's second term ended, almost no one outside the Government—and far from everyone inside—was satisfied with its record in welfare policy. A CPAG evaluation concluded:

> Although . . . it introduced a number of reforms, poverty remains on a considerable and perhaps even greater scale than when it assumed office. Many of the Government's own

actions have exacerbated poverty and a general strategy of planning has not been in evidence. Low income families have been the group which has benefitted least from the actions of the Government—at least in its period of office so far.[41]

Had the poor become poorer since 1964? "If true," replied David Ennals, who was now Minister of State at the new Department of Health and Social Security, "there could hardly be a more damning indictment of the Labour Government."[42] He did not think the accusation was true, nor did the Prime Minister, as he rejected a suggestion that he establish a Royal Commission on Poverty:

> I do not accept that the position of the low-incomes group is worse than when we came into office. It has been a question of priorities and I think we have *now* got our priorities right.[43]

His Government had indeed nearly doubled spending on the social services, introduced some significant structural changes in the social insurance programs, and, through its tax policy, shifted the cost of the "welfare state" toward higher-income households. All this was done, moreover, amid a series of economic crises that severely restricted government actions.

Nonetheless, Wilson's critics maintained, the overall record illbehooved a socialist party. The increased outlays for social welfare, they contended, were illusory, due more to the growth of the eligible population and the demands of middle-income families for higher education and similar programs than to any real improvement in assistance for the poor. In any case, the Government's economic policies were said to cancel out its social ones, and thanks to revenue-retrieving changes like clawback, the net effect of benefits and taxes on income distribution was estimated to be minuscule.[44]

What really happened to the poor during Labour's two terms of office prompted a lengthy and often complicated debate in Britain.[45] But the details of the matter were in a sense less important than the fact that after six years of Labour rule, there could be a serious dispute at all. Notwithstanding the party's traditions and beliefs, the heirs of Attlee, Bevan, and other founders of the "welfare state" had seemingly run out of will or ideas.

Conclusion

During the first half of the 1960s, both the United States and Britain acquired governments committed to social reform. The rediscovery of

51

poverty presented each with a welcome opportunity, but each soon found out that it was also a potential pitfall. Other issues—an overseas war, a staggering economy—limited the amount of effort and money policy-makers could devote to assisting the poor. Even worse, traditional welfare policies seemed unlikely to be productive and, some thought, caused social and political problems of their own. Yet, unless they could come up with better ways of reducing poverty, Democratic and Labour governments of which much was expected stood to be blamed not just by their opponents but by their own supporters.

It was in this context that the negative income tax emerged as an attractive idea. Developed by academics and reformers as an alternative to the "welfare state," it seemed initially a vehicle for expanding it. But this was not to be a simple expansion. Because it incorporated a test of means, the negative income tax offered the prospect of giving more help only to those who truly needed it. At the same time, its "incentive theory" gave reason to think it would not induce dependency and, some Americans hoped, might even encourage recipients to become self-supporting. In short, linking benefits and taxes seemed to be a policy-maker's dream: a way of accomplishing desirable but contradictory goals.

Nonetheless, this turned out to be a vision few people in the Wilson or Johnson governments were eager to realize. Only a partial and inadequate step toward the negative income tax was taken in Britain, and in the United States, it was Congress more than the White House that was responsible for introducing incentives into welfare policy. By the end of their terms, both reformist governments were still hunting for new ideas to aid the poor.

Part of the reason was that, to many officials in the two countries, the negative income tax resembled a nightmare rather than a dream. Although concentrating help on the most needy, the plan still amounted to an increase in aid and, depending on the actual figures chosen, a quite costly one, even if less expensive than providing equivalent benefits through existing programs. Moreover, it raised an enormous number of new and hard-to-answer questions about its likely consequences and feasibility. In the United States, the Internal Revenue Service decided it could adapt a tax-collection system to pay benefits; its British counterpart claimed it could not. Who was right was not just a matter of administrative detail but also of political disposition. The negative income tax would have altered responsibilities as well as programs, and some officials, such as Cohen in the United States and Callaghan in Britain, were not eager to cede authority in order to assist the poor.

As the debate over clawback revealed, such objections could be overcome, at least partially. Much more resistant were the views on welfare policy handed down among Democratic and Labour politicians. The predecessors of the Johnson Administration believed in providing opportunities, not income support; the forebears of the Wilson Government trusted universal programs, not selective ones. The negative income tax was not only new and complicated, but alien to the traditions of policy-makers in Britain and the United States during the 1960s. And while times may have changed, older notions still lingered. Not surprisingly, the fact that each nation was governed by the party that had created its welfare policy proved to be a major obstacle to adopting an idea born as an alternative to that policy.

Notes

1. Bentley B. Gilbert, *The Evolution of National Insurance in Great Britain: The Origins of the Welfare State* (1966), pp. 226–32.
2. George Stigler, "The Economics of Minimum Wage Legislation," *American Economic Review* (1946), pp. 358–65.
3. Milton Friedman, *Capitalism and Freedom* (1962), chap. xii.
4. U.S. Congress, Joint Economic Committee, *Hearings: Income Maintenance Programs* 2 (1968):675–90.
5. Joseph A. Kershaw, *Government Against Poverty* (1970), p. 40.
6. Franklin D. Raines, "Presidential Policy Development: The Genesis of the Family Assistance Plan" (1971), pp. 38–39; Vincent J. and Vee Burke, *Nixon's Good Deed: Welfare Reform* (1974), pp. 20–21.
7. Robert A. Levine, *The Poor Ye Need Not Have with You: Lessons from the War on Poverty* (1970), p. 62.
8. Walter Williams, *The Struggle for a Negative Income Tax* (1972), p. 4.
9. Raines, p. 37.
10. Hazel Erskine, "The Polls: Government Role in Welfare," *Public Opinion Quarterly* (1975), pp. 268–70.
11. Memo of September 8, 1965, from Robert A. Levine to Joseph Kershaw on September 7 meeting of White House Task Force on Income Maintenance, cited by Burke and Burke, p. 19.
12. Lyndon B. Johnson, quoted by Daniel P. Moynihan, *The Politics of a Guaranteed Income* (1973), p. 131.
13. Levine, p. 209.
14. James L. Sundquist, ed., *On Fighting Poverty* (1969), p. 250.
15. Gilbert Y. Steiner, *The State of Welfare* (1971), p. 45.
16. Lyndon B. Johnson, quoted by Moynihan (1973), p. 359.
17. Ibid., p. 360.
18. F. W. S. Craig, ed., *British Election Manifestos, 1918–66* (1970), pp. 223–24.
19. Ibid., pp. 239–40.
20. Ibid., p. 243.
21. Samuel Brittan, *Steering the Economy* (1971), p. 302.

22. Lady Juliet Rhys Williams, *Something to Look Forward To* (1943), p. 141.

23. Ibid., p. 156.

24. Great Britain, Royal Commission on the Taxation of Profits and Income, *Second Report* (1954), p. 17.

25. Douglas Houghton, *Paying for Social Services* (1967), p. 12.

26. Frank Field, "A Pressure Group for the Poor," *Family Poverty: Programme for the Seventies*, ed. David Bull (1971), pp. 145–57.

27. Ibid., p. 150.

28. Great Britain, *Hansard's Parliamentary Debates* (Commons), 723 (January 25, 1966), cols. 20–21.

29. Craig, ed., pp. 261 and 277.

30. *Hansard*, 725 (May 24, 1966), col. 345.

31. Harold Wilson, *A Personal Record: The Labour Government, 1964–1970* (1971), p. 420.

32. Great Britain, Ministry of Social Security, *Circumstances of Families* (1967), chap. ii.

33. *Poverty: Journal of the Child Poverty Action Group*, no. 4 (Autumn 1967), p. 1.

34. *Hansard*, 753 (November 8, 1967), col. 1057.

35. Ibid., 756 (January 17, 1968), col. 1800.

36. Ibid., 762 (April 2, 1968), col. 194.

37. Ibid., cols. 223 and 225.

38. Cited by Margaret Wynn, *Family Policy* (2d ed. rev.; 1972), p. 204.

39. Bull, ed., pp. 125–27.

40. Personal interview with the author.

41. Child Poverty Action Group, *Poverty and the Labour Government*, "Poverty Pamphlet," no. 3 (1970), p. 18.

42. Ibid., p. 22.

43. *Hansard*, 796 (February 17, 1970), cols. 209–211. Emphasis added.

44. Peter Townsend and Nicholas Bosanquet, eds., *Labour and Inequality: Sixteen Fabian Essays* (1972), pp. 274–301 *et passim*.

45. Wilfred Beckerman, ed., *The Labour Government's Economic Record: 1964–1970* (1972), chap. ii.

4

The Proposal of FAP and FIS

If the duty of an opposition is to oppose, both British Conservatives and American Republicans have been notably derelict in the area of welfare policy. Into the 1960s, neither party offered much more than token dissent from the directions laid out by their political foes. Early on, the Tories had made peace with the idea of the "welfare state," extended it in some notable ways during their thirteen years in office, and when Labour returned to power in 1964, prepared to defend the "national minimum" against the egalitarian schemes of the "Left." Much the same occurred in the United States, where the first Republican administration since the New Deal essentially ratified the framework established by the Social Security Act. Later, when a Democratic president declared an all-out "war on poverty," the GOP for the most part went along, complaining that victory was unlikely to be achieved but not that government should forsake the effort. To be sure, each party could be counted on to vote dutifully against the plans of its opponents and to criticize excessive costs and administrative bungling. However, apart from scattered groups of ideologists on their fringes, neither the Conservatives nor the Republicans were prepared to suggest any major alternative to the generally accepted approaches to welfare policy.

Devising such a substitute would, in any case, have been difficult for a party in opposition. In the first place, a substantial political risk was involved. Until well into the 1960s, neither the British nor the Americans seemed particularly unhappy with their version of the "welfare state." Even afterwards, discontent was by no means widespread. For most politicians, bidding for support by promising to preserve and expand the existing programs appeared to be more sensible and less hazardous than proposing to experiment with pensions, sickness benefits, and other forms of relief.

Furthermore, being out-of-office made designing an alternative policy considerably more difficult. Accurate information about the impact of proposed changes on costs and recipients was harder to obtain. Until possible reforms were under serious consideration, the likely reaction of the press and key political groups was not easy to gauge. Not least important for parties of the "Right" was the tendency of most prominent thinkers and writers about welfare policy to be disposed toward the "Left." Even if the Republicans and Conservatives had been willing to risk the political consequences of taking on the "welfare state," they would have been hard-pressed to figure out how to do so.

It might be expected that this was less of a problem in Britain than in the United States. British political parties have been more ideological than their American counterparts and have well-developed traditions of opposition. Indeed, within each of the major parties were units expressly designed to criticize and produce alternative proposals when the opposing party was in power. The Conservative Party's research department, dating back to Disraeli, was virtually an in-house think-tank, brimming with Oxbridge graduates, who saw writing and debating about issues as ways to begin a political career. Nonetheless, in welfare policy, little came of all this. During the 1960s, as we will see, the Tories discussed and publicized a variety of initiatives, but never committed themselves to any fundamental change in the "welfare state."

The underlying difficulty was that welfare policy as it had evolved in Britain and the United States proved to be rather compatible with Republican and Conservative views. The existing programs did provide help to the needy, without seeming to impoverish those who were not in need. At least in principle, they sought to encourage thrift, work, independence, and similar Tory virtues. The acceptance of government responsibility for promoting public well-being had led the parties of the "Right" to expect much worse. As it turned out, while defects in particular measures could easily be found, the shape of the "welfare state" in Britain and the United States gave most Conservatives and Republicans little ground for wanting a thorough overhaul.

Despite this, within months of returning to power at the end of the 1960s, both parties proposed a radical break with one of the bedrocks of the existing policy: the tradition of not providing income on the basis of need to those able to work. The vehicle for doing this was inspired by the negative income tax and relied heavily on the "incentive theory." How and why Republican and Conservative governments decided to endorse what their presumably more progressive predecessors had rejected will be described in this chapter.

Conservatives in Opposition

While the Wilson Government struggled to appear fiscally prudent after 1964, the Conservative opposition began to examine its own policies. The last years of the Macmillan era had not been pleasant ones. Internal disputes over budgetary issues (culminating in the dismissal of Selwyn Lloyd and six other Cabinet ministers in 1962), together with General DeGaulle's veto of Britain's application to the Common Market, seemed to underline the exhaustion of the party after a dozen years in office. The ascension of Sir Alec Douglas-Home after a divisive contest, then the defeat at the polls, spurred the sentiment that rejuvenation was needed.

In addition, the replacement of Home by Edward Heath shortly after the election marked a significant change in the nature of Tory leadership. A carpenter's son, Heath not only was the first party leader in a century to come from a lower middle-class background, but also had been the first to be chosen by something resembling a democratic procedure. Although not the most distinguished of the group of self-made men who had entered Conservative politics in the 1950s and were now taking charge, Heath was particularly interested in issues of policy. After serving under Home as chairman of the party's Advisory Committee on Policy, he retained the post until the end of 1968, when much of its work had been completed. During this period, a thorough look at Tory commitments, including support of the "welfare state," was undertaken with much fanfare, but few real results.

The focal point of the Conservative reassessment was the Economic Policy Group. One of some thirty committees composed of members of Parliament, peers, and outside experts, with staffing provided by the research department, the group was charged with finding ways to realize the central item of the party's platform: a higher rate of economic growth. In short order, its main interest became the reduction and reform of taxation. Reflecting the party's new middle-class ethos, the group's first report, as Nigel Fisher has written, was ". . . based on the premise that economic growth depends upon human energy and ingenuity and that the tax system in Britain has discouraged these qualities and therefore must be changed."[1] In 1965, the "shadow" Chancellor, Iain Macleod, told the party conference that "The key to the door of excellence lies in a modern taxation policy."[2] But even with the enormously ambitious techniques which the Conservatives ultimately employed—including a computerized trial of the effects of forty-eight tax packages on twenty-eight different types of households—the key was not easy to find.

Although the British tax burden was heavy, rather drastic reductions in public spending were first required in order to permit large savings through lower taxation. This presented a formidable political problem, which some Tories hoped to avoid at least in part by restructuring the ways British government raised revenue. "It is the tax system itself which is wrong," Macleod conceded privately, "and not the total tax burden."[3] Accordingly, the Economic Policy Group began to examine alternatives—a Value-Added Tax, a reform of corporate levies, modernizing the administration of the income tax, and even, for a time, a tax on wealth—which could maintain existing revenue-levels while being less destructive of risk-taking and other activities conducive to economic growth. By November 1968, a lengthy report on taxation had been presented to Heath, outlining, in Fisher's words, "an old Socialist dream—the transformation of society by means of the tax system."[4]

Not even a reformed tax system, many Tories agreed, would support the level of public spending Labour was establishing. Thus, some proposed to dispense with the seeming "extravagances" of government, particularly in the areas of health and education. But this idea ran into opposition from the party's leadership. Such cuts, they feared, would be less burdensome to the loyal Tory voter than to the "floater," whose support the party needed to return to power. Moreover, Heath, Macleod, Reginald Maudling and others now in charge had labored too hard to secure Conservative acceptance of the "welfare state" in the 1950s and were too committed to the Beveridge idea to agree to any major turnabout. A plan to replace grammar school subsidies with education vouchers was dismissed by Heath as a "return to 1870."[5]

Increasingly, Conservative thinking about government expenditures concentrated on reform rather than retrenchment. Many of the new recruits brought into the party by Heath had been successful businessmen; rather than eliminating public programs, they proposed to administer them better. (American innovations, like planning-programming-budgeting systems and policy evaluation staffs, attracted much interest.) Public spending was to become more selective and efficient. "The true problem in social policy," the party's 1970 manifesto declared, "is not that we spend too much but that with Labour stagnation we can afford too little."[6]

This was also how income support programs were being viewed. Initially, Heath seemed to be listening to the arguments put forth by Geoffrey Howe and the members of the Bow Group. In his first major address as leader, he told the annual party conference:

> After 20 years, the Welfare State, by its very success has made itself in part obsolete. People with higher incomes, with new horizons, with more time and more money and more opportunity to develop their family life are seeking a new approach to so many of the services which are provided

by the State. The old struggle to maintain the minimum standards is now receding into the past.[7]

A few months later, he outlined "a new charter for the social services" that proposed to "use our resources more flexibly, so that they are better directed to the real needs." A second goal was ". . . to lessen the dependency on the State and give back to individuals wherever we can the freedom and opportunity to provide for themselves."[8] Yet, immediately afterwards, Heath denied he was changing the Conservative Party's traditional reluctance to define "need" strictly in financial terms. The Tories, he averred, were not advocating a "means-test state," but "are extending the welfare state to help those who are at present overlooked, not abandoning it."[9]

Although most of the interest within the party was still devoted to pensions and the elderly, the evident difficulty the Labour Government was having with its own policy made the "pockets of poverty" an attractive opportunity for partisan attack. However, unless they were willing to earn the presumably harmful reputation of wanting to revive the means-test, the Conservatives could say little. Their references to "remodelling the welfare state" during the 1966 campaign had not been understood by the electorate and they seemed to have nothing more concrete to offer.[10]

Conservatives and the Negative Income Tax

With the Wilson Government's decisions to raise family allowances and to introduce clawback, the absence of a Conservative alternative became more embarrassing. Labour's complicated approach to selectivity was an easy target. Giving benefits to all while increasing taxes for most was a strategy, Tory spokesman Sir Marcus Worsley, said, which combined "the maximum of expense with the maximum of disincentive."[11] But he was quickly challenged by Labour's Douglas Houghton:

> HOUGHTON: Is the hon. Gentleman's remedy, therefore, to subsidize low wages?

> WORSLEY: No, my remedy is not to subsidize low wages. The right hon. Gentleman will know the history of the Speenhamland system and the difficulties into which it got.[12]

In the preceding two or three years, however, some of his colleagues had seemed to suggest exactly that. The "answer" to poverty that was due to low earnings, Sir Keith Joseph had written, "may well have to take the form of extra family allowances for these particular children paid through the Supplementary Benefits Commission."[13] Although other Conservatives had disavowed such intentions, they were still having difficulty saying precisely what they would do.

Fortunately, the discomfort of the Wilson Government with its own proposals eased the task of the opposition. But with little more than the suggestion that their own brand of selectivity would be more effective than Labour's, the Conservatives were scarcely in a position to exploit their advantage. In this context, the negative income tax again came under scrutiny.

Labour's proposal (and later abandonment) of the "minimum income guarantee" for the elderly had aroused Conservative interest in the possibility of using the income tax system to pay social benefits.[14] In November 1966, Brendon Sewill, director of the party's research department, published a description of such a scheme: the Automatic Unit for National Taxation and Insurance, or AUNTIE.[15] His concern was primarily for streamlining the public sector:

> Most families pay out in taxation, insurance contributions and local rates. In return, they receive back free health services, free education, free medicine, family allowances, school meals and school milk, possibly a housing subsidy and other social benefits such as paternity grants, widows' pensions, retirement pensions and ultimately death benefit. . . .
>
> The Ministry of Social Security, the Ministry of Health and the Inland Revenue together employ some 120,000 civil servants—five officials to every GP doctor! They cost the taxpayer at least £200 million a year—enough to build two hundred new hospitals every year, or to double our whole annual road building programme. Yet much of it goes in routine administration.[16]

By amalgamating all these operations and employing one large, central computer to record all transactions, duplication could be avoided and public spending reduced.

However, Sewill was not unmindful of AUNTIE's potential to concentrate social services on those in need, including large families with low incomes:

> At the beginning of this pamphlet an example was given of the number of forms involved in the process of childbirth. If AUNTIE were in existence, the notification of the pregnancy and a further notification of the birth would suffice. All the appropriate benefits would follow automatically—and the

pension, subject to a sufficient contribution record, would automatically be paid sixty or sixty-five years later.[17]

"Computermania," Titmuss dubbed the idea, as he dissected its "administrative, technical and real-life complexities."[18] Tax specialists, including Conservative ones, doubted that the procedures of the income tax could be used for paying welfare benefits, especially to people who were still in the labor force and whose earnings fluctuated. Nonetheless, the research department continued to work on the scheme and in 1967, Sewill himself travelled to the United States to study, among other things, American plans for a negative income tax.

Elsewhere in the policy baggage of the Conservative Party was another version of this idea. In 1960, Sir Brandon Rhys Williams, standing as a Conservative candidate for Parliament in Wales, promised to push for the enactment of the "social dividend" plan which he as a schoolboy had helped his mother develop. Although he did not enter the House of Commons until 1968, he vigorously promoted his proposal—now called the "new social contract"—within the party in connection with its reassessment of policy. Finally, Macleod gave in and appointed a special committee to study it.

As in 1951, the cost of providing everyone with benefits or tax credits equal to "basic needs" appeared too vast and the consequences of radically changing the income tax system too uncertain for the plan to be considered seriously. Moreover, the chief Conservative adviser on taxation, Sir Arthur Cockfield, was particularly indisposed toward it. As a member of the Board of Inland Revenue, he had presented the case against the "social dividend" to the Royal Commission on the Taxation of Profits and Income. As a member of Parliament, Rhys Williams continued to lobby for his mother's ideas, but while Tory backbenchers did become more familiar with it, they remained unconvinced.

The most fully developed proposal to emerge was unveiled just as clawback was being enacted in a party pamphlet entitled *Must the Children Suffer?*[19] The work of Barney Hayhoe, a mechanical engineer who had served in the Ministry of Aviation before joining the staff of the research department in 1965, it outlined a "family benefit scheme" that would have used the income tax system to pay a portion of the difference between a family's earnings and the amount at which its tax liability began. For most families, the size of the proposed grant would have been enough to lift them above the poverty-line, but at a cost below the £30 million which Labour planned to spend on family allowances after clawback. Only those who needed help would have received it; yet, it would have come not after a means-test, but automatically through PAYE—the mechanism through which most British employees paid their weekly or monthly tax bill. Since additional earnings would not have been offset by an equal decline in aid, the plan contained an incentive to work. The "family benefit scheme" was, in short, a negative income tax for families.

Despite Hayhoe's pamphlet, the Conservative leadership was still unsure about endorsing the idea. In part, this was because they were not certain it would really work. Although by confining the program to families who came under PAYE, Hayhoe had simplified the administrative problems of the negative income tax, considerable difficulties persisted, including the exclusion of the self-employed (who do not use PAYE), some 20 percent of the working poor.[20] Moreover, the lowering of the point at which tax liability commenced—a result of the 1968 and 1969 budgets—diminished the plan's attraction. In order to bring families above the poverty-line, the rate of payment would have to be increased, but this, in turn, meant that as a worker earned more, his net gain would be less, since the benefit would have to be withdrawn at a faster rate. Under these conditions, the likelihood that the "family benefit scheme" would actually reduce poverty without inducing dependency seemed doubtful.

In any case, many high-ranking Tories were uneasy about breaking with the tradition of not providing assistance based on need to anyone capable of self-support. Their indecision can be traced in the proceedings of the annual party conference. In 1968, the "family benefit" plan was included in a policy document, *Make Life Better*, and Heath told the audience, ". . . Let nobody underestimate the radical nature of the changes we propose . . . for handling family allowances."[21] The following year, there was hardly any reference. Although selectivity was again the theme of the social services debate, neither the negative income tax nor the working poor was mentioned in the leadership's summation. Instead, emphasis was placed on the contrast between the Conservatives' policy of individualism and Labour's alleged desire to promote dependence on the state. This may have been just mandatory pre-election posturing, but even in private meetings, such as the Selsdon Park conference at the beginning of 1970, no small number of future Tory Cabinet ministers and key advisers were prepared to assert that the Hayhoe Plan—and indeed, the other ways of aiding the working poor which had been discussed— were more likely to achieve their opponents' goals than their own.[22]

The Conservatives' dilemma—having an issue but no real alternative policy—was dramatically exposed during the budget debate just before the 1970 election. Responding to the Government's presentation, Macleod observed that the "main omission" of the budget was "any relief directly aimed at child poverty." He then summarized his party's view:

> The long-term answer, if there be one, is probably a form of negative income tax, or a device of that nature. I am certain that the Government has studied this. We have given a great deal of study to it, but we have not yet found a wholly satisfactory method of automatic identification, which would be its great advantage, of those below a given line.

"In the meantime," the Tory shadow Chancellor continued, ". . . although it quite likely is not a very popular thing to do, I think that if we operate in this matter we should do so on the family allowances with the claw-back."[23]

The Labour front bench was incredulous. Dick Taverne, a junior minister at the Treasury, challenged Macleod to rescind his previous characterization of clawback as ". . . a new principle and a thoroughly bad one."[24] He replied that in the short-term, and with the amount of money the government had to spend, "Although I do not like it, I believe [clawback] to be the right answer."[25] No doubt gratefully, Taverne averred this was the Chancellor's reasoning too. A month later, the press was reporting that if a Conservative government were elected, the elimination of child poverty using clawback as the vehicle, would be a main objective of its first budget.

For a party already under attack by Labour for having moved too far to the "Right," endorsement of the Wilson Government's own strategy for aiding the low-income family made political sense. If accused now of favoring a return to the "means-test state," the Tories would not have to begin a complex explanation of the negative income tax. In some areas, the reassessment of party policy had been fruitful; ideas for new pensions and housing legislation, as well as tax reforms, were ready in time for the election. However, on an issue that epitomized both the failings of the Beveridge plan and the Labour Party's exhaustion in social policy, six years of work in opposition had seemingly left the Conservatives with no distinctive proposal of their own to offer.

Republicans in Opposition

Nothing so elaborate as the Conservatives' policy reassessment occurred within the Republican Party. Indeed, in the 1960s, Republicans acted as though they hardly needed an official program at all; between quadrennial conventions, they even lacked a clear-cut leader. Only after they returned to office in 1969 did the task of devising specific proposals really begin.

Neither poverty nor dependency had been a major issue of the 1968 campaign. In fact, both parties had taken similar positions, differing primarily in their willingness to extol or decry the record of the previous eight years. The Republicans promised a drastic revision of welfare and poverty programs "to liberate the poor from the debilitating dependence which erodes self-respect and discourages family unity and responsibility." Their specific recommendations included more job training, extension of the 1967 amendments to the Social Security Act, and "creative and responsible participation" by the poor.[26]

The Democrats made a seemingly more radical pledge. "Every American family whose income is not sufficient to enable its members to live in decency" was to be given aid "free of the indignities and uncertainties that still too often mar our present programs." As a practical matter, however, this seemed to mean improvements in the Federal-state programs of public assistance and a repeal of the 1967 AFDC freeze (though not of the work-incentive measures, which were endorsed). For the working poor, the Democrats promised no more than to give "highest priority attention" to a "thorough evaluation" of proposals for income support.[27]

The candidate whose stand on social policy seemed most distinctive was not from either of the major parties, but rather was George C. Wallace, who campaigned as an independent. His was a platform of retrenchment, mixed with racism; he promised less government and at the same time stricter government, ready to curb the disorderly behavior of the 1960s. Although his record as governor of Alabama was not an illiberal one, his state was almost last in the generosity of its AFDC payments and his basic constituency was thought to consist of people strongly attached to the virtues of independence and self-support. In the 1968 election, Wallace carried only five states, but the size of his vote—13.5 percent nationwide—combined with that of the Republican victor was widely interpreted as a mandate *against* the goals and programs of the Great Society.

So far as anyone knew, the President-elect, Richard M. Nixon, was a traditionalist in matters of welfare policy. He was skeptical about the way public assistance was administered and suspected that the growth of dependency might be due to overly liberal standards. But the goals he had set out for welfare policy during the campaign were no different from those of his Democratic predecessors:

> First, it should meet the immediate needs of those who cannot help themselves—the poor, the disabled, the aged and

the sick. And it should do this in a way that preserves the dignity of the individual and the integrity of the family.

Second, it should offer opportunity and incentive, for those who can, to move off the welfare rolls onto private payrolls.[28]

The negative income tax had received some consideration within the Republican Party. Milton Friedman's version had come to the attention of a number of officials, including Representative Melvin R. Laird of Wisconsin, the chairman of the House Republican Conference, whom Nixon would choose as Secretary of Defense. The Ripon Society, a group of young and generally liberal Republicans, had endorsed the idea in 1967 as an alternative to "the mismanaged, miscellaneous, and ineffectual War on Poverty that has been put forth by the Johnson administration."[29] Yet, in May 1968, candidate Nixon told a meeting of the Association of American Editorial Cartoonists that while not ruling out such action, he did not see a "reasonable prospect" of his recommending a "guaranteed annual income or a negative income tax."[30] Although some advisers continued to urge him to back the idea, Nixon went no further than supporting Federal—implicitly, tighter—standards for the existing public assistance programs.

His pre-inaugural task force on public welfare—one of many appointed to develop proposals for the new Administration—endorsed this approach. Chaired by Richard P. Nathan, a liberal Republican on leave from the Brookings Institution, it was composed of people who had long been associated with the design and management of welfare policy. Its report of December 28, 1968, which canvassed a variety of possible ways to assist the poor, came down in favor of national standards for AFDC and the other public assistance programs, including a minimum benefit level. The recommended direction was toward complete Federal financing of welfare, reflecting the special interest of Nathan in reforming intergovernmental finance (and precisely opposite from the position of the Eisenhower Administration, which had wanted to increase the state and local role). The negative income tax and other structural changes were described as "longer-run alternatives" to be considered only if the more "incremental gains" recommended by the task force should prove unsatisfactory.[31]

In truth, the task force's agenda was hardly a cautious one. It would have added at least $1.5 billion to the federal share of expenditures for public assistance and substantially broadened the extent of national influence in the conduct of the program. But the agenda was also a familiar one, part of the unfinished business of welfare administrators, and signified the inability of the Republicans while out of

65

office to devise an alternative to a system that even the Johnson Administration had acknowledged was in need of fundamental change.

The Nixon Administration and the Welfare Crisis

Task forces are just one source of advice for an incoming administration. Also important are internal channels developed after the inauguration. As the first Republican government in eight years, the Nixon Administration was especially wary of relying on the Washington bureaucracies, not least among them the new array spawned by the Great Society. Accordingly, in his first executive order, Nixon created a White House staff arm called the Urban Affairs Council, which was intended to be a counterpart of the National Security Council. Its membership consisted of the Cabinet secretaries responsible for domestic programs; it possessed its own staff; and to direct it, Nixon chose Daniel P. Moynihan, a Democrat and prominent supporter of Robert F. Kennedy during the 1968 campaign, who was known to be critical of liberal dogma in social policy, especially its unwillingness to consider seemingly conservative ideas for reform. Moynihan's views implied a judgment of those who had governed during the 1960s; partly for that reason, and partly because Nixon lacked an approach of his own, the new President found Moynihan's ideas attractive.

At its first meeting, the President charged his new Council to formulate a policy:

> . . . [C]oherent, consistent positions as to what the national government would hope to see happen; what it will encourage, what it will discourage. Having a policy in urban affairs is no more a guarantor of success than having one in foreign affairs. But it is a precondition of success.

He also added: "We don't want the record written that we were too cautious."[22] His was to be an aggressive Republican administration; its actions were to be strategic, analytic, and coordinated.

More by circumstance than by design, welfare policy provided the first major test of this new approach. Even before his inauguration, Nixon had singled out the "welfare mess" for immediate action. In a letter to Moynihan and several other appointees, he demanded a thorough investigation:

> I do not want this swept under the rug or put aside on the ground that we want to have an "era of good feeling" with the bureaucrats as we begin. This whole thing smells to high heaven and we should get charging on it immediately.[33]

A subcommittee of the Urban Affairs Council was set up to work on the subject and to it was referred the report of the pre-inaugural task force. By February, an initial commitment had been made to the creation of national standards for public assistance. It was a feasible first step, and had the support of many of the nation's governors and mayors, whose case for relief from the increasingly burdensome costs of welfare had been effectively presented by Nelson A. Rockefeller, the leader of the Republican Party's liberal wing.

Also responsible for assessing the pre-inaugural reports was a member of the conservative wing, Arthur F. Burns, an economist and former official of the Eisenhower Administration, who held a seat in the Cabinet and a general brief to coordinate domestic policy. For him, and perhaps for most of those who had voted for Nixon, welfare reform meant reducing the number of people on relief. The recommendations of the Nathan group, Burns predicted, would have the opposite result, further increasing government spending and straining the national economy. He warned the President against hasty action.

Moynihan joined Burns in questioning whether the Administration should proceed with the task force's program. In a series of memoranda, he argued that the nation's welfare system was in such serious disarray that a major presidential initiative was required. Central to his message was a restatement of the thesis he had advanced nearly five years earlier while serving in the Department of Labor: AFDC was a program which discouraged work, weakened the family, and was having a grave effect on the social and economic status of blacks and hence, the entire nation. Although he supported national standards for public assistance, Moynihan also wanted to appoint a commission to study what had gone wrong with the existing programs.

This soon appeared to be unnecessary. As early as 1966, the policy planning staffs in the Office of Economic Opportunity and the Department of Health, Education, and Welfare (HEW) had discussed the possibility of devising a limited and less costly version of the negative income tax as a vehicle for reforming AFDC. By paying benefits only to needy families with children, such a plan could have replaced a portion of welfare payments with a national program that assisted the working poor too. A new set of principles, those of taxation, not relief, would be applied to both groups, perhaps as many as nineteen million people. "We believe," the staffs wrote in an internal document, ". . . this is an important beginning in the necessary work of dismantling the present welfare structure within a framework which aids rather than penalizes the beneficiaries of that system."[34]

Implied in this was the belief that an "income strategy" could be used to solve the problem of dependency as well as poverty. For the policy planners, the route to welfare reform lay not through rehabilitation but through changing the economic incentives facing the poor.

When the task force report was routinely referred to them for comment, the HEW planners had little reason not to submit their own proposal as an alternative approach. Most of these individuals expected to leave government service by the time the transition to a new administration had been completed; nothing would be lost by one last effort to promote the "income strategy." Moreover, the climate at HEW had changed perceptibly. The new leadership—Robert H. Finch as Secretary, and John G. Veneman, a former California legislator who had specialized in welfare matters, as Undersecretary—had no personal stake in defending New Deal programs and were sympathetic to the President's desire for bold measures. The proposals of the Nathan task force could easily have appeared any time during the preceding eight years; the negative income tax, as the planners well knew, could not. Its unorthodox quality, one of the idea's chief liabilities during the Johnson Administration, now loomed as one of its greatest assets.

Furthermore, this particular measure seemed not just bold but reasonable. It would be a step, the planners argued, towards federalizing welfare programs, while also getting rid of the now controversial requirement that only families headed by a female (or in some states, an unemployed male) were eligible for assistance. The right benefit level—$1,200 for a family of four with no other income had originally been suggested—would not only increase the incomes of most of the poor, but also provide additional Federal funds to states which already paid more through AFDC. In short, this version of the negative income tax had all the attractions of the Nathan task force proposals, and more—and at a not much greater cost (estimated at $2 billion in 1966).

With Finch and Veneman persuaded by the planning staff, a series of meetings was convened to convince others to support the scheme. (One consequence of these meetings was to increase the basic benefit to $1,500, an amount greater than the Federal share of AFDC costs in all but two states.) Nathan, who had joined the Administration as assistant director of the Bureau of the Budget with responsibility for "human resources" programs, was willing to forsake the recommendations of his task force when he saw that a more comprehensive scheme could be had at about the same cost. Similarly, Moynihan, one of the early proponents of the incentive theory, was prepared to urge it upon the Administration if only to assure that lesser measures, such as national standards for the existing programs, would not be lost. Others in the White House, however, were not so encouraging; for several months, the Republicans seemed to have a new idea for welfare policy but not the will to propose it.

The Debate Over the "Family Security System"

On March 24, 1969, Finch presented the program, named the "Family Security System" (FSS), to the welfare policy subcommittee of the Urban Affairs Council. Almost immediately, Burns' deputy, Martin Anderson, criticized it. FSS, he charged, was really a negative income tax and would not only have a detrimental impact on work incentives but also contravene Nixon's campaign position against the idea. Also present was Moynihan; confident that the President was beginning to appreciate the economic causes of welfare dependency, he challenged each of Anderson's arguments and implied that the idea might now interest Nixon. None of the other Cabinet members was so sure. What they did know was that Finch's plan seemed a far-reaching, politically ambitious, and potentially expensive venture, and no one was prepared to make a commitment without further study.

The weekend of April 5 had been set aside by Nixon to review proposals for his long-overdue domestic program. His interest in FSS had already been aroused by a memorandum from Moynihan:

> *The essential fact about the Family Security System is that it will abolish poverty for dependent children and the working poor.* The cost is not very great. *Because it is a direct payment system.* The tremendous costs of the poverty program come from *services. . . .*
>
> The Family Security System would enable you to begin cutting back sharply on these costly and questionable services, and yet to assert with full validity that it was under your Presidency that poverty was abolished in America.[35]

An outline of the plan was placed high in the briefing book for Nixon's review, together with a note from Moynihan reporting that FSS had not yet been approved by the Urban Affairs Council subcommittee. Adding his support was the President's long-time ally, Secretary Finch, who told him that FSS would be a "revolutionary" reform of the welfare system.[36]

As his aide had done, Arthur Burns opposed the plan on the grounds that it was a guaranteed income and would increase the number of Americans receiving assistance. (Anticipating this, Finch proposed to add an expanded job training program to complement FSS.) Although he recommended no major initiatives, Burns was known to favor the idea of revenue-sharing. Instead of providing

69

funds to state and local governments that were earmarked for specific uses, the Federal government under this plan would distribute a portion of its revenue and let governors and mayors decide how to spend it. Moynihan and others seized upon this notion to argue for FSS; just as the latter proposed to give income rather than direct services to the poor, revenue-sharing offered more money in place of particular programs to state and local officials. By combining the two, the Nixon Administration could have the makings of a distinctive and coherent approach to domestic policy, and, not unimportantly, Burns would have at least one major achievement to show for his tenure in the White House.

At the weekend meetings, the President apparently accepted this suggestion. His counsel, John D. Ehrlichman, relayed the news informally to Moynihan, who set his Urban Affairs Council staff to work at preparing the necessary documents. On April 14, Nixon informed Congress of his intention to submit a major reform of public assistance:

> Our studies have demonstrated that tinkering with the present welfare system is not enough. We need a complete reappraisal and re-direction of programs which have aggravated the troubles they were meant to cure, perpetuating a dismal cycle of dependency from one generation to the next. Therefore, I will be submitting to Congress a program for providing for reform of the welfare system.[37]

Within a week, newspapers began reporting the details of the Administration's "dramatic proposal."[38]

In fact, matters remained unsettled in the White House. Partly by design and partly because of the press of other events, Nixon allowed the task of translating FSS into a legislative program to become an occasion for opening up issues of policy and for involving participants from within and outside his Administration. This semi-public dispute among his aides conveyed a lasting impression, especially among Republican conservatives, that Nixon was really undecided about the plan in the first place. Of more immediate consequence, a presidential message on FSS was not delivered for four months, and a proposal was not ready to go to Congress for six.

Once again, Arthur Burns took the lead. In a memorandum to the President on April 21, entitled "Investing in Human Dignity: A Study of the Welfare Problem," he repeated his now familiar judgment of FSS:

> The so-called Family Security System is a plan for guaranteeing incomes of people. In its technical form, it is simply a

specific application of the negative income tax, as formulated by Milton Friedman.

He was concerned about the shift in principle which this decision implied, away "from a welfare policy aimed at those who cannot help themselves" and "toward a policy of income maintenance." According to his own analysis, the rise in welfare rolls was due to higher benefits and lax administration, and would soon pass away. FSS, he predicted, was likely to cost the President political support, not least because a scheme so complex and unfamiliar would be easy to misrepresent. Instead, Burns urged Nixon to consider adopting some of the recommendations of the Nathan task force, along with a program of job training and placement for the "welfare-prone." Special emphasis should also be given to enforcing the work-requirements of the 1967 Social Security Act amendments.[39]

Others offered different advice. From Moynihan, the President continued to receive memoranda extolling the virtues of incentives and the "income strategy." Finch and Veneman persisted in their advocacy of the plan and assigned some of those who helped design FSS to the White House technical group that was wrestling with its costs and other technical details. At meetings of the Urban Affairs Council, Nixon heard civil rights leaders and mayors emphasize the urgent need for replacing the existing welfare system; a private poll of businessmen, as well as newspaper and magazine commentary, made the same point. Allied with those favoring FSS was nearly a decade's concern about the problems of poverty and dependency which had produced, at least among the highly selective group that was consulted, a willingness to endorse the kind of bold plan the President had before him. At a Cabinet-level review on April 26, the Administration's top officials, though mindful of the expense and the possible political risks, agreed to press on with the scheme. "It may be," legislative counsel, Bryce Harlow, concluded after a pessimistic review of the plan's Congressional prospects, "this is a crisis decision."[40]

Indeed, the fate of FSS would rest on its acceptability to Congress and public opinion. If new options in welfare policy suddenly seemed appealing in the White House and the conference rooms of business groups like the Committee for Economic Development, the readiness of legislators and the public to depart from well-established traditions concerning aid to the poor could not be assumed. To the contrary, a Cabinet composed mostly of cautious men was more prone to think that the objections raised by Burns and others would be especially forceful on Capitol Hill and in the nation. For that reason, if for no other, answers had to be found.

71

This task ultimately fell to George P. Shultz, a former colleague of Milton Friedman at the University of Chicago and now Secretary of Labor. In May, he was asked by the President to provide an independent assessment of the plan. His report, delivered on June 10, began by asserting: "The AFDC program has brought the welfare system to the point where it is less a solution than a contributor to dependency." FSS, in contrast, "seeks to restore to the welfare system the purpose of reducing dependency," Shultz noted, "by including the male *in* rather than forcing him out, by supplementing the earnings from low-wage employment, and by building a Federal floor." As then constituted, however, it did not seem to offer sufficient incentives for recipients to enter or stay at work.

Accordingly, Shultz recommended two principal changes. Both had already been authorized for AFDC recipients in the 1967 amendments: a fixed allowance for work expenses and expanded training and day care programs. Along with penalties for those who refused suitable employment and retraining provisions for some of the working poor, these additions would have added over $1 billion to the cost of FSS, but without them, Shultz warned, the new reform plan would be "wasted":

> The initial acceptance and long-range success of this program will depend in large part on the extent to which the American people believe that the FSS approach will not seriously erode the incentive to work, but rather would strengthen it.
> Welfare reform has two sides—welfare payments and work incentives. The combined objective is to have people move up and out of poverty, and into the freedom of self-sustaining jobs.[41]

In effect, the Labor Secretary had added rehabilitative and preventive measures of the sort long favored by welfare professionals and implicit in Burns' arguments. Although FSS was still unmistakably a product of the "income strategy," it now had a rationale and features which gave it some continuity with more traditional beliefs about welfare reform.

The Proposal of FAP

The Shultz memorandum effectively ended the debate on policy in the White House. Although Nixon also had an option, fashioned by Paul W. McCracken, chairman of the Council of Economic Advisers, that outlined a series of modest changes in the existing assistance programs, he chose the more radical and expensive plan put together by Shultz. His decision had much to do with the nature and politics of welfare in 1969.

In the less than six months his Administration had been in office, the growth-rate of the welfare rolls had accelerated. By the end of 1969, nearly two million families would be on relief, an increase of one-quarter million within a year.[42] State and local officials—no longer exclusively from the Northeast and the Far West—as well as businessmen and others were urging Nixon to give high priority to welfare reform. Under Moynihan's tutelage, he had also come to see that the design of AFDC was itself a contributor to the problem of dependency. It seemed a prime example of the sort of well-meaning but counter-productive government program which had seemingly enraged so many of November's voters.

In FSS, Nixon thought he had an acceptable substitute. It was not AFDC, but it was also, the Administration would maintain, not a "guaranteed income." By incorporating the changes suggested by Shultz, FSS would be a program emphasizing jobs, not income support. The President could say he was proposing not a negative income tax but rather a new form of assistance for families with children which increased the number receiving aid while also improving their incentives to obtain or remain in employment. To be sure, there was an element of self-deception here; no one at the White House could really be confident that FSS would not weaken work incentives instead of enhancing them. Yet whatever happened, AFDC seemed certain to make the welfare crisis worse.

Another matter was nearly as predictable. The Democrats controlled Congress and could be expected to persist in trying to expand the programs of the Great Society. The Nixon Administration could either resist, seeking to curtail public spending, or it could try to preempt Congressional action with a proposal of its own. Moynihan urged the latter course:

> I am really pretty discouraged about the budget situation in the coming three to five years. I fear you will have nothing like the options I am sure you hoped for. Even more, I fear that the pressure from Congress will be nigh irresistible to use up what extra resources you have on a sort of ten percent across-the-board increase in all the Great Society programs each year. . . .
>
> Therefore I am doubly interested in seeing you go up now with a genuinely new, unmistakably Nixon, unmistakably needed program. . . . We can afford the Family Security System. Once you have asked for it, you can resist the pressures

endlessly to add marginal funds to already doubtful programs.[43]

President Johnson's Commission on Income Maintenance Programs, he also advised, was preparing to recommend a scheme like FSS within a few months. A less ambitious plan from the White House would inevitably risk seeming feeble and being ignored.

As vice-president under Eisenhower, Nixon had not lacked opportunity to observe the political hazards of a policy based on budgetary restraint. Nor had he sought to become president in order to ratify the decisions of a Democratic Congress. Moreover, the first months of his term were a period of ascendance for men like Moynihan, Finch, and particularly, Shultz; Burns was in a kind of limbo, en route to the chairmanship of the Federal Reserve System's Board of Governors. By championing the Shultz plan, Nixon and the Republican Party could at last claim credit for a major, even historic, initiative in social policy, and one that their opponents might have produced in any event.

Before the end of June, the President had instructed his aides to draft a bill and a message based on the report of the Secretary of Labor. However, within his Administration the arguments continued. Burns and other senior officials now objected to FSS on the ground that it was too costly to propose at a time when the Administration was committed to cutting back on public spending. (With the additions proposed by Shultz, an increase in the benefit level to $1,600, and a new formula to provide more "fiscal relief" to state and local governments, the price of the plan approached $6 billion.) The Vice-President, Spiro T. Agnew, judged that the proposal "will not be a political winner" and would be called "niggardly" in comparison to the far more expensive versions the Democrats would immediately put forth.[44] This proved to be a reasonably accurate prediction, just as the questions raised by Martin Anderson and others in the staff meetings dealing with the technical features of the measure reappeared after it had gone to Congress. But the moment for reconsideration had passed. Staying with the existing welfare system was costly too, both financially and politically. The efforts of opponents of FSS to reverse the President's decision now served only to delay it.

At the final Cabinet meeting before the plan was revealed to the public, Nixon himself took charge and instructed the junior officials in attendance to explain the rise in welfare dependency and the advantages of the proposed reform. He next sought the views of his Secretaries, Budget director, and other advisers. Most could be described as, at best, lukewarm toward the idea, some still did not understand it, and a few repeated their well-known objections to it. The

President announced that he was not prepared to continue the existing welfare system and would proceed with the plan. No further compromises would be made; nothing would be changed but the program's name. "Family Security System," complained Melvin Laird, who supported the proposal, seemed too "New Dealish"; the next day, a speechwriter invented the less traditional title, "Family Assistance Plan."[45] Although the Cabinet remained divided, the decision stood. In a nationally televised address on August 8, 1969, Nixon announced he was offering a replacement for the existing welfare system, the like of which no one would have predicted when he was elected.

The Proposal of FIS

In Britain, the triumph of the negative income tax was not nearly so difficult. When the Conservatives returned to office in June 1970, they were unsure what they would propose to do for families in poverty. By the end of October, without much debate inside the Government, they had produced a plan.

As in 1966, both major parties thought family poverty was important enough to mention in their election manifestos. Labour promised to "review the present system of family allowances and income tax child allowances," while the Conservatives pledged to "tackle the problem of family poverty and ensure that adequate family allowances go to those families that need them."[46] Largely at Barney Hayhoe's insistence, however, Macleod had prevailed upon the shadow Cabinet to include a codicil:

> A scheme based on the negative income tax would allow benefits to be related to family need; other families would benefit by reduced taxation. The Government have exaggerated the administrative problems involved, and we will make a real effort to find a practical solution. If this can be done, it will increase incentive for those at work, and bring much-needed help to children living in poverty.[47]

This was hardly a strong commitment, and little was made of it during the campaign.

Moreover, on June 1, Heath had responded to a request from the Child Poverty Action Group (CPAG) to clarify the party's pledge on family poverty by reaffirming Macleod's budget-debate statement in favor of clawback. The Conservative leader added:

> In the future it may be possible to introduce some kind of negative income tax which would provide more help for the

families that need it, while other families would benefit by reduced taxation. This needs a good deal more examination by experts before a firm commitment can be made.[48]

If this reply caused some disappointment at the research department, it nonetheless served the purpose of assuring that CPAG would continue to criticize Labour, particularly after Wilson, in response to the same request, referred the group to his Government's record. And only those who were attentive to the issue of family poverty—in the campaign of 1970, as in earlier ones, not a large group—would have realized that the Conservatives were still confused over selectivity.

Events immediately after the Tories' unexpected victory further muddled the new Government's intentions. Little more than a month after the election, Iain Macleod died. His replacement as Chancellor was Anthony Barber, the party's chairman and the first tax lawyer to preside over the Exchequer since the Second World War. Unlike Macleod, though, he had not been greatly involved in the reassessment of Conservative policy and had made no specific commitments regarding welfare programs.

In addition, Heath had somewhat surprisingly asked Sir Keith Joseph to become Secretary of the Department of Health and Social Security (DHSS). Although Joseph had briefly served as opposition spokesman for social services, since October 1965 he had been chiefly concerned with employment and industry and was thought likely to head the Board of Trade. Regarded as one of the party's ideologists, he had been active in the policy study groups, albeit not usually in those dealing with welfare programs. Insofar as his views on these matters were known, they seemed close to the ideas of the Bow Group and the neo-Liberals, but moderated both by his background— his family had established a charitable foundation—and by his constituency, the manufacturing city of Leeds.

Shortly after taking office, the Conservatives also learned that the party's main commitment for aiding the poor was likely to prove unworkable. Although the Labour Government had not concealed the problem, it was only after the election, when the senior members of the civil service began to brief their new superiors, that the Heath Government came to understand how a new round of clawback would take benefits away precisely from the families who needed them most. In order to use clawback to concentrate an increase in family allowances on the needy, the Conservatives would have to raise the point at which tax liability started (for example, by hiking up personal tax deductions). This would be almost as costly as simply boosting family allowances for everyone and would likely prevent a quick reduction in the income tax rate, the major priority. The scheme Heath and Macleod had endorsed because it seemed to be the only feasible one now appeared to be improbable.

On the other hand, the proposals which the Conservatives had all but given up on started to acquire new life. In the customary fashion, the election of a new government had set the civil service at work translating the language of its election manifesto into position papers. Orders went from Whitehall to the party's central office for copies of *Must the Children Suffer?*, while Hayhoe, who had won a seat in the House of Commons, was consulted about the discussions of family poverty in opposition. During the preceding six years, the civil service had also invested considerable effort in studying the potential of the negative income tax and, if anything, had a more pessimistic opinion of its feasibility than did the Tories. Not just the Treasury and Inland Revenue, but also DHSS agreed that even if a workable scheme could be devised, the negative income tax offered the prospect of vast changes in public programs for relatively limited improvements in government performance. Of all the manifesto items, the endorsement of still more study of this idea was among the least welcomed in Whitehall. With a program of tax reform already on the agenda, plus intimations of reorganizations for the social services and central government, the civil service felt the Conservatives had presented it with enough to do.

Nonetheless, the Heath Government had promised to deal with family poverty, and it took the commitment seriously. In office, Sir Keith Joseph compensated for his lack of exposure to the issue during opposition by an eagerness to take action rapidly and a willingness to consider a fresh approach once he had been shown that clawback was no longer useful. One possibility was simply to increase family allowances, but since not much of a raise could be afforded, many families would remain below the poverty-line. Furthermore, since this benefit went only to families with two or more children, no help at all would go to one-child families, who made up one-third of the working poor and were of special concern to the new Secretary. CPAG again proposed replacing children's tax deductions with larger family allowances, modified to include the single-child family. However, even this, at a minimum net cost of £80 million, was far more than what the Government was prepared to spend.[49]

Another option emerged from civil service efforts to solve a related problem. To prevent Supplementary Benefits from encouraging low-paid workers to quit their jobs, a provision known as the "wage-stop" precluded those who had exhausted their unemployment insurance from receiving more in public assistance than they had previously earned, even if this was below the "minimum requirements" as judged by the Supplementary Benefits Commission. Since that standard was the generally accepted poverty-line, the wage-stop amounted to government-sanctioned impoverishment of the jobless, and was widely disliked. To avoid using it during the periods of prolonged unemployment of the 1960s, different procedures for calculating wages were studied, as were "earnings-related equivalents" of Supplementary Benefits scales. Providing means-tested assistance to full-time workers had also been discussed, but was abandoned in light of the problem of maintaining incentives and the Labour Government's lack of enthusiasm for such measures.

After the Conservatives were elected, Hayhoe's scheme and another version of the negative income tax developed by D. S. Lees, a University of Nottingham economist who had studied at the University of Chicago, suggested a solution.[50] By providing aid equal to just a portion of the gap between a worker's normal earnings and a modified Supplementary Benefits scale (instead of, in Hayhoe's plan, the income tax threshold), total income in employment could be lifted above the "minimum requirements." At the same time, an increase in wages would always result in a reduction of less than the same amount in assistance. Without much difficulty, the program could be run by the Supplementary Benefits Commission and be extended to aid the one-child family. If adopted, such a plan would assure that far fewer workers were subject to the wage-stop and that all families in poverty would realize an increase in their standard of living.

Called a "supplementary family allowance," the idea was outlined to Joseph in July. Once he had advocated a similar scheme, which even his own party had disavowed.[51] Now he could argue that his civil servants had managed to give substance to the Conservative principle of selectivity. (DHSS officials were not unaware of what was happening in the United States; however, a request to the American embassy for details about FAP failed to elicit information for nine months, by which time it was no longer useful.) As it was likely that an October budget would contain both tax reductions and the imposition of user charges for some of the social services, making good as soon as possible on the pledge of more aid for the neediest was a matter of some political consequence. The plan devised by Joseph's bureaucracy not only was the most practical way but also promised to be the least costly. After six years of fruitless study in opposition, to have produced a solution to the problem of family poverty so quickly would be a coup for someone who had come unexpectedly to the subject, and to his department.

The scheme which Joseph approved was not as elaborate as most of those which had been discussed, and this was a considerable advantage. Since it was no more than a response to the narrow problem of the low-paid worker, the proposal aroused little concern either in Whitehall or in the Cabinet. Its passage through the Home and Social Affairs Committee of the Cabinet was uneventful; indeed, Joseph's colleagues were generally delighted that a potentially troublesome election commitment could be redeemed so swiftly and at a cost of only £8 million, one-quarter of what Macleod had estimated for clawback. (Joseph's main issue in Cabinet was his proposal for an annual review and uprating of pensions, a far more expensive undertaking.) The procedures of the Inland Revenue were not to be affected by it, nor were the fiscal controls of the Chancellor to be complicated by any linkage of taxes and social security payments. While some older Tories, like Lord Hailsham (Quintin Hogg), muttered about Speenhamland, younger ones viewed the plan as either a first step toward restructuring social benefits completely, or as a major achievement in its own right. Although Heath was largely uninvolved in the deliberations, he apparently held the latter opinion, for he would refer to the plan later as a "radical new measure, which brings help in a most effective way to those who really need it."[52] Renamed the Family Income Supplement (FIS) to be more euphonious, the Conservatives' new approach to aiding the poor, which had seemed so hard to discern when they entered office in June, was laid before the House of Commons on October 27.

Conclusion

With the proposal of FAP in the United States and FIS in Britain, the Republican and Conservative parties assumed the unaccustomed role of initiating a change in social policy, virtually for the first time since the advent of the "welfare state" in each country. From their period out of office in the 1960s, neither seemed likely to do this. Although the Conservatives searched for new ways of helping the poor, they never quite succeeded in finding any. The Republicans were not set up to do so and hardly tried at all.

However, each party returned to office at a time of mounting discontent with the existing programs. In the United States, an atmosphere of crisis turned welfare reform into an issue of urgent priority for the incoming Nixon Administration. If matters were not quite so grave in Britain, Labour's record in aiding the poor had nevertheless been a vulnerable spot which the Tories had exploited in fashioning their surprising victory at the polls. Moreover, the Heath Government shared the view that misguided and excessive social spending was a contributing factor in the nation's economic malaise. Although neither the Republicans nor the Conservatives were inclined to question the popularity of most aspects of welfare policy, trying to fix that part which was in the greatest disrepair and which their predecessors had been unable to improve (to say the least) was an opportunity too attractive to resist.

But what to do? In each country, the answer ultimately came from within the government. Sensitive to the political changes that had brought the two parties to power, bureaucrats in the United States and Britain revived ideas that had been discussed in the preceding years, adapted them to the views of the elected officials now in charge, and advocated them as solutions to problems regarded as most pressing. In this sense, FAP and FIS were indeed "civil servants' bills."[53]

Yet they were also more than that. In fact, in each country, important elements in the bureaucracies had been *opposed* to the negative income tax when it was first broached. That FAP and FIS were not full-blown versions of such a tax helped. Neither seemed as complicated or costly as the original idea. Since the plan was to be limited to families and administered as a welfare, not a tax, program, its radical nature was made to appear more conventional.

Even so, FAP and FIS were departures from the longstanding tradition of not giving assistance based on need to the able-bodied poor. The reason two presumably cautious governments agreed to this departure was that the logic of the incentive theory made it seem consistent with traditional goals. To be sure, people capable of self-support were to be given money. But this was to be done through a formula that would encourage them to become less dependent. Indeed, under the new programs, even those who had always been considered eligible for relief—mothers with children, the long-term unemployed—would have a financial reason to look for work. Understood this way, the aim of FAP and of FIS was not to establish a new objective for welfare policy but rather to create a new and possibly better way of achieving old objectives.

To Republican and Conservative politicians accustomed to playing second fiddle in matters of social reform, the novelty of this approach was its greatest appeal. Unlike their predecessors, they were not tied by bonds of parentage to the existing "welfare state." They wanted to do something, and only lacked agreement as to what. To them, FAP and FIS afforded a chance to make a stunning innovation in welfare policy while maintaining fidelity to its widely accepted virtues.

Notes

1. Nigel Fisher, *Iain Macleod* (1973), p. 264.
2. Quoted by Fisher, p. 265.
3. Quoted by David Butler and Michael Pinto-Duschinsky, *The British General Election of 1970* (1971), p. 72.
4. Fisher, p. 305.
5. Quoted by Butler and Pinto-Duschinsky, p. 71.
6. *A Better Tomorrow: The Conservative Programme for the Next 5 Years* (1970), p. 6.
7. National Union of Conservative and Unionist Associations, *Verbatim Report of 83rd Annual Conference* (1965), p. 126.
8. *The Sunday Times* (London), February 6, 1966, p. 4.
9. *The Times* (London), February 10, 1966, p. 5.
10. David Butler and Anthony King, *The British General Election of 1966* (1966), pp. 189–90.
11. Great Britain, *Hansard's Parliamentary Debates* (Commons), 762 (April 2, 1968), col. 277.
12. Ibid., col. 281.
13. Sir Keith Joseph, *Social Security: The New Priorities* (1966), p. 26.
14. Geoffrey Howe, *In Place of Beveridge?* (1965), p. 4.
15. Hilary Sewill, *AUNTIE* (1966), p. 4. Concerned that the idea was too radical even for some Conservatives, it was credited to the real author's wife.
16. Ibid., pp. 3–4.
17. Ibid., p. 7.
18. Richard M. Titmuss, *Commitment to Welfare* (1968), p. 116.
19. Barney Hayhoe, *Must the Children Suffer? A New Family Benefit Scheme* (1968), pp. 10–19.
20. *Hansard*, 762 (April 2, 1968), col. 187.
21. National Union of Conservative and Unionist Associations, *Verbatim Report of 86th Annual Conference* (1968), p. 126.
22. Author's personal interviews with participants.
23. *Hansard*, 799 (April 15, 1970), cols. 1,399–1,400.
24. *Hansard*, 761 (March 20, 1968), col. 437.
25. *Hansard*, 799 (April 15, 1970), col. 1,413.
26. "Complete Text of the 1968 Republican Platform," *1968 Congressional Quarterly Almanac*, pp. 989–90.
27. "Complete Text of the 1968 Democratic Platform," ibid., p. 1,037.
28. Cited in Report to President-Elect Nixon by Task Force on Public Welfare, "Programs to Assist the Poor" (December 28, 1968), p. 4.
29. "The Negative Income Tax: A Ripon Research Paper," *The Ripon Forum* (April 1967), p. 1.
30. Richard M. Nixon, Audio Transcript of Remarks to Meeting of the American Association of Editorial Cartoonists (May 17, 1968), p. 6.
31. Report to President-Elect Nixon by Task Force on Public Welfare (December 28, 1968), p. 20.

32. Quoted by Daniel Patrick Moynihan, *The Politics of a Guaranteed Income* (1973), p. 74.

33. Quoted by Franklin D. Raines, "Presidential Policy Development: The Genesis of the Family Assistance Plan" (1971), pp. 5–6.

34. Ibid., p. 42. These ideas had already influenced the work incentive portions of the 1968 amendments to the Social Security Act.

35. Moynihan, *The Politics of a Guaranteed Income*, pp. 147–48.

36. Raines, p. 66.

37. U.S., President, *Weekly Compilation of Presidential Documents* (April 21, 1969), p. 559.

38. Cited by Moynihan, *The Politics of a Guaranteed Income*, pp. 165–66.

39. Ibid., pp. 181 and 183.

40. Ibid., p. 172. The President was not present.

41. George P. Shultz, Memorandum for the President (June 10, 1969), pp. 1 and 11.

42. U.S., Bureau of the Census, *Statistical Abstract of the United States* (93d ed.; 1972), p. 299.

43. Moynihan, *The Politics of a Guaranteed Income*, p. 176.

44. Spiro T. Agnew, "Welfare Reform," Memorandum for the President (August 4, 1969), p. 3.

45. Cited in Moynihan, *The Politics of a Guaranteed Income*, p. 216.

46. For Labour, see, *Now Britain's Strong—Let's Make it Great to Live In* (1970), p. 20; for the Conservatives, see, *A Better Tomorrow*, p. 23.

47. *A Better Tomorrow*, p. 22. Hayhoe was a principal drafter of the manifesto.

48. "Correspondence with the Prime Minister," *Poverty*, no. 16/17 (n.d.), 30.

49. Peter Townsend and Tony Atkinson, "The Advantages of Universal Family Allowances," *Poverty*, no. 16/17 (n.d.), 18–19.

50. D. S. Lees, "Poor Families and Fiscal Reform," *Lloyds Bank Review* (October 1967), pp. 1–15.

51. Joseph, p. 26. Joseph's proposal did not make any reference to work incentives.

52. Edward Heath, Speech at the Free Trade Hall, Manchester (February 20, 1974), p. 6.

53. The phrase was used by Richard Crossman during the debate over FIS. See, *Hansard*, 806 (November 10, 1970), col. 260.

5

Incentives and Disincentives

Of all the circumstances surrounding the proposal of the Family Assistance Plan (FAP) and the Family Income Supplement (FIS), perhaps none was more extraordinary than the willingness of two different governments to stake their reputations upon what was, in truth, an unproven theory. Neither British nor American policy-makers could really be sure that an incentive policy would succeed. Indeed, in the United States, hardly any evidence existed to support the view that the growth of dependency was due to the nature of the existing welfare programs. Nonetheless, both Richard M. Nixon and Edward Heath were prepared to make radical departures in social policy on the assumption that offering a financial reward to work would induce FAP and FIS recipients to do so.

This was a lesson that could reasonably be drawn from the Speenhamland experience.[1] Although it provided aid to the able-bodied, Britain's Napoleonic-era welfare system did not reward efforts at self-support. For every extra amount earned, an equal amount of assistance was taken away. In the economist's terminology, the program entailed a "benefit-reduction rate" (or "marginal tax rate") of 100 percent for additional income. It made sense to suppose that a lower tax rate would not have such debilitating effects. Just that idea governed FAP and FIS.

However, no one really knew what rate was necessary to forestall dependency. Both FAP and FIS assumed it was about 50 percent, largely because that seemed "right" and easy to understand. But applied to the other end of the income distribution, a levy of that magnitude would be close to the maximum deemed feasible, if not above it. Even worse, at the lower end, the *real* tax rate was apt to be greater than 50 percent. In addition to losing a portion of FAP or FIS benefits as they earned more money, the working poor might have to pay social insurance and, possibly, income taxes, as well as face a decline in aid from other programs (such as food stamps in the United States or rent rebates in Britain) for which they were eligible. When fully calculated, the net gain from extra effort could turn out to be uninspiringly small.

In any event, just as plausible as the theory that people would seize any opportunity to earn more money was the alternative view that they were more interested in attaining a "satisfactory" level of income. Even with the right incentives, work would not be all gains and no losses; it would mean less leisure time, accepting job rules and other restrictions, and, particularly for the low-paid, a certain amount of unpleasantness. If their current income met their needs, economists speculated, many people might decide not to seek more. And if a government program provided part of the desired amount, so much the better. How those eligible for FAP and FIS would react was impossible to predict, but the chance existed that financial incentives might not be enough to prevent welfare dependency.

Because of the mathematics of the negative income tax, not even lowering the marginal tax rate was sure to be an improvement. At any particular benefit level, strengthening the incentive to work necessarily meant increasing the number of people who were eligible for at least some assistance. Thus, a negative income tax paying $2,000 to a family with no other income and with a benefit-reduction rate of 50 percent would provide help to all families with less than $4,000 in earnings; if the rate dropped to 25 percent, it would cover everyone with an income up to $8,000, a much larger number. The rewards for extra effort would be greater in the latter case, but more people would be tempted not to try by the availability of public support. Although a smaller, initial benefit could mitigate this problem, it would inevitably lead to charges of insufficient generosity toward the most needy.

The designers of FAP and FIS generally knew of these issues. In light of the apparent lack of better ways to aid the poor, they judged the possibility that the incentive theory would not work to be a risk worth taking. However, the political success of FAP and FIS would depend on the ability of these policy-makers to persuade others to agree. In the United States, the separation of powers between the executive and legislative branches (and party control) made the enactment of FAP problematic. In Britain, although the Parliamentary majority enjoyed by the Heath Government assured the passage of FIS, it could not safeguard it from criticism. Under this scrutiny, the "disincentives" of each measure became the focus of attention, creating a major obstacle for FAP and seriously wounding FIS. This chapter will explain what happened.

FAP and FIS

The measures proposed in the United States and Britain seemed uncomplicated. FAP was to guarantee every American family a minimum income based on its size and need. For example, a family of four with no other income would be assured $1,600; each additional member (up to a total family size of seven) would be worth an extra $300. In determining need, the first sixty dollars per month of earnings would not be counted; thereafter, one dollar of aid would be subtracted for every two dollars of wages, a tax rate of 50 percent. A family of four would thus be able to receive some help until its income passed $3,920 per year, which was approximately the official poverty-line. The typically larger poor family could earn even more without losing all aid.

FIS employed the same principles in a slightly different manner. Whereas FAP was available to all families, its British counterpart was only for the working poor. It also provided extra income based on family size and need. For example, a family of four would be eligible for a grant equal to half the difference between its earnings and a "prescribed amount," which was set initially at twenty pounds per week; each additional child increased the income ceiling by two pounds. To limit program costs, a maximum benefit of three pounds per week (raised to four shortly after FIS was proposed) was set. Since the official "minimum requirements" for a four-person family were just below fourteen pounds, FIS assured that such families with at least eleven pounds in earnings would not be poor, while Supplementary Benefits gave the same guarantee to those without anyone able to work.

Yet, if relatively straightforward to calculate, FAP and FIS were far more difficult to implement. In the United States, some of the problems lay in design: what was "income," how often should need be assessed, who were the members of the "family," and so on. Although these were not unfamiliar questions to students of the negative income tax, putting answers into legislative language was a new experience. Ultimately, many matters were not decided at all, but were left to the discretion of the Secretary of Health, Education and Welfare (HEW) and the Social Security Administration, which was to run the program.

As a result, operational details reflected the relatively liberal standards of the welfare professionals. Eligibility for FAP, for example, was to be determined by a simple declaration of need. Mothers with preschool children—a sizable proportion of the projected recipients— were not to be required to register for work or training. (The 1967 amendments to the Social Security Act had allowed no exceptions.) The penalty for others who failed to register, $300, was even less than the one under the existing law (which provided that an uncooperative individual's *needs* would not be considered in computing a family's AFDC grant). So remote had been the prospects for a guaranteed in-

come that the only way anyone could think of running the new program was like the old.

For a somewhat different reason, liberal standards finally prevailed in Britain too. Unlike the proposals of Hayhoe and others, FIS
did not operate "automatically." Families eligible for it would have to
submit a special application to obtain assistance; no large computer
would be sifting tax returns to determine who should pay and who
should receive. If, as a result, benefits would not be claimed by many
of those who needed them, the Tory version of selectivity might turn
out to be no more efficient at reducing poverty than the universally
obtainable program of family allowances.

In the hope of encouraging the working poor to "take up" FIS,
the Department of Health and Social Security (DHSS) sought to make
the getting of it as easy as possible. To verify their income, for example, applicants would have to show only five pay slips; employers
would not be queried. Single-page forms were to be available in post
offices and mailed to a central location for processing. Once approved, the benefit would not normally be reviewed again for six—
later, twelve— months, regardless of fluctuations in earnings. A publicity campaign would be mounted to urge eligible families to apply,
and, to avoid any political interference with the program, the independent Supplementary Benefits Commission would oversee it. The
guiding principle of FIS, British officials would say, was to be "rough
justice," not the scrupulous regard for individual needs and resources
that was normally associated with means-tested assistance.

Because it did not duplicate any existing programs, FIS was
spared one set of complications that persistently vexed its American
counterpart. FAP was meant not just to assist the working poor but
also to put a Federal floor under public assistance benefits. However,
in all but eight states, AFDC provided grants above the FAP maximum. Should these forty-two be required to supplement the national
guarantee even though the Federal government would no longer
share in any costs of public assistance beyond those of FAP itself? In
proposing the measure, Nixon pledged that no AFDC family would
be harmed by the change and that every state would be able to reduce
its spending on welfare by at least 10 percent. Even with the $1 billion
revenue-sharing program he announced at the same time, accomplishing these twin goals would not be simple.

A related issue concerned the working poor. Although not generally eligible for welfare, some did take advantage of other forms of
assistance, especially food stamps, which, in 1969, were worth as
much as $800 per year to a family of four. Were such programs to be
continued? Or should they be included in FAP's cash grant, as Friedman's original design for a negative income tax contemplated? Torn

between interest groups, such as the farm lobby, which wanted to preserve programs subsidizing particular expenditures, and the policy planners, who were in favor of a single, efficient system of income support, the Nixon Administration was unsure. After some public vacillation, it opted for keeping the in-kind programs. (The British government made a similar choice in continuing and later expanding rent rebates, a housing allowance for low-income people who did not live in publicly-owned housing). The working poor, as well as AFDC families, would thus be able to add food stamps to the help they received from FAP. Though at the price of increased complexity, the Nixon Administration was able to say it was providing assistance more generous than FAP alone.

Not that exaggeration was really necessary. By giving an additional $2.5 billion to the poor, FAP would have a far-reaching impact.[2] Nearly twenty million people would become eligible to receive aid, more than double the number on AFDC. One-third of the families helped by FAP would have been headed by someone who worked full-time; three out of five would have been headed by a man; 62 percent would have been white.[3] The Southern states especially stood to gain. Half of FAP's potential beneficiaries lived in the nation's poorest region, and the Nixon Administration's welfare reform meant an influx of Federal money that would have had a profound effect on its economy.[4] Overall, FAP was expected to provide an average payment of almost $1,000 per family. Along with food stamps, that amount was sufficient to reduce the "poverty gap"—the difference between the total income of the poor and the sum that would be needed to eliminate poverty—by nearly 60 percent.[5]

FIS, too, would have made a substantial contribution to improving the lot of the needy. According to the Government, it would have provided up to £156 per year to approximately 190,000 households, containing about one-half million children.[6] Moreover, it could begin doing so by August 1971, a relatively short span in which to launch a major welfare program. But how much FIS would have actually reduced poverty was difficult to predict. Since the British poverty-line varied with the amount of rent paid, two families of the same size and the same income might not be considered equally impoverished if they had different expenditures for housing; an equal benefit from FIS could have left one poor and the other not. Even so, during the parliamentary debate, Sir Keith Joseph indicated the Government expected the program to cut the number of families in poverty by half and added that adjustments in benefits (as well as rent rebates) were "highly likely."[7]

Yet neither the British nor the Americans wanted to say too much about the money they were giving to the poor. Responding to the traditional objections to supplementing the wages of full-time workers, Joseph asserted that the means-test for FIS was to be "simple" and "very rarely will this involve a visit to the home."[8] To reduce further any chance of stigmatizing recipients, a "most elaborate take-up campaign" was promised, and to the dismay of the civil service, a target of enrolling 85 percent of the eligible families was announced.[9] Nonetheless, since only a small proportion of the population would be eligible, massive dependency along the lines of Speenhamland, the DHSS Secretary contended, would not arise, epsecially since the labor force was no longer rural and unorganized. As long as the benefit equalled only half the gap between earnings and the "prescribed amount," the incentive to obtain higher wages would remain. However, a rate higher than 50 percent, he warned, could endanger the motivation to work. "The vast majority of cases that we intend to help under the Bill," Joseph said at the end of the debate, "will be simple, straightforward cases of very poor families indeed, working full-time and trying to bring up children to reasonable standards."[10] As long as not too much was expected of it, he was confident FIS would succeed.

In his television address, Nixon similarly tried to dispel any fears his listeners might have about FAP:

> Under the guaranteed income proposal, everyone would be assured a minimum income, regardless of how much he was capable of earning, regardless of what his need was, regardless of whether or not he was willing to work.
>
> During the Presidential campaign last year, I opposed such a plan. I oppose it now and I will continue to oppose it, and this is the reason: A guaranteed income would undermine the incentive to work; the family assistance plan that I propose increases the incentive to work.
>
> A guaranteed income establishes a right without any responsibilities; family assistance recognizes a need and establishes a responsibility. It provides help to those in need and, in turn, requires that those who receive help work to the extent of their capabilities.[11]

To this end, his proposal contained work requirements, financial incentives, and expanded day care and manpower training programs. FAP, the President insisted, would provide more "workfare," not more "welfare."[12]

The Reaction to FAP

Nixon's portrayal of FAP as a scheme to encourage self-support helped produce an overwhelmingly favorable reaction to it. Of those respondents who had heard or read about "President Nixon's new welfare proposals," the Gallup Poll found that 65 percent approved and only 20 percent did not. (Just a year earlier, Gallup had reportedly nearly 60 percent *opposition* to a "guaranteed minimum income" of $3,200 per year, but almost 80 percent support for a program assuring everyone jobs paying that amount in wages.)[13] The Harris Survey also found about half of its sample in favor of the President's plan, with the most attractive features being its work incentives as well as the belief that "up to now, welfare has been a colossal failure."[14] Virtually all of the newspaper editorials were positive, while the syndicated columnists employed adjectives like "historic," "bold," and "sweeping" in approving the new plan.

From the unions, whose opposition Wilbur Cohen had feared, came additional support. After first criticizing FAP as a subsidy to low-wage employers, the AFL-CIO's president, George Meany, was soon commending Nixon for "bringing this welfare situation to the public from the White House."[16] (Ironically, businessmen's groups, like the United States Chamber of Commerce, labelled FAP a "socialist strategy" and tried to defeat it.)[17] Part of the reason for this about-face was that labor could hardly oppose a measure so committed to promoting the "work ethic." Perhaps more importantly, except for those active in low-paying industries like textiles and the service trades, most unions would not be directly affected by any consequences FAP might have for wages. Indeed, the Administration's proposal was most worrisome to the public employees' union, which demanded assurances that the move toward federalization of public assistance would not result in a loss of jobs for its members in state and local welfare offices. Although the AFL-CIO would have preferred national standards for AFDC (and a higher minimum wage), it decided it could live with FAP and placed the program on its list of legislative priorities.

Within this symphony of praise, two important discordant notes could be detected. One came from the South. An opinion poll taken late in 1969 by the University of Michigan Survey Research Center found, as expected, national endorsement of FAP, but also that Southerners were less likely to support it than residents of other regions.[18] Likewise, in assessing the scheme, Southern editors turned out to be more reserved or worried about the fine print. It was in the former Confederacy that this version of the negative income tax would have its most profound impact and if the ideas underlying it were not going to succeed, Southerners wanted to find out before it was tried.

A sharper protest came from a new pressure group, the National Welfare Rights Organization (NWRO). Formed in 1967, it consisted of

AFDC recipients, chiefly female, overwhelmingly black, and mostly from the major cities of the North and the West. Any reforms proposed for public assistance were matters of immediate consequence for it. The group's first public reaction to FAP was unequivocal: "This plan is anti-poor, and anti-black. It is a flagrant example of institutional racism."[19] Despite its rhetoric, however, the NWRO's specific complaints were those of a conventional interest group. Since most of its members lived in states that paid relatively high welfare benefits, for them FAP meant no additional assistance and possibly a reduction if the states were not required to supplement the Federal grant. By altering the rules concerning employment, eligibility, and the like, FAP also struck at the heart of the group's activities: the manipulation of the existing procedures in order to increase aid for welfare clients. Although the NWRO was not against raising benefits or creating a national minimum, it wanted to be sure that doing so preserved (or expanded) such advantages as its members already enjoyed.

Thus, as FAP was transmitted to Congress, a curious situation prevailed. The public approved of the measure, but the people whose region stood to gain the most from its enactment were the most cautious. Liberal pressure groups were in favor of it, but none had any vital stake in seeing it become law, while the conservative organizations that normally supported the Administration were opposed, or were backing it only because the President was. At the same time, the few organizations that would be directly affected were likely to criticize FAP for not doing enough for their members, or alternately, for doing too much to them. Meanwhile, no one spoke for the main beneficiaries of the proposal, the working poor. Insofar as bargaining among such groups would determine its fate, FAP seemed headed for trouble.

FAP and the Ways and Means Committee

The prospects in Congress did not look encouraging either. According to a survey done at the beginning of 1969, most members of the legislature were opposed to the principle of a guaranteed income and believed it would be politically suicidal to advocate one, no matter how much they disliked the welfare system or desired to help the poor.[20] Only "safe-seat liberals" seemed prepared to endorse a major change in welfare policy, although even they agreed it would have little chance in the 91st Congress. Like the rest of the public prior to the proposal of FAP, Congressmen preferred plans to give jobs to the poor. Although most were sympathetic to efforts to eliminate hunger, without grassroots support or strong presidential leadership they were not ready to do much more about public assistance than trying to improve the existing programs.

Even White House backing was of mixed value to FAP. In submitting the proposal, a Republican President was, in effect, asking a solidly Democratic Congress to enact a law that would permit him (and his party) to usurp the Democrats' historic role of leadership in social reform. Moreover, because of their generally conservative views on policy, legislators from his own party might offer the greatest resistance. Since FAP had emerged from a White House expected to be conservative, such opposition could be overcome. However, Congress was a different kind of institution, a representative body, not a policy-making one. Presidential support notwithstanding, any Congressman who voted for FAP would still face the difficulty of explaining to his constituents why, in order to reduce welfare dependency, he endorsed a measure that would double the number of Americans receiving assistance.

If any part of the legislature possessed some of the features of a policy-making group, it was the Ways and Means Committee of the House of Representatives, in which, as a proposed amendment to the Social Security Act, FAP would be considered first. Because it had primary responsibility for originating tax bills, Ways and Means was a busy, powerful, and normally cautious body. Although its members formed a cross-section of Republicans and Democrats in the chamber, their partisanship within the committee was "restrained."[21] Its leaders, Wilbur D. Mills, a Democrat from Arkansas, who was chairman, and John W. Byrnes, of Wisconsin, the ranking Republican, were capable and serious men, who had established a close working relationship over the years. They were accustomed to controlling the committee's business, permitting as much debate as seemed advisable, and above all, seeking positions that would command the support not just of a majority of the members, but of nearly all. When the Ways and Means Committee endorsed a bill, the rest of the House of Representatives was almost certain to do so as well.

However, the committee was primarily a revenue-raising body, not a spending one. Despite its authority over the Social Security Act, its main interest was taxation. Ways and Means had resisted presidential efforts to establish health insurance for the elderly until, following the Johnson landslide of 1964, its enactment seemed inevitable. But except for that, the committee's only other contribution to the Great Society had been the controversial Social Security Act amendments of 1967. Earlier in the decade, Mills and some of his colleagues had become alarmed about rising welfare rolls and their resultant claim on the federal treasury; public assistance seemed an affront to their sense

91

of fiscal responsibility and a challenge to Congressional control. Their aim in adding work requirements, earnings incentives, training programs, and most notably, the AFDC freeze was to force state and local officials to establish more rigorous standards. Now, just two years later, Ways and Means was being asked to endorse a proposal that could double the number of people receiving aid.

Predictably, the first reaction of committee members was not favorable. No sooner had HEW Secretary Robert H. Finch finished testifying on the first day of hearings, October 15, than the fourth-ranking Democrat, Al Ullman of Oregon, professed to being ". . . shocked, frankly almost to the point of being speechless, by the recommendations that you have made."[22] Others, such as Representative Martha Griffiths, a liberal Democrat from Detroit, who had once chaired a Congressional study of income transfer programs, joined in:

> . . . [M]y viewpoint is that all you have added to this program is money and I believe that money is never going to do it. You are going to have to do something far different if you are ever going to cure the problem of welfare. I just think you are not looking at it from the right standpoint.[23]

She wondered, as Ullman had, what FAP would do to rehabilitate individual recipients. That the Nixon Administration was proposing an entirely different strategy had, at least on its first airing, not been understood.

If the committee had voted then, it would likely have opted for steps to federalize the AFDC program. Some consensus on such a move already existed: it would have provided financial help to a few governors and mayors, and it would have given the committee more leverage over the work programs established in 1967. But Ways and Means was not accustomed to acting hastily, and a related bill, a series of proposed changes in the old-age insurance programs and the other titles of the Social Security Act, had to be considered too. Most of the testimony during a month of hearings pertained to these measures, not to FAP. In the meantime, a process not unlike what had occurred in the White House commenced, geared to convincing the committee of the logic behind the Administration's proposal.

Part of this effort took place in public. The questioning of Byrnes and other Republicans drew attention to a point the Administration wished to emphasize:

> MR. BYRNES: I would like to move in a little bit on the welfare area. I really did not get from the Secretary's statement this morning the correlation that you intend to develop between the family

assistance program and your program of training for work and putting people to work. The real effect, it seems to me, is to develop further beyond what we tried to develop in a starting sense in the 1967 act—the movement of welfare people into the economic stream rather than staying in the welfare stream as a way of life. . . .

MR. VENEMAN: It is almost the key part.[24]

Once again, the Secretary of Labor, George P. Shultz, was called upon to play a central role. Repeating his discussion of work incentives and his department's experience with manpower programs, he emphasized both the need for change and continuity with the past:

> I believe very deeply, Mr. Chairman, that the time has come to start over on providing assistance to needy families. We should not be content just to mend AFDC; the record is clear that AFDC doesn't work.
> The family assistance plan is a new start.
> I believe the changes we propose are consistent with the forward-looking changes made recently by this committee with regard to training opportunities, and the treatment of earned income. Family assistance, in a sense, builds on the foundations already laid by recent amendments to AFDC.[25]

Of the public witnesses who dealt with the proposal at all, most commended the Administration and supported FAP in principle, while expressing some reservations about the details. Finally, as the hearings concluded, President Johnson's Commission on Income Maintenance Programs issued its report, advocating substantially the same plan President Nixon had offered. For a consensus-seeking body, this demonstration of agreement was important.

More significant, though, were the activities occurring in private. Over the years, Ways and Means had become accustomed to working closely with executive branch officials in fashioning legislation, both during hearings and afterwards in executive session. On welfare matters, such collaboration was almost a necessity, since the committee's own staff consisted primarily of specialists in taxation. During a period of four months, Veneman and other officials were able to participate in closed-door meetings, restating the arguments in behalf of FAP to the legislators, defending it against objections, and employing the full range of analytic tools and information available to them. At least in taxation, members of Ways and Means already understood how financial incentives were supposed to operate, and many were aware of the problem of dependency and the history of efforts to deal with it. In addition, the states where welfare caseloads had risen most rapidly were well-represented on the committee. This was not a group unwilling to consider a new approach, and in private, the Administration's policy planners began to convince them that FAP was serious and well-conceived.

Nonetheless, the committee's action would ultimately depend upon its chairman. On FAP, Mills' own views were conflicted. More than any of the committee's members, he was sensitive to the failures of previous welfare programs. ". . . [P]erhaps we haven't done enough in the past—certainly we haven't—in trying to prevent the need for assistance," he observed on the final day of public hearings. "Why can't we develop some kind of program that would tend to motivate these people?"[26] He was not against spending more money, if the result would be a reduction in the number of families on relief. FAP, however, offered the certainty of higher costs and more recipients, but only the possibility of a long-run solution to the problem of dependency. His close associate, John Byrnes, was supporting the Nixon Administration's proposal, as were others whose judgment he trusted (including, now that he was out of office, Wilbur Cohen). Yet, Mills was from Arkansas, among the least generous states in providing AFDC, and hence, among the ones to be most affected, for good or ill, by the measure before him. For the chairman, FAP was more than a matter of committee politics; it could be of personal consequence as well.

Above all at this stage in his career, Mills was a realist. A Republican president had put forth a guaranteed income. It was endorsed by the public and the press. Important Congressmen and interest groups favored it. Moreover, unless he wished to champion the discredited AFDC, he seemed to have no other alternative. At some point after executive sessions of the committee began on November 17, Mills decided to report FAP to the full House of Representatives.

As was his custom, Mills withheld his own view while trying to build a coalition for the measure that could carry it through both his committee and the House. For conservatives, the "workfare" provisions were strengthened. For liberals, states or cities which paid benefits above the FAP maximum would be required to supplement them for AFDC families, with the Federal government paying 30 percent of the cost. Food stamps and other in-kind aid would be continued. To enhance the appeal of the bill as a whole, a more generous program of public assistance for the elderly, blind, and disabled was added. Even with these changes, the committee's report was careful to note the plan being recommended was "essentially patterned after the pro-posals of the President."[27]

Although a high price had to be paid, the effort within Ways and Means to obtain a consensus on FAP was successful. By a vote of twenty-one to three, the committee approved the welfare reform bill. Only Ullman and two Southern Democrats dissented, urging that the existing programs be made more effective before ". . . we consider bringing millions more into the system."[28] Their colleagues had come to believe either that the incentive theory might work or that FAP contained adequate provisions for job training and social services. Most could also find other reasons for supporting the bill: loyalty to the President, fiscal savings for their states, or the prospect of more Congressional control over welfare expenditures. The endorsement given by influential members of the committee like Byrnes and Hale Boggs, the second-ranking Democrat and the party's Whip, helped too. Yet, in the end, the crucial point was probably that FAP was not AFDC. As Veneman observed when the committee finally acted, "Many members of Congress finally realized where we were going under the present system."[29] What made the difference in Ways and Means was what had mattered most in the White House too.

Just as it had taken time for President Nixon to reach his con-clusion, so too with the Ways and Means Committee. Nearly five months elapsed before, on March 5, 1970, it completed work on FAP. Another week would pass before its report was ready for considera-tion, first by the Rules Committee and then by the entire chamber. The Administration had tried to get quicker action. On January 13, in a speech at the National Press Club, Secretary Finch had warned, "the odds for reform are running against us."[30] Nine days later, in his first State of the Union message, the President listed FAP as his most urgent priority among domestic proposals. None of this had much effect. The timing of the Ways and Means Committee's business was the prerogative of its chairman, and Mills was not willing to sponsor a measure until he felt it stood a real chance of passage. As a result, if FAP did win approval by the House, little time would be left for con-sideration in the Senate, and even that would be complicated by the 1970 elections.

The House Acts

The more immediate problem was the vote in the House of Repre-sentatives. Although both Mills and Veneman averred they were con-fident FAP would pass, their behavior suggested otherwise. After initially suggesting he was not even sure he would vote for the measure, Mills appeared at the Rules Committee hearing on April 7 and flamboyantly told of his conversion to the incentive theory. He was emphatic in warning that "the biggest mistake we can make is to assume that a majority of [the poor] don't want to help themselves," and in pledging that he would recommend a presidential veto before accepting any Senate action that would raise the benefit level. When a member of the committee, recounting criticisms of both AFDC and FAP, opined "We're damned if we do and damned if we don't," Mills corrected: "No, sir, we're saved if we do and damned if we don't."[31] Whether or not his conviction was genuine, FAP now appeared to be Mills' proposal, as well as the President's.

At the same time, the Administration was assembling its supporters. Part of the effort was directed at Republican stalwarts, many of whom had been surprised by the proposal of FAP and were being urged by groups like the Chamber of Commerce to vote against it. Obligations to party and to the President were invoked, as well as the urgent need to reform the existing welfare system.

Even if all backed the measure, House Republicans could not pass FAP by themselves. Votes from the other side of the aisle were necessary, and to obtain them, Administration officials concentrated on the members of the Democratic Study Group, a caucus of liberal Congressmen. Although they would have preferred more generous benefits and less stringent work requirements, they were prepared to support FAP on the assumption that improvements could be made in the Senate. Moreover, the chairman of the group's Health and Welfare Task Force, Philip Burton, a San Franciscan who had served with Veneman in the California State Legislature, was not averse to compromise. On April 2, in return for stronger Administration support of the new provisions for the elderly, blind, and disabled, the task force recommended approval of FAP. With that, substantial Democratic support was all but assured for the Republican Administration's pathbreaking plan.

On April 15, the debate on FAP began, and the next day, the House of Representatives voted to approve it by a comfortable margin of 243 to 155.[32] The proceedings had been restrained; much of the allotted time had been used by Mills, Byrnes, and their colleagues on Ways and Means to explain the new approach to welfare reform. A "closed rule" was in effect, prohibiting amendments except those acceptable to the bill's sponsors. For the most part, the chamber was nearly empty. The most persistent objections came from Southern Congressmen, such as William M. Colmer, a New Dealer when elected and now in his nineteenth term representing Mississippi, who sought to portray FAP as a guaranteed income:

> Unquestionably, it is the most controversial, it is the most important, it is the most complex and disturbing piece of legislation that I have had occasion to consider in my whole career here as a Member of this body.
>
> I am very much disturbed about this bill. I am very much disturbed about the threat that it poses to our system of government, to our way of life.[33]

In rebuttal, Mills emphasized that half of the working poor lived in the South, but his effort was in vain. Of 102 Southerners voting, only seventeen were recorded in favor of FAP. Overwhelming support from the wealthier states, the ones that would be less affected by the plan but were more liberal in the area of welfare, accounted for the passage of FAP.

This was a forewarning of what was to come in the Senate. FAP had been successful in the House of Representatives not because of any change in attitudes toward a guaranteed income, but as a result of a particular set of legislative conditions—a workmanlike committee with a concern about the problem of dependency, a pragmatic chairman, support for the measure from senior Republicans, the provision of a vehicle for organizing liberal Democrats, and procedures for restricting debate in the House chamber—all of which enabled the Nixon Administration to explain and build support for the theory upon which FAP was based. Since few of these circumstances were likely to be repeated in the Senate, a new political strategy was necessary. What was not anticipated was the possibility that the incentive theory itself might be discredited. But it was.

The Passage of FIS

The passage of FIS required nothing like the political maneuvering necessary to secure FAP's approval by the House of Representatives. Since a majority of the members of the House of Commons were Conservatives, party opposition to the Heath Government's proposal was not sufficient to keep it from being enacted. However, the criticisms levelled at FIS, both during Parliamentary consideration and afterwards, did concern the Tories and caused them to begin rethinking their strategy for welfare policy.

The main threat to the adoption of FIS would have been objections from Conservative Party backbenchers, but for the most part, their judgment was favorable. Few, if any, really understood the details of the plan. Nonetheless, most were able to appreciate that FIS did embody the principle of selectivity and gave some help to the poor at a time when the Government's policies were accused of too much favoritism toward the rich. In any case, the scheme was their party's proposal and to oppose it would have been a grave decision indeed.

Even so, two notable Conservatives spoke out against the measure. Enoch Powell, having long since parted company with Heath and the new Tory leadership, declared FIS to be a "momentous and fateful step" toward—in a phrase that had been used to describe Speenhamland—" 'relief in supplementation of wages.' " After recounting the assessment of that system by the noted historian, G. M. Trevelyan, Powell voiced his fear that "all the temptations and stresses which we in this House know so well" would make the Government's modest plan so generous that it would end the same way. "We shall no doubt give the Bill a Second Reading tonight," Powell intoned in his most Cassandra-like manner, "but many of those who vote for it or let it go through will live to regret what we have done."[34]

If Powell spoke for the Old Tory, the second dissenter, Sir Brandon Rhys Williams, evoked the memory of the Old Whig in criticizing FIS not for its principle but for its design. Because of his indefatigable efforts in behalf of his mother's "social dividend" plan, he was regarded as an expert on this topic, "the Maharishi of the cult of the negative income tax," as one backbencher called him.[35] His reaction to the Heath Government's proposal was to term it an "oxymoron— something which is partly agreeable and partly extremely sour." Drawing on his knowledge, Rhys Williams proceeded to list a half-dozen objections to FIS. Although acknowledging he would still support the measure as a first step, he urged Sir Keith Joseph to "dare the ultimate," to proceed toward a real negative income tax, and—in a reference to Sir Arthur Cockfield, who had joined the Government as a special adviser to the Chancellor—to beware of "men who have not convinced themselves that they have the political will to solve the problem."[36]

Across the aisle, the reaction was far more critical. To the Labour Party, the proposal of FIS seemed to justify the charge that the Conservatives really favored a return to the "means-test state." "Nothing was more pathetic," Harold Wilson observed, "than his [Anthony Barber's] wriggles and evasions in explaining why . . . the Government have lost no time in reneging on that promise" of another round of clawback.[37] For Richard Crossman, FIS was "the first phase of the great counter-revolution in the social security sector," and he chided

Joseph for capitulating to both the Chancellor and the civil service in accepting it.[38]

Other members of the opposition attacked the plan's details. "This Bill is being introduced in a background of inflationary, repressive and irrelevant proposals," charged Brian O'Malley, one of Labour's spokesmen for social services. The application forms will make it "a full-time job to be poor," while the limitations on the size of the grant will create a new poverty-line, lower than the Supplementary Benefits scale plus rent.[39] The amount of aid, the likely administrative difficulties, the implicit subsidy to "bad employers," and the extent to which key features were to be defined by regulations instead of by statute were all challenged. Several Labour speakers also noted that reducing FIS benefits at a rate of 50 percent imposed a high tax on low-wage workers. Together with social insurance contributions, they would have less of an incentive to obtain higher earnings than the much-criticized (by Tories) tax system gave to the better-paid.

Nonetheless, the tone of the opposition seemed to reflect normal standards of partisanship more than deep displeasure with what the Heath Government proposed to do. Although numerous amendments were offered during the debate, Labour's aim, according to its shadow minister for DHSS, Shirley Williams, was to make "a bad Bill better." She added, "This is likely to be the best we can hope for in respect of poverty from this Government."[40] More than bending to Parliamentary reality was involved in this tactic. FIS, Williams averred, was "a very, very small triumph . . . in [the] war against poverty" and "at best a crutch which can keep the poor just walking but no radical solution."[41] If it did not succeed, the Conservatives could be blamed and their version of selectivity brought into disrepute. However, if FIS proved reasonably effective, a future Labour government would not be committed to abandoning a tool for achieving its social objectives.

Indeed, if Labour had still been in office, it might have done just what the Conservatives did. The Wilson Government had known of—in fact, was responsible for—the limited utility of clawback, and Crossman's detailed critique of FIS strongly suggested it had been given no little consideration when he was heading DHSS. The 1966 replacement of the promised "minimum income guarantee" with an upgraded public assistance program (Supplementary Benefits) even gave Labour a precedent of sorts. In light of its much greater sensitivity to CPAG's assessment of its record, the value of FIS as a speedy solution to the problem of family poverty might have been appealing to a re-elected Wilson Government. In opposition, Labour could not help realizing that the Conservatives had introduced a program which they themselves could have implemented, but did not dare to propose.

On Novemberr 10, 1970, FIS was given a Second Reading and approved by a vote of 221 to 188.[42] After the consideration of a series of technical amendments, final passage occurred on December 1. Following an uneventful stop at the House of Lords, the measure received the Royal Assent on December 17 and became law less than two months after it had been proposed. Winding up the last debate, Joseph's deputy, Paul Dean, announced:

> We regard this as a first step in dealing with family poverty. . . . a first step in an unfolding social programme to which the Government are committed, and as such I commend it to the House.[43]

That this was sincere need not be doubted. What the Heath Government did not know, however, was that the second step would have to be hastened in order to correct troubles that were besetting FIS.

The Limits of Selectivity

FIS began to pay benefits in August 1971, as scheduled. At the Conservative Party conference that autumn, Joseph defended the Government's record in helping the needy, but admitted it was still too soon to tell whether FIS would succeed. By the end of December, *The Times* of London had pronounced it a failure, and even the more conservative *Daily Telegraph* was reminding the Heath Government that the measure was designed to be "a palliative rather than a cure."[44] Even when it had been announced, some thought (and hoped) FIS would not work. "An inappropriate method," *The Times* had called it, and CPAG declared it to be "questionable or worse."[45] But it was not only ill will which made FIS into a controversial measure and forced the Government's officials to devote much attention to it. Rather, in implementing FIS, the Conservatives began to learn about the limits of selectivity.

One problem—enrolling the families who were eligible for benefits—had been anticipated, but proved intractable. Despite a major publicity campaign, costing £650 million by the fall of 1973, rarely did more than half of those thought to have incomes below the "prescribed amount" ever receive FIS. The Government tried a variety of tactics. It hired an advertising specialist from Benton and Bowles and employed market research techniques to "sell" its new program. It increased the income limits and size of the benefit regularly. It made

FIS a ticket of eligibility for other types of assistance, such as free school meals, prescriptions, dental treatment, and eye glasses.

As Joseph and Dean frequently tried to point out, these efforts did produce results. The larger the benefit, the higher the rate of enrollment in FIS. Moreover, the program had become a major source of support for single-parent families, who accounted for nearly half of all recipients; under Supplementary Benefits, the heads of such households were not allowed to work more than part-time. Nonetheless, these accomplishments did not conceal the fact that even at the upper amount claimed (75 percent), the total take-up of FIS was not near the Government's avowed target of 85 percent.

In truth, how well the program was doing was impossible to say for sure. Neither DHSS nor anyone else had a definitive way of determining how many families were really eligible. Estimates of the number of low-income families were subject not only to normal sampling errors, but also to the tendency for people to under-report their actual income when asked in an official inquiry. (The size of the sample used to forecast the number of eligibles was forty-five. This yielded an estimate of 70,000 to 210,000 families whose incomes qualified them for FIS, and when the program began the Government chose the midpoint as the official figure.) Moreover, since the incomes of low-paid workers fluctuated considerably, the number counted as poor in the course of a year was larger than the number in poverty at any particular time. In its first months of operation, half of the applicants for FIS were found to be unqualified largely because their earnings varied widely during the five-week period needed to prove eligibility.

In any welfare program, identifying those who should receive assistance is a problem. But using income as the main criterion makes for greater difficulty than relying on relatively objective and easily ascertained characteristics like unemployment, retirement, and family size. Unless estimates of take-up can be spurned entirely—a procedure which the civil servants who designed FIS recommended to their colleagues who were preparing rent rebates—no operator of a purely means-tested program is likely to be able to claim success. After a while, the Heath Government gave up trying and accepted low take-up as an inherent limitation of FIS.

In the meantime, another defect had been uncovered that seemed more serious and politically more harmful. At the end of the 1960s, several writers on social policy had demonstrated how the benefit-reduction rates, or "tapers," in means-tested programs would be cumulative if a family obtained more than one at the same time.[46] At the time, this was mostly a problem for local governments, which ran a variety of programs assisting the poor with meals, special health needs, and educational expenses. The major national benefits either were unrelated to income or went to people not normally in the labor force and whose incentives would be little affected by these tapers.[47] The introduction of FIS changed this situation; as several members observed during the debates in the House of Commons, its 50 percent tax rate, added to a 4 percent social insurance contribution, constituted a heavy burden that might discourage some workers from seeking higher earnings.

As the Heath Government soon learned when FIS began to operate, this was an under-estimate. Not only were low-paid workers to lose half as much in benefits as they gained in wages, but those who were also obtaining help from their local governments were apt to have a further reduction. The Government's rent subsidy, which started in 1972, added another taper, and until that year's budget, some families receiving all these types of aid might have been paying income taxes as well. It was not difficult to demonstrate that as a result of these overlapping tapers and taxes, most low-income families faced an "implicit" tax of 67 percent, quite a few paid at a rate near 80 percent or above, and for some, each pound earned meant *more* than a pound lost in social benefits and taxes.

This "surtax for the poor" turned out to be more theoretical than real. Not all programs were adjusted at the same time to reflect changes in earnings, nor did all deduct (as FIS did) some assistance for every additional pound in wages. "Their effects on marginal rates of tax," wrote one observer, "are . . . unpredictable and capricious."[48] Moreover, not all families claimed the benefits—and the implicit taxes—for which they were eligible. (Ironically, to the extent the Heath Government improved its take-up record, it would exacerbate its taper problem.) There was no evidence that the low-paid worker was aware of the cumulative tax burden he supposedly faced and no certainty as to how much these high rates really affected his motivation. Yet, for a Government that had entered office on a theme of restoring incentive to British economic life, even a theoretical surtax looked like a willingness to create disincentives for the neediest.

Even more than low take-up, the discovery that FIS helped produce high cumulative tax rates put the Conservatives in an awkward position. Not surprisingly, the Labour Party and CPAG were the sharpest critics. Calling the situation a "poverty trap" (since total rates of more than 100 percent occurred just as a family's income neared its poverty-line), they charged it was another instance of the socially divisive results of the Tory approach to welfare policy.[49] But disquiet could also be found among Conservatives, few of whom had originally shared Enoch Powell's forebodings. A former leader of the Young Conservatives, now a member of Parliament, singled out, as a major danger of the Heath Government's approach to social services, its concentration "upon the electorally advantageous business of dealing with temporary deprivation at the expense of those in permanent need." While FIS was an important addition, he looked forward to an alternative that would ". . . simplify the general administration and cut the amount of means testing to the lowest level consistent with the aim of channelling help to the needy while encouraging independence and self-help."[50] Not all Conservatives were as worried, but the possibility that selectivity was producing dependency had been raised and could not be ignored.

Indeed, before long, the problem of financial disincentives in welfare programs became an important issue in the Heath Government's troubled relations with the Trades Union Congress. Although the TUC had wanted an increase in family allowances and thought that FIS fell "far short," it was willing to accept the plan for "a relatively small number of exceptional cases," even though it was a subsidy to low-wage industries.[51] The poverty-trap was a different matter. The possibility that the gains of collective bargaining could be eroded by a combination of taxes and tapers threatened the most basic union interest. "We believe," Alf Allen, the head of the shop and distributive workers, told the 1972 TUC meeting, "that, after the abolition of the Industrial Relations Act, the elimination of the effects of the poverty trap is the single greatest challenge to the trade union movement."[52] He favored the idea being urged by CPAG and others that the solution lay in replacing means-tested benefits with universal ones, like family allowances.

Other union leaders took a different line. While not opposed to higher social security benefits, Jack Jones, the transport workers' leader, argued that the TUC's responsibility was to obtain higher wages for its members:

> . . . [G]overnment policies must not be permitted to create a situation where workers become dependent upon the good will and kindliness of the State for major elements of their standard of living—that way lies continued poverty.[53]

If this view took hold, the measure of successful negotiations would become an increase not in gross earnings, but, especially for the family man, in take-home pay. For a Government that believed its anti-inflation efforts required moderation in union wage-demands, FIS seemed to have added a further complication to the already numerous difficulties of developing an incomes policy.

Nonetheless, if disappointed with its new welfare program and a bit apologetic in its public statements, the Government stood by FIS. It was no surprise that a new program initiated in little more than a year, particularly one which served an entirely new group of beneficiaries, should create problems. By the start of 1972, however, FIS was aiding up to 75,000 families with relatively little administrative bother. The troubles that remained, like the cumulative tax rate issue, were blamed on ill will, misunderstanding or ivory-tower theorizing. (CPAG's stance was regarded as exceptionally muddled; to civil servants, the group seemed to be demanding that take-up be increased, while criticizing spending on publicity as excessive.) Plans were being made to have FIS included in the annual indexing of social benefits and this, as well as other actions, suggested that it was on its way to becoming a routine feature of the British "welfare state."

Inside Whitehall, it was a different story. The problems encountered by FIS encouraged the Heath Government to speed up its search for the next step. At DHSS, the civil servants continued to work on "super-FIS," a plan which would have merged the application process for a variety of programs and integrated their marginal tax rates. Sir Keith Joseph began to examine the causes of poverty and urged studies of the "cycle of deprivation." To reduce some of the political pressure, the Chancellor opened the poverty-trap a little by raising the tax threshold in the 1972 budget.

None of these seemed likely to offer more than a partial solution. For the foreseeable future, the Government appeared to have no concrete plans for replacing a program that many believed was increasing dependency without doing much about poverty. Yet, in fact, by the end of 1971, an idea had been developed which would have virtually eliminated FIS.

The Disincentives of FAP

In the United States, the same criticisms were made about FAP as would be made about FIS. The Nixon Administration's plan, it was said, did not do enough for the poor, but at the same time did too much by weakening their incentives for self-support. Unlike in the British experience, however, these allegations were put forth even before FAP had become law, and they left the President's most important domestic policy proposal in serious trouble.

After passage by the House of Representatives, FAP next went to the Senate Finance Committee. Like Ways and Means, it too was chiefly a revenue-raising body. But (since tax measures originate in the House), its jurisdiction was appellate. To the hearings of the Finance Committee came parties seeking redress from actions taken, or omitted, in the other chamber. Its bills were fashioned through accommodation, not consensus. And before its legislation was approved by the entire Senate, numerous amendments were apt to have been added. If Ways and Means could be said to have some likeness to a policy-making body, the Finance Committee was more one where private interests affected by pending bills could be represented.

Yet the committee itself was not a particularly representative group. Half of its ten Democrats were Southerners, two more came from the Southwest, and only one—Abraham Ribicoff of Connecticut—was from an industrial state. All but one of the seven Republicans were elected by Western or Midwestern constituencies. Tariffs and mining, not welfare dependency, were the dominant concerns of the members of the Finance Committee. With few exceptions, their states provided AFDC benefits that fell below the national average. As a result, a majority of the Senators spoke for jurisdictions that would be among those most affected by the Nixon Administration's proposal.

Nonetheless, the committee's composition did not necessarily foreshadow opposition to FAP. In considering the 1967 amendments to the Social Security Act, it had softened some of the work rules written by Ways and Means and objected to the AFDC freeze. As a member of the Democratic leadership during the 89th Congress, the committee's chairman, Russell B. Long of Louisiana, had played an important part in enacting legislation for the Great Society. In Ribicoff, the group possessed a former HEW Secretary, whose views about social policy commanded respect within the Senate. Moreover, the committee had recently added its own specialist on welfare, Michael Stern, who had once been an assistant to Wilbur Cohen. If a conservative lot, the Republican Senators were loyal to the President and from some of them, as well as from others on the committee, the Administration understood that a welfare reform bill would receive favorable consideration.

A week after the House vote, the prospects began to change. In a Senate speech, Long raised some questions about FAP:

Do we want to pass a bill which develops the course of public welfare in such a way as to provide fantastic, illogical incentives for people to quit work, or do we want to pass a bill which helps those who have need and have a problem—a bill which encourages them to find constructive employment

105

for their own advantage, and to move up the economic ladder?[54]

His doubts about the Administration's bill had been prompted by a staff briefing on April 22. Charts had been produced demonstrating that a family headed by a full-time worker could wind up with *less* income under FAP than one headed by a part-time employee. The cause of this anomaly was not the new welfare plan, but rather the existing one, which in half of the states assisted households where the father worked less than thirty or thirty-five hours per week. The bill enacted by the House not only extended this provision to all the states, but also required those which paid generous benefits to maintain them. The working poor would be eligible for FAP alone; those who worked a few hours less, FAP plus a state supplement. Thus, judged Long, "The bill before the Committee on Finance . . . would provide an incentive for many low-income working people to quit work, rather than try a little harder to improve their condition and that of their families."[55]

The Senator from Louisiana had other concerns as well. The apparent laxity of government agencies in implementing the work provisions of the 1967 amendments caused him to question their sincerity about those in the new bill. The estimates of FAP's cost and coverage, he also suggested, might be too low. But the novelty of his remarks lay in the examples he presented. Under certain circumstances, Long was telling his colleagues, the Nixon Administration's new approach to welfare made dependency more attractive than self-support.

When hearings began on April 29, the committee's ranking Republican, John J. Williams of Delaware, exploited this line of criticism with great skill. Before HEW Secretary Finch had concluded speaking, Williams interrupted to ask that charts be prepared, showing the effect of FAP on the income of a family in different circumstances. Unlike Long, he was interested in the female-headed family, with four members and with seven, at various levels of income. Other welfare benefits, like AFDC and food stamps, were to be included too, according to their availability in four locations: Phoenix, New York City, Chicago, and Wilmington, Delaware. When completed to specifications, the resulting charts were devastating.[56]

Because of the piecemeal development of the existing welfare system, diverse rules or administrative practices, and the particular arrangements in each city, various points could be found where a rise in earnings would theoretically be exceeded by the combination of lost benefits and higher taxes. Williams led Robert E. Patricelli, Veneman's deputy, through each example:

SENATOR WILLIAMS: . . . If they increase their earnings from $720 to $5,560 under this bill, they have a spendable income of $6,109, or $19 less than if they sit in a rocking chair earning only $720. Is that not correct?

PATRICELLI: That is correct, Senator; they would have less if they earned $5,560 than if they earned $720, provided they get public housing, medical payments, and so forth.

SENATOR WILLIAMS: They are penalized $19 because they go out and earn $5,500.
   Is that correct?

PATRICELLI: That is correct.

SENATOR LONG: . . . What possible logic is there to it?

PATRICELLI: There is none, Senator.[57]

FAP now stood accused of being a disincentive not only for the working poor but for the dependent as well.

There was nothing especially startling in the revelations of the Long and Williams charts. Those familiar with the mathematics of the negative income tax understood how overlapping, income-related benefits could produce these "notch effects." During White House consideration of FAP, they had been discussed, but judged atypical. To lower marginal tax rates a little, the Administration decided to disregard a portion of income for work expenses, as Secretary Shultz proposed.

The Ways and Means Committee likewise knew of this potential problem. Milton Friedman had described it in his testimony, and during executive sessions the Administration had produced some preliminary findings from the first of the Office of Economic Opportunity's income maintenance experiments, which claimed that a negative income tax did not result in a decline in work effort. In any case, solving the problem presented political difficulties. Unless it was willing to revise (or "cash out") programs like food stamps, or raise the cost to states and cities of supplementing FAP's maximum benefit, the committee could do little. Accordingly, both it and HEW were disposed to postpone such adjustments until after the new strategy for welfare was in place.

The leaders of the Senate Finance Committee had a different inclination. "I am not trying to discredit anybody or embarrass anybody," said Senator Williams. "It has been my position throughout life," he added, "that if you have a problem, you have to lay the problem out cold in its worst light and then we can sit down and intelligently start working out a plan to solve the problem. . . ."[58] For a family with earnings in a certain range, living in a specific city, and claiming all the benefits to which it was entitled, the rewards of work could indeed be less than those of relief and thus dependency would be encouraged. That there were relatively few such families did not make the situation less worrisome to the members of the Finance Committee.

In hindsight, some Administration officials wished they had not so readily agreed to prepare the charts for a body that was proving to be much less cooperative than Ways and Means had been. Although that might well have been the safe course, they probably had no alternative, since in opposing FAP, the Finance Committee chairman and top Republicans had seized upon an issue the plan's defenders could not avoid. The incentive theory had been employed to show why welfare rolls would not likely decrease, and might even rise, if FAP were enacted. Only by maintaining that families would not respond as expected—that they would prefer to work despite large disincentives or a financial loss—could the Long and Williams charts have been effectively refuted. But doing so would also have undermined the rationale advanced in behalf of FAP. In effect, the Nixon Administration had been trumped with its own cards.

The Nixon Administration Retreats

Even before the Long and Williams charts had appeared, other conservatives on the Finance Committee had criticized FAP's cost and coverage, its liberal administrative procedures, and the discretion it granted to the HEW Secretary. Like their leadership, they could not respond enthusiastically to what seemed to be an expansion of welfare or be unconcerned about the prospect of vastly enlarging the number of recipients in their own states. In Louisiana, one-quarter of the population would have been eligible for FAP; elsewhere, approximately one out of five constituents could have obtained grants.[59] In other parts of the country, such generosity might have been rewarded by votes, but in the South and Midwest, AFDC had been the stepchild among the offspring of the Social Security Act. Neither the citizens nor state and local officials in these regions were anxious for more Federal funds or standards for relief; to the contrary, many thought the rise in dependency was caused by the overly liberal policies of national agencies like HEW. In FAP, they believed the President had been deceived into accepting the wrong kind of welfare reform. Although such views had been represented on Ways and Means, those who held them were more numerous on the Finance Committee, and with staff assistance could turn them into a pointed critique of the Administration's plan.

Strangely enough, conservative opponents of FAP received considerable help from liberals, who objected to the proposal for different reasons. Part of this was expected, since groups like the AFL-CIO judged their chances of obtaining amendments to be greater in the Senate. On April 20, Ribicoff introduced a package of such changes, the most important of which were raising the benefit level over three years to $2,000 for a family of four and including childless couples and single individuals in the program. To White House officials, these proposals seemed a reasonable opening to negotiations.

Not so with those offered by two other liberal Democrats on the Finance Committee. On February 10, even before FAP had reached the Senate, Fred R. Harris of Oklahoma introduced a new bill, the National Basic Income Benefits Act, which would have set the benefit level at $2,520 for a family of four and raised it to the poverty-line (then $3,720) in three years. Two months later, on April 30, Eugene J. McCarthy of Minnesota sponsored the NWRO's Adequate Income Act, which would have established a $5,500 benefit level. Since both men aspired to the presidency, these actions were partly an attempt to win additional supporters. But more than personal politics was involved.

When fully implemented, Harris' measure would have cost more than $25 billion and McCarthy's over $70 billion.[60] Few, perhaps not even the two sponsors, would have seriously considered such expenditures had they not been concentrating instead on the amount that would be provided to each recipient. Harris wanted to assure a minimum income not below what the government defined as necessary for subsistence, while McCarthy aimed at the more generous "lower living standard" for urban families computed by the Bureau of Labor Statistics. By contrast, FAP's basic benefit of $1,600—or, with food stamps, $2,400—looked miserly indeed. In proposing their alternatives, Harris and McCarthy were accusing the Nixon Administration's program of not doing enough for the poor.

What they were also doing was showing a serious misunderstanding of how the negative income tax worked. Under the Nixon

Administration's proposal, except in those states where AFDC benefits were lower, no families would have been expected to live on $1,600, or even $2,400. FAP was designed not to replace income, as traditional relief programs did, but rather to supplement it. The average low-income family, headed by someone in the labor force, would have had earnings, Finch testified, of $3,400; with additions from FAP and food stamps, its total income would have been slightly above the poverty-line.[61] Other families would have either gained or been guaranteed no loss, if they were receiving AFDC benefits higher than FAP's maximum.

In addition, because of the work-incentive features of the negative income tax, increasing its generosity for families without any income meant expanding drastically the number eligible to receive at least some help. If a 50 percent benefit-reduction rate was maintained, the plans offered by the two Senators would have turned half of all American families into potential grantees. Although most could have obtained only small amounts of aid, the total cost of such a scheme would have been enormous, with the bulk going to people who did not really need assistance.

Nonetheless, many politicians (and editorial writers) were accustomed to thinking about traditional welfare programs and had great difficulty grasping the subtleties of the proposed new approach. In counterpoint to the Senate conservatives, Harris, McCarthy, and a growing number of social welfare organizations were successful in disparaging the generosity of the Nixon Administration's plan. As a result, a substantial hike in the basic benefit became the touchstone for liberal support of welfare reform.

The Nixon Administration appeared unable to respond effectively to this two-pronged assault on FAP. In part, this was because it was preoccupied with other matters. On April 30, the second day of the Finance Committee's hearings, the entry of American soldiers into Cambodia was announced. The President now had little time for the relatively minor crisis in welfare nor any desire to affront the sensibilities of those conservatives who rallied to his support by pressing for the enactment of FAP. Finch, Shultz, Moynihan, and other architects of the plan also had other controversies to deal with or had gone on to other assignments in the Administration.

But over-confidence was partly to blame as well. The margin by which FAP had passed the House of Representatives and the greater notice paid to liberal concerns by officials like Moynihan had led to a neglect of the sort of inconsistencies uncovered by Long and Williams. Moreover, White House and departmental staffs most closely in touch with the Senate misjudged the prospects for a compromise on welfare reform—as they would do consistently throughout FAP's history. Sooner or later, they felt, the logic of the incentive theory and the absence of better alternatives would be understood. In fact, after the Williams charts had been presented, not one of the seventeen members of the Finance Committee—not even Ribicoff—appeared willing to support FAP.

On May 1, Finch yielded to a suggestion by Chairman Long that the hearings be recessed to enable the Administration to revise its proposal. Since the pending changes in the social insurance programs had not yet been referred to it, the committee had no other bill to consider. Nor did it wish to undertake the task of rewriting the legislation, as Ways and Means might have done. The work required was too extensive for a Congressional staff, as Long's remarks indicated:

> We would like to pass a bill which takes into consideration everything that private employers can be expected to do; everything that State governments can be expected to do; everything that other Federal agencies can be expected to do as part of this overall effort.[62]

Indeed, even the Administration could have had difficulty making these changes before the 91st Congress adjourned. Yet, Finch predicted that new proposals would be ready within a few days and affirmed that he was still optimistic about the prospects for welfare reform. Unless he wished FAP to remain blocked in the Finance Committee, he had no real choice but to revise it.

Conclusion

Despite the planning that had gone into their development, FAP and FIS proved to be readily vulnerable to criticism. Using examples more theoretical than real, opponents of the two measures were able to suggest that each would create significant disincentives to work. At the same time, compared to imaginary programs costing more and reaching everyone in need, neither seemed to do enough for the poor. In little more than a year, the radical departures from traditional welfare policy proposed by an American and a British government were made to appear potentially harmful and ineffective.

Both FAP and FIS deserved better. Their alleged deficiencies inhered in existing welfare programs to an even greater degree. For Americans and Britons receiving public assistance, notches and the poverty-trap were not new phenomena. Nor did the existing efforts to help the needy reach all of them or provide sufficient aid so that they would no longer be poor. Indeed, FAP and FIS were meant to be responses to these problems and did offer the prospect of some improvement. Ironically, the fact that neither measure went far enough in reforming welfare turned out to be a source of opposition to their doing anything at all.

However, FAP and FIS also would have visited the disabilities of the current welfare system on a new, large, and potentially sensitive group, the working poor. While enhancing their incomes, both programs truly would have raised the effective "tax" they paid on additional earnings. A repetition of Speenhamland, or something like it, was not unimaginable. And for all the analysis and discussions of the negative income tax that had occurred in Britain and the United States, no one knew for sure what combination of benefit levels and reduction rates would avoid such a calamity.

The British political system was more willing than the American one to suspend doubt and take the risk of enacting FIS, although not without objections. The Heath Government's program was simpler and less obtrusive than FAP, and this no doubt helped. When the latter benefitted from a degree of bi-partisan sympathy and a sense of urgency about doing something to reform welfare—as in the Ways and Means Committee—skepticism about its merits receded in importance. Yet, once FIS became law and questions arose again, the Heath Government was forced to scurry for answers, just as the Nixon Administration had to do after the defects of FAP were exposed by the Finance Committee.

To no small degree, the theoretical advantages of the negative income tax induced in its supporters an over-confidence in its political attractiveness. Even though nominally conservative governments were prepared to gamble on an untested idea, those who would have been most directly affected by FAP and FIS were not. Some, fearing real harm, would charge that the measures went too far. Others, more afraid of partisan disadvantage, would maintain they did not go far enough. Amid such doubts, the institutions of British politics proved somewhat more capable of producing a decision, but in neither country could agreement be reached on how to proceed.

Notes

1. Mark Blaug, "The Poor Law Reexamined," *Journal of Economic History* (June 1964), pp. 229–45.

2. The rest of the program's cost went for fiscal relief, job training, and day care.

3. U.S., Department of Health, Education, and Welfare, Office of the Assistant Secretary for Planning and Evaluation, "Selected Characteristics of Families Eligible for the Family Assistance Plan, 1971 Projections," February 2,

1970, reprinted in Daniel Patrick Moynihan, *The Politics of a Guaranteed Income* (1973), p. 219.

4. John F. Kain and Robert Schafer, "Regional Impacts of the Family Assistance Plan," Program on Regional and Urban Economics, Harvard University (June 1971), p. 31, *et passim;* Richard Armstrong, "The Looming Money Revolution Down South," *Fortune* (June 1970) pp. 66ff.

5. Statement of Robert H. Finch in U.S., House of Representatives, Committee on Ways and Means, *Hearings: Social Security and Welfare Proposals* (1969), p. 42.

6. Great Britain, *Hansard's Parliamentary Debates* (Commons), 806 (November 10, 1970), col. 217.

7. Ibid., col. 227.

8. Ibid., col. 223.

9. Ibid., col. 227.

10. *Hansard,* 807 (December 1, 1970), col. 1222.

11. Richard M. Nixon, Text of the President's Domestic Speech (August 8, 1969), p. 4.

12. Ibid., p. 8.

13. *The Washington Post,* August 31, 1969, p. 2; cf., George Gallup, "Public Opposes Guaranteed Minimum Income, Supports Guaranteed Work Plan," *The Gallup Report,* June 15, 1968.

14. Cited in Moynihan, *The Politics of a Guaranteed Income,* pp. 268–69.

15. U.S., Department of Health, Education, and Welfare, Office of the Secretary, "Analysis of Initial Editorial, Columnist, Magazine and Public Opinion Reaction to the President's Welfare Message," October 21, 1969.

16. AFL-CIO, Transcript of Interview with George Meany (August 28, 1969), p. 2.

17. Karl T. Schlotterbeck, "Jobs for Welfare Clients Seen as Alternative to Guaranteed Income," Chamber of Commerce of the United States, *Washington Report* (June 23, 1969), p. 4.

18. Otto A. Davis and John E. Jackson, "Representative Assemblies and Demands for Redistribution: The Case of Senate Voting on the Family Assistance Plan" (unpublished paper, October 1972), Table 2, p. 8.

19. Johnnie Tillmon and George A. Wiley, Letter to President Richard M. Nixon (August 6, 1969), p. 2.

20. Bill Cavala and Aaron Wildavsky, "The Political Feasibility of Income by Right," *Public Policy* (Spring 1970), pp. 323–29.

21. John F. Manley, *The Politics of Finance: The House Committee on Ways and Means* (1970), p. 64.

22. U.S., House of Representatives, Committee on Ways and Means, *Social Security and Welfare Proposals* (1969), p. 160.

23. Ibid., p. 168.

24. Ibid., pp. 212–13.

25. Ibid., p. 258.

26. Ibid., p. 2357.

27. U.S., House of Representatives, Committee on Ways and Means, *Family Assistance Act of 1970,* 91st Cong., 2d Sess., 1970, H. Rept. No. 91-904 to accompany H.R. 16311, p. 2.

28. Ibid., pp. 84–85.

29. George P. Shultz et al., Transcript of Press Conference (March 5, 1970), p. 2.

30. Cited by Moynihan, *The Politics of a Guaranteed Income*, p. 423.

31. *The New York Times*, April 8, 1970, p. 31.

32. U.S., *Congressional Record*, vol. 116, no. 61 (April 16, 1970), H3220–21.

33. Ibid., H3163.

34. *Hansard*, 806 (November 10, 1970), cols. 261–62 and 265.

35. Ibid., col. 313.

36. Ibid., cols. 282–86 and 288–89.

37. *Hansard*, 805 (November 5, 1970), col. 1278.

38. *Hansard*, 806 (November 10, 1970), col. 259.

39. Ibid., cols. 320–25.

40. Ibid., col. 239.

41. Ibid., col. 234; *Hansard*, 807 (December 1, 1970), col. 1235.

42. *Hansard*, 806 (November 10, 1970), col. 340.

43. *Hansard*, 807 (December 1, 1970), col. 1238.

44. "The Wrong Method of Helping Families," *The Times* (London), December 22, 1971, p. 13; "The Deserving Poor," *Daily Telegraph* (London), December 22, 1971, p. 12.

45. "No Attack on Welfare," *The Times* (London), October 28, 1970, p. 13, Frank Field, "Poor People and the Conservative Government," *Poverty*, no. 16/17 (n.d.), 16.

46. Mike Reddin, "Local Authority Means-Tested Services," in Peter Townsend, Mike Reddin, and Peter Kaim-Caudle, *Social Services for All? Part One*, Fabian Tract 382 (1968), pp. 7–15; A. R. Prest, *Social Benefits and Tax Rates*, Institute of Economic Affairs Research Monograph 22 (1970), *passim*; David Piachaud, "Poverty and Taxation," *The Political Quarterly* (January–March 1971), pp. 31–44.

47. Rate, or property-tax, rebates were means-tested and did go to the working poor, but their value was exceedingly small.

48. David Barker, "The Family Income Supplement," *Family Poverty: Programme for the Seventies*, ed. David Bull (1971), p. 80.

49. Frank Field, *One Nation: The Conservatives' Record since June 1970*, Child Poverty Action Group Poverty Pamphlet 12 (September 1972), pp. 6–7.

50. John Selwyn Gummer, "The Social Services," *The Political Quarterly* (October–December 1973), pp. 430–31.

51. Trades Union Congress, *Report of 103rd Annual Congress* (1971), pp. 111–12.

52. Trades Union Congress, *Report of 104th Annual Congress* (1972), p. 500. The Industrial Relations Act regulated strikes and other aspects of union conduct; the TUC had essentially adopted a policy of non-compliance with it.

53. Jack Jones, "Wages and Social Security," *New Statesman* (January 7, 1972), p. 7.

54. U.S., *Congressional Record*, vol. 116, no. 65 (April 23, 1970), S6104.

55. Ibid.

56. U.S., Senate, Committee on Finance, *Hearings: Family Assistance Act of 1970* (1970), pp. 371–79.

57. Ibid., p. 278. This particular example was from Chicago.

58. Ibid., p. 279.

59. U.S., Senate, Committee on Finance, *Material Related to Administration Revision of H.R. 16311* (1970), p. 5.

60. Charles L. Schultze et al., *Setting National Priorities: The 1972 Budget* (1971), pp. 186–88.

61. U.S., Senate, Committee on Finance, *Family Assistance Act of 1970*, p. 199.

62. Ibid., p. 397.

6

The Defeat of The Negative Income Tax

"The bane of all pauper legislation," observed the Royal Poor Law Commission of 1834, "has been the legislating for extreme cases."[1] Trying to account for every case of need, no matter how improbable, seemed a formula for producing laws full of loopholes and open to widespread abuse. Far better, they advised, to adopt a program based on sound principles and to leave exceptional cases to individual charity.

Nearly one and one-half centuries later, welfare reformers in Britain and the United States would have done well to remember this lesson. In FAP and FIS, they proposed measures that would give more help to the poor while providing incentives for self-support. Before long, the programs were being attacked for failing to do either well. The weight of the charge rested upon atypical examples: people who faced unusually high cumulative tax rates over a portion of their earnings, who failed to claim the benefits which they presumably needed, or who lived in the least generous, lowest-paying regions of the United States. What FAP and FIS would have done for the average recipient seemed not to be at issue.

Nonetheless, both American and British policy-makers tried to modify their programs to deal with the objections that had been raised. To have done otherwise would almost surely have doomed FAP and probably left FIS vulnerable to drastic alteration, or even abolition, at the next change of government. These new proposals were more ambitious, expensive, and complicated than what had originally been put forth. Indeed, in a matter of months, the British were able to develop a full-blown negative income tax, which would have used the tax system to pay social benefits. But in attempting to adjust FAP and FIS to fix out-of-the-ordinary situations, the Nixon and Heath Governments wound up in precisely the predicament forecast by the Poor Law Commission.

Despite their efforts, opposition to restructuring welfare policy continued and even intensified. The broader scope of the new measures only meant that more people would be concerned about how their situations were to be affected. At the same time, the proposals were not so all-encompassing that exceptional cases of hardship or disincentives could not still be found. They were sufficiently bold, though, to be unmistakable departures and to lose the backing of those who might once have thought that this approach to welfare policy was just a better way to achieve traditional goals. Since such people were particularly numerous within Republican and Conservative ranks, their growing dismay over what their leaders were seeking was especially significant.

This time, both the Nixon and Heath Governments were defeated. After nearly four years of planning and debate, only FIS became law, and then as something of a step-child among British welfare programs. Although it continued to be discussed, the idea of establishing a negative income tax, or a version of it, was no longer novel or appealing. As a practical matter, it was all but dead. This chapter will explain how these once-promising schemes met their end.

The Finance Committee Revisited

Although the history of FAP would not be concluded for at least another three years, the rebuff administered by the Senate Finance Committee in May 1970 effectively sealed its fate. In part, this was because the initiative had now passed to Long, Williams, and their colleagues. They would dictate when hearings would be resumed and what issues would be discussed. Although the Administration's revisions were ready by June 10, the committee did not begin reconsideration of FAP until July 21, and it continued to take testimony until September 10. With some Senators still dissatisfied, a "revised revision" was readied and presented by HEW's Veneman at an executive session on October 13. Not until November 5, two days after the midterm elections, was the committee's staff analysis issued, and two more weeks would elapse before the October version of FAP would come to a vote.

The Administration could do little to speed up this schedule. Nixon did meet with the committee's members and publicly urged that the full Senate be allowed to vote on his program. Both Williams and Senator Mike Mansfield, the Democratic leader, from Montana, assured him it would. But the Senate was not disposed to interfere with one of its committees, unless it was neglecting a matter of compelling national importance. Thanks to the revisions of FAP placed before it, the Finance Committee gave every impression of having plenty left to consider.

After the first round of hearings was recessed, the White House created a Cabinet-level working party, composed mostly of the same officials who had been responsible for the original welfare proposal (with the exception of Burns, who had gone to the chairmanship of the Federal Reserve Board). Their initial disposition was to modify FAP less extensively than Long had directed and resubmit it to the Finance Committee within a fortnight. Yet, after nearly six weeks of continual staff meetings, they had decided to include a new health insurance program for the poor, changes in the social services provided for welfare recipients, a revision of food stamps, and plans for closer coordination of FAP with public housing rules. These steps, the planners had argued, along with several smaller ones, responded to the criticisms raised during the hearings and improved the credibility of the incentive theory. Only by making such a broad overhaul of the American "welfare state" could the prospects for defending FAP and winning Finance Committee approval be enhanced.

However, each proposed change also opened up new areas of controversy. For example, partly to eliminate the notch described by Long in his first speech about FAP and partly to contain the total cost of the proposal, the Administration decided to eliminate AFDC grants to unemployed fathers. Under the President's plan, families headed by a full-time worker and those headed by one who was employed part-time, or less, would have been eligible for the same benefits. In the more generous states, the result could have been less income for approximately 90,000 families, leading Senator Harris to remark:

> . . . I believe in every instance that you have mentioned here during the last days, when you have made an effort to rationalize what is a very irrational system, and avoid these notches that apply, disincentives to work which presently exist, you have done it to the detriment of the recipient. He winds up being the victim of rationality.[2]

Although the Administration offered to add a "grandfather clause," the admission that a considerable number of families might be harmed by the transition to FAP seemed to be damaging confirmation of what liberals like Harris and the National Welfare Rights Organization (NWRO) had been asserting all along.

Furthermore, even the June revisions had not really solved some of the work-incentive problems. Although the notches facing earners at the upper end of the FAP income scale had been reduced, the rewards of employment had seemingly diminished for the lowest-paid workers. As the Administration's witnesses sought to explain, this was a consequence of the dynamics of the negative income tax. Unless the total cost or number of people covered was to expand, lowering the rate at which benefits were withdrawn as wages increased for some families required raising it for others. To the skeptical Senators, however, the mathematics mattered less than the continued presence of strong disincentives to work. "I am not claiming that the Administration bill does not eliminate some of the notches," said Williams:

> . . . but I am trying to get the statistical results. The average welfare recipient is not interested in notches and charts. He is interested in what he has to spend, and that is what we are trying to get the answer on.[3]

To the critics on the Finance Committee, the June revisions only reinforced their view that FAP was hastily planned, incomplete, and unclear, while giving them ample excuses for postponing formal action on it.

Not that these Senators needed much additional reason for delaying. For the overwhelming majority of Finance Committee members, the major problem with FAP was not its technical details, but the vast changes it portended for their states. The staff analysis of the June revisions began with charts showing the potential increase in "welfare recipients" under the Administration's proposed reform; all but three of the committee's members represented states where the gain would have been above the national average.[4] This would not be well-received at home, nor could these Senators afford to be unconcerned about the consequences of FAP for local labor markets. (A General Accounting Office study, commissioned at the request of Senator Williams, questioned the optimistic "preliminary findings" of the Office of Economic Opportunity's income maintenance experiments with regard to the likely work-effort of recipients.)[5] Of the public witnesses who testified, few supported the Nixon Administration's bill without reservations, and all but one of the governors who appeared withheld endorsement of FAP in favor of the less radical step of increasing Federal funding for the existing welfare programs.

In short, the measure before the Finance Committee seemed to have many political difficulties. When the time to vote could no longer be avoided, the Senators had no trouble reaching a decision. Taking their appellate duties seriously, on October 8, fourteen cast their ballots against the House-passed version of FAP, while only one—Harris—was in favor of it.[6]

The Liberals' Hour

The Nixon Administration was not surprised by this result. After hearings had resumed in July, the extent of hostility or doubts about FAP on the Finance Committee had become unmistakable. Consequently, the White House had already begun to think about ways of bringing the bill before the full Senate, where journalists and legislative aides predicted that fifty to sixty Senators might support it.

At first, the Administration tried to fashion a "moderate" bloc on the committee which would be willing to report out some version of welfare reform. Meetings with top officials were arranged, Cabinet members like Moynihan were dispatched to deliver speeches in members' constituencies, and on September 3, a group of Senators, including Long and Ribicoff, were flown to the Western White House in San Clemente, California, to attend a state dinner and participate in a discussion with the President. But this meeting did little more than remove doubts about Nixon's commitment to the measure. After explaining that he was for FAP because it was only a "possible disaster," while AFDC was a "certain" one, he insisted that the committee pass a bill along the lines he had proposed, or else he might have to veto it.[7] To a group that was already hesitant about endorsing the plan and had rather different notions about how to deal with dependency, the President's threat was less a spur to take action than another reason to avoid it.

The mid-term elections further complicated the prospects for welfare reform. On the one hand, the Administration had campaigned aggressively—and sometimes, successfully—against liberals, including some who had been expected to support FAP in the Senate. On the other, its campaign references to the measure carefully emphasized its work-inducing provisions rather than its income guarantee. The result was to give FAP a more partisan and more conservative appearance. And in an election that could not have passed unnoticed in the Finance Committee, Representative George Bush, a Texan who was one of the few from his region to vote for the Administration's proposal in the House of Representatives, lost his bid for the Senate.

When the Congress reassembled for its first lame-duck session in twenty years, a new version of FAP awaited Finance Committee action. During the summer hearings, both Ribicoff and Long had asked whether the plan could first be tested in several locales. After initially dismissing this as "temporizing," the Nixon Administration perceived a use for the idea in order to bring FAP before the full Senate.[8] On August 28, the President announced his willingness to accept Ribicoff's amendment; it was the major change incorporated in the October revisions.

Unlike the Office of Economic Opportunity's experiments, these tests would only have postponed nationwide implementation of FAP for twelve months while studies of its effects were conducted. If Congress wished to prevent full operation of the program in July 1972, it would have had to enact another bill. With time needed for securing an appropriation, undertaking the tests, and completing a report, this procedure, noted the committee's staff, would leave less than four months in which changes could be made, time only "perhaps for minor changes affecting administrative procedure."[9] Since no welfare reform legislation was expected before the end of 1970 anyhow, the Nixon Administration had essentially agreed to trade its anticipated start-up time for support from the more cautious Senators.

This ploy might well have succeeded, had not liberal disaffection with FAP become a factor. The October revisions were to be offered by Ribicoff and Senator Wallace F. Bennett, the second-ranking Republican, from Utah, as an amendment to the bill hiking social insurance benefits, which was then before the Finance Committee and virtually certain to be reported to the full Senate. Administration officials intensified their efforts to gain support for FAP, as did the interest groups which favored it.

Those opposed to the measure also became active. On November 18, the NWRO began two days of "people's hearings" in one of the Senate office buildings. With several Senators in attendance, FAP was passionately denounced as inadequate and repressive, a plan aimed at forcing mothers with young children to work at low-paid jobs.[10] Since most of the summer had been spent strengthening the program's "workfare" features (as, for example, by increasing the penalty for refusing to register for work or training), a case could be made for these claims.

Nonetheless, on November 19, Elliot L. Richardson, who had succeeded Finch as Secretary of Health, Education, and Welfare (HEW), informed the President that eight members of the Finance Committee—including the two main targets of the NWRO's campaign, Harris and McCarthy—could be counted on to vote for assisting the working poor. If one more supporter could be found, FAP would be reported to the Senate floor. The next day, Senator Len. B. Jordan, a Republican from Idaho, responded to an appeal for party loyalty by agreeing to vote for the President's bill.

His switch was to no avail. On November 20, by a margin of ten to six, the Finance Committee rejected the October revisions. Harris cast his own ballot and proxies for McCarthy and Senator Albert Gore, a Tennessee Democrat who had lost his seat in the mid-term elections, against the proposal; Clinton P. Anderson of New Mexico, the second-ranking Democrat, followed his lead. Afterward, by a thirteen-to-three tally, the committee adopted a different Ribicoff amendment, authorizing tests of FAP and several other plans for welfare reform, but requiring Congressional approval before any could be implemented nationwide. Once again, the dissenting votes were those of Harris, McCarthy, and Gore.[11]

"It is difficult to know," stated the White House press secretary, Ronald L. Ziegler, in answer to the question of why the only Senator to have supported the House-passed version in October had turned against FAP in November.[12] The reason, Harris explained to reporters, was that the Administration's efforts to forge a "moderate" bloc in the committee had ". . . continually compromised the people's interest." Citing provisions which, he claimed, were "worse than the regressive features of the Social Security amendment [the AFDC freeze] that Senator Robert Kennedy and I successfully fought against in 1967," he concluded: "They've made this bill worse and worse, and finally the straw broke the camel's back."[13] But since Ribicoff had helped fashion the measure and found it suitable, this seems unlikely to have been the primary reason Harris turned against FAP.

Rather, in his vote could be seen the confluence of both major strands of opposition to the Administration's proposal. Harris was one of several liberal Democrats contemplating a campaign for the Presidency. Possible supporters, like the NWRO and its allies, had served clear notice they were against FAP, while most other liberal interest groups had been restrained in their endorsement of it. At the same time, Harris was still a Senator from Oklahoma, one of the states that would have been most affected by the passage of the Administration's bill. One in seven residents would have become, as other Southerners on the committee were fond of putting it, "welfare recipients." As long as FAP stood no chance of becoming law, his vote did not matter; when it did stand a chance, the safest course was to oppose. For Harris, this new approach to welfare reform did too little, yet also too much, and the Administration's revisions did not alter this underlying reality.

To the Senate Floor

Despite the defection of the liberals, the Administration and its Senate allies continued to press for enactment of FAP. The Finance Committee's second vote on November 20 assured that welfare reform provisions would be included in the pending Social Security bill. But Richardson estimated that testing the alternatives before seeking Congressional approval would delay real changes for at least several years. Unlike the White House, HEW lobbyists had believed that the best place to build a coalition for FAP would be in the full Senate, not in the Finance Committee. Now they began work in earnest with

Ribicoff and Bennett to fashion a coalition for a measure that would do more than increase the number of income maintenance experiments.

On December 3, Richardson revealed the results. The Administration would agree to restoration of House-passed provisions, like the program of aid for unemployed fathers, and to adding new titles creating public service jobs and declaring a national goal of an adequate income for every family. However, for budgetary reasons, it insisted on retaining a $1,600 benefit level for a family of four, which was acceptable to Ribicoff. This latest revision of FAP was introduced as an amendment to the Social Security bill on December 9 and eight days later, HEW lobbyists reported that fifty-three senators favored it, with only twenty-six opposed.

Nonetheless, it never came to a vote. The Social Security bill did not leave the Finance Committee until December 11 and did not go before the Senate for nearly another week because a debate was underway on providing military aid to Cambodia. The measure was a typical end-of-session bill, containing not only changes in the old-age insurance program and the welfare reform tests but also a health insurance plan for "catastrophic" illnesses, a series of provisions seeking to restore public assistance rules overturned by the Supreme Court, and a major trade act. Any one of these could have prompted a prolonged discussion, and the trade quotas did.

As the Senate lingered, the prospects for passing FAP declined. Although a motion by Long, on December 19, to table the Ribicoff-Bennett amendment failed on a margin of sixty-five to fifteen, a chance to vote on it again did not occur until the 28th.[14] By then, both the White House and the leadership of Ways and Means had concluded that the task of reforming welfare would have to be carried over into the next Congress. (Mills, in fact, had let it become known he would not even discuss the subject in a conference committee, even if the Senate did approve a bill.) A number of Senators, including Bennett, agreed, but did not want to adjourn before raising social insurance benefits. When Long proposed to remove all the welfare provisions (as well as the trade quotas) from the pending Social Security bill, Ribicoff agreed not to press his amendment. On a division of forty-nine to twenty-one, Long's motion was carried, and the history of welfare reform in the 91st Congress came to an end.[15]

For Senator John J. Williams of Delaware, this outcome was the triumph of his final—his 24th—year in the Senate. Just as he had led the Finance Committee to the notch problem at the beginning of the hearings, so he dominated the parliamentary maneuvering at the close of the floor debate. His next-to-last insertion in the *Congressional*

Record would be a defense of his stand against the measure, complete with charts of benefits and incentives. Throughout his career, he had cultivated a reputation as the Senate's "watchdog," diligently pursuing official corruption and battling farm subsidies, oil depletion allowances, and even increased pay for Congressmen. The Administration's plan seemed of that ilk:

> . . . [N]ot one welfare recipient in America will get a dime less than that which he is now getting under existing law. We must therefore proceed on the premise that there is no reform in this bill. Quite the contrary, all inequities in the existing law will be frozen into the new program.[16]

Although he was willing to test other ways of reforming welfare, Williams could see no compelling reason for adding the working poor to, in his view, an already overly long list of public dependents, and he fought passionately against doing so.

The Administration's problems in the Senate were due not just to one man's crusade, but also to the failure of its political strategy. To offset conservative opposition, it had counted on winning votes for FAP from Republicans who wished to be loyal to the President and Democrats who favored greater help to the poor. In the House of Representatives, such a coalition emerged. In the Senate, it did not.

To no small extent, the Finance Committee's hearings were to blame. FAP had been made to appear uncertain and premature, while at the same time its merits as a replacement for the existing system were questioned and the possibility was raised of better alternatives. Even with presidential backing, support for a guaranteed income was still a risky proposition, possessing little electoral appeal except to those Senators under pressure to find a solution to the problem of dependency. (And they might have been satisfied with federalizing the existing programs.) Support for a solution with as many problems as FAP seemed to have was nearly suicidal. Perhaps the most surprising aspect of the measure's history in the 91st Congress was that so many Senators were even willing to put it to a vote.

At the end, contrary to the Nixon Administration's hopes, too many Republicans had become concerned with the principles of FAP and too many Democrats with its partisan implications. Men like Bennett and Ribicoff were too few to offset the likes of Williams and Harris. The demolition of the incentive theory had also destroyed the political motivations that had enabled FAP to win approval in the House of Representatives.

The Invention of the Tax-Credit Plan

Unlike what happened in the United States, plans for revising Britain's version of the negative income tax came not from its supporters at the Department of Health and Social Security (DHSS), but from one of its most consistent foes. Moreover, the scheme this person designed was warmly received not just by those who had favored FIS but also by many who had been opposed to it. Even so, the Heath Government wound up with no more to show for its efforts than the Nixon Administration.

When the Conservatives entered office in 1970, their main objective was to make the British tax system more conducive to economic growth. Within two years, they had merged a surtax for the wealthy with the personal income tax, restructured company taxes, and created a Value-Added Tax that was to become effective in April 1973. Much of this was the work of Arthur Cockfield, the special adviser on taxation to the Chancellor of the Exchequer.

Cockfield had a reputation as perhaps the only person who fully understood the complicated arrangements of British taxation. After joining the Inland Revenue Service in 1938, he had risen rapidly to become in 1951, the youngest commissioner in the service's long history. Two years later, he left public life to become finance director of a drug firm, but he returned in 1967 to advise Edward Heath on tax policy. A former student of Friedrich A. Hayek, Cockfield had long been concerned with the effects of taxation on the rate of national growth. ". . . [W]hen the history of our age comes to be written," he argued in 1955,

> one of the most striking features which will emerge will be the way that broadly speaking the Tory Party have accepted the vast and fundamental changes made by the Labour Governments in the whole fabric of our social and economic system—not always for the better—and there is no field in which this is more true than that of taxation.[17]

However, he was not disposed toward retrenchment, but rather toward a more careful balancing of what the state provided and how it raised revenues. "We have ended up," he wrote in 1968, "with the worst of both worlds: bad taxes and heavy taxes. What we really want are good taxes and light taxes."[18]

This was one reason he was against the various negative income tax schemes that had been proposed during the period of the 1960s. He still believed, as he had when he presented the Inland Revenue's critique of the Rhys Williams plan to the Royal Commission in 1951, that far from simplifying and reducing taxation, such ideas would have the opposite effect. When he became one of a handful of political appointees in the Heath Government, no one could have predicted he would change his mind.

The Conservative tax program, although it aimed mainly at reducing levies on "economic pacemakers" and shifting from direct to indirect taxation, was also interested in improving the efficiency of the basic revenue-collecting mechanism, the "pay-as-you-earn" system (PAYE).[19] The Labour Government had made some efforts to do this, largely by trying to transfer the operation of the system from clerks to computers. But since PAYE had been designed during the Second World War, when a much lower proportion of the population paid taxes and the sources of income and exemptions were less varied, simply automating the system was difficult and brought few improvements in efficiency.

In opposition, the Conservatives primarily examined the possibility of importing the American practice of self-assessment. Under PAYE, most British families submitted a yearly declaration of their probable financial obligations (like the number of dependents), were assigned an appropriate code—there were 450 at the start of the 1970s—and had their tax deducted entirely from their wages or other sources of income. By allowing the payer to figure out his own tax liability, the Conservatives hoped to realize savings in staff costs. However, they also were aware that this procedure might increase tax evasion and be harder for the public to understand.

Cockfield had another idea, which except in a brief outline to Heath and Macleod, he had not much developed before the election. PAYE was distinctive in being a "cumulative" system; tax deducted was kept in line with total earnings, so that at the end of the year, refunds or additional payments were usually not needed. In effect, this penalized wage-earners who increased their income, since they would immediately pay tax at the marginal rate in order to reach the correct average rate for the year. Moreover, for workers whose wages declined near the end of the tax year, a sizable refund could be forthcoming, which, some Conservatives believed, trade unions used in planning strikes. Cockfield's idea, which had been discussed intermittently in Inland Revenue since 1942, was to put the system on a non-cumulative basis. In much the same way the American withholding tax operates, the amount deducted would be based simply on income during the pay-period, using a rate which assumed the payer would have the same earnings throughout the year.

To avoid having to make a large number of year-end adjustments, Cockfield thought two other features were necessary. A single rate of tax would have to apply across a wide band of income, and some means would have to be found for providing refunds during the year to those payers whose after-tax earnings dropped below an acceptable level (such as the poverty-line). To achieve these objectives, while also making the system as a whole modestly progressive, Cockfield proposed replacing children's and personal tax deductions with a refundable tax credit. Thus, an individual's tax liability would be calculated by applying a single tax rate to his income. If the credit to which he was entitled was larger, he would receive the difference as an addition to his pay; if smaller, the amount owed would be subtracted from his pay. Even if earnings fluctuated, the tax due on total income in a year would equal the amount actually paid on a weekly or monthly basis. At the same time, those whose pay dipped below the poverty-line could have their actual income increased.[20]

After the first round of tax reforms had been completed, Cockfield set to work on simplifying PAYE. From the beginning of the Heath Government, the Treasury had been studying the possibility of using the negative income tax to alter the tax system, but had made little progress. (Brendon Sewill had joined the Government to advise Anthony Barber and was encouraging this work.) Cockfield, however, was working independently and was primarily interested in transforming PAYE into a non-cumulative system. Only after he had determined this was feasible did he begin to examine which welfare objectives, if any, could also be attained. By the summer of 1971, Cockfield was able to give a fifty-page paper to Barber and Sewill detailing his plan.

They reacted excitedly when they saw that someone—particularly someone whose dislike for the idea was well-known—had finally managed to devise a workable negative income tax. The three discussed at length whether the "tax-credit plan" would achieve its objectives and was worth the large cost, which Cockfield had put at nearly one billion pounds. After concluding that it was, they began to consult with members of the Cabinet in October.

For most of the ministers in the Heath Government, the idea seemed like another tax measure, important and pathbreaking to be sure, but relevant to their own interests only insofar as it preempted funds in the budget. To some degree, this was also the view at DHSS. The tax-credit plan had more to do, some civil servants thought, with a "hole in the ground in Skipton," one of the future sites for an Inland Revenue computer, than with welfare policy.[21]

Quickly, though, the potential of the scheme for resolving some of the Department's problems with FIS and other programs became evident. Cockfield himself had suggested that the value of FIS as well as of family allowances and other social benefits might be included in the refundable credit. Moreover, by treating pensions as a form of income, extra help could be provided to the elderly, who were generally reluctant to claim Supplementary Benefits.

Yet DHSS officials were also aware that the negative income tax had been discussed before. One version—Labour's minimum income grant—had even been advanced by Cabinet members, but was found to be unworkable. In devising the tax-credit plan, Cockfield had operated alone. The cautious men at Inland Revenue had not had much to do with its design or assessment. Until it survived their scrutiny, no one was ready to embrace Cockfield's work as the second step in the Conservative program to end family poverty.

In November 1971, a Treasury committee was established to study the tax-credit plan. Composed of civil servants from Inland Revenue and DHSS, as well as an outside tax expert, it met almost daily and in secrecy, exploring the details of the scheme and the numerous items that were necessarily omitted from Cockfield's initial formulation. To be sure, this was standard procedure for the civil service, and did not suggest any animosity toward the plan. On the contrary, Inland Revenue's initial reaction had been that it could be helpful in a variety of ways. However, trial-by-detail had stifled major government initiatives in the past, ex-ministers always claimed, and the bureaucracy had no reason to share the Conservatives' desire for a tax reform as sweeping as the one now before it.

Indeed, if anything, British civil servants had more reason to be wary of an undertaking so enormous. DHSS officials had just seen several years of work on the Titmuss group's pension reforms go unrewarded because of a change in government, while few in Inland Revenue had forgotten the outcry that occurred the last time the tax system had been used to relieve family poverty, in the unpopular clawback. As always, the Treasury was alert to prevent any restrictions on the Chancellor's ability to manage the economy, which both the cost and mechanics of Cockfield's scheme would almost certainly have imposed.

That the tax-credit plan survived the intensive questioning to which it was subjected was partly tribute to the simplicity and logic of the idea itself. In addition, Cockfield was actively and persuasively involved in responding to the issues raised by the study group. Since his knowledge of taxation extended to the finer details as well as encompassing the broader concepts, his views were impossible to dismiss; since he was from but not of the Inland Revenue, he was not about to be deferential. Finally, it was understood that the Chancellor favored the idea and wanted to announce it in his next budget. With that commitment, the most troublesome issue of the plan's cost became secondary.

In short order, the study group endorsed the scheme. These civil servants, younger men and still assistant secretaries, proved not to be the "enlightened amateurs" on whom many of the recent failings of British government had been blamed. Rather, not unlike Cockfield himself, they were administrative specialists, who were aware of the need to improve the operation of Britain's tax and welfare programs and who became convinced that the tax-credit plan was feasible and advantageous. Indeed, so committed did they ultimately become that they came as close to being partisans of the Heath Government's scheme as the code of the British civil service would allow.

In his budget address of March 1972, the Chancellor of the Exchequer, Anthony Barber, announced the Government's intention to propose the tax-credit plan. "This new system," he said,

> . . . represents the most radical reform, improvement and simplification of the PAYE and social service systems for a quarter of a century. Not only that, but it would also mean a considerable improvement in the position of very many people in the more hard-pressed sections of the community.[22]

However, he gave little more than the outlines of the plan and an account of its development. The main personal tax deductions would be replaced by the new credit, as would family allowances and FIS. Using a non-cumulative system, a basic tax rate of 30 percent would be applied to all income. With pensioners and other recipients of social insurance benefits included, the plan would cover 90 percent of the population, with the self-employed being the major group excluded. A saving of ten to fifteen thousand civil servants was also envisioned.

Help would be directed, the Chancellor said, to "many people in need," while at the same time the scheme ". . . would avoid some of the worst features of what has become known as the poverty surtax, with all that that implies by way of disincentive to earn more."[23] Barber acknowledged that the tax-credit plan was the culmination of interests expressed by members of all parties, as well as people outside of politics. "Over the past twenty years or so," he recounted, "so many different schemes have been put forward, yet each one has served only to demonstrate the immense difficulties that there are of making progress on this area."[24] Now, he suggested, a breakthrough had occurred. His plan was selective; only the low-wage worker or pensioner, whose tax credit exceeded his tax liability, would receive a cash grant. Yet it was also universal; everyone included in the scheme would obtain a tax credit of equal value. And for both those who received and those who paid, the incentive to work—the tax rate on earnings—would be the same.

Insofar as it had any precedents, the Heath Government's new proposal seemed reminiscent of the Rhys Williams plan. However, the tax-credit plan differed in two significant ways from the "social dividend." Benefits were to be paid net of taxes, in a single transaction, not in two stages, as Lady Rhys Williams had suggested. More importantly, no commitment had been made to setting the refundable tax credit at a "subsistence" level. Indeed, by deciding to treat pensions and other social insurance benefits as a form of income, Cockfield had managed to avoid the difficulties and costs of providing, in the context of a tax system, adequate grants to those outside the labor force. (For those with neither earnings nor pensions, Supplementary Benefits would remain the primary source of assistance.) Nonetheless, the resemblance of the tax-credit plan to the "social dividend" was sufficient to give Sir Brandon Rhys Williams, and the not insubstantial number of other parliamentarians he had converted, a sense of having at long last made progress, which Barber graciously endorsed.

In truth, what the new proposal was like was much less important politically than what it was not. For Conservatives, the tax-credit plan meant an escape from the worrisome and embarrassing effects of selectivity, as revealed in FIS. For Labour, it was, to paraphrase Roy Jenkins on clawback, universality in an efficient and affordable form. The Heath Government, it appeared, had invented a new way of helping those most in need, while treating everyone equally. Thus, it was especially surprising that the tax-credit plan was not enacted.

The Debate over Tax Credits

A major reason was delay.

In opposition, the Conservatives had repeatedly protested the Labour Government's practice of using the budget message to introduce changes in the tax system. Since Chancellors have traditionally not revealed their budget proposals even to other members of the Cabinet until they are presented in the House of Commons, this procedure drastically limited the opportunity for advance comment on possible tax reforms from interested parties. Accordingly, though not by preference, the Heath Government felt obliged to present its tax changes in "Green Papers" for discussion. In this case, moreover, since the tax-credit plan was expected to require several years to implement, both the opportunity and the incentive existed to create an all-party Select Committee of the House of Commons to study it and perhaps reach a consensus on its desirability that would outlast a change of government. Although this is what the Conservatives did, the results were different from what they intended.

After working throughout the summer, the Heath Government presented its Green Paper on tax credits to Parliament on October 10, 1972. In a foreword, Barber and Sir Keith Joseph described the plan as

> . . . a radical new approach—in which this country is leading the world. . . . It is a development of great importance and one which we believe will be widely welcomed. Because it would affect the everyday lives of so many it merits widespread public interest and discussion.[25]

By the first of December, a Select Committee had been appointed, consisting of five Conservatives, four Labour members of Parliament, and one Liberal. Its chairman was William Clark, a Conservative back-bencher who specialized in tax matters. During the next six months, it received evidence from a variety of individuals and groups. Since the committee was nominally operating as a non-partisan group considering the tax-credit plan only on its merits, the Cabinet secretaries responsible for it were not called to testify and had little formal contact with its members. However, the civil servants who had been working on the plan—now called the Tax-Credit Study Group—did present extensive evidence and commented on the testimony of other witnesses.

Since most of the witnesses favored the scheme, not much commentary was necessary. Although he regretted that more emphasis seemed to have been placed on rationalizing the tax system than on social benefits, nonetheless, the Labour party adviser, Brian Abel-Smith, nonetheless joined the Heath Government in viewing the tax-credit plan as the "largest single step forward in nearly universal provision for the poor and for social dependents" since the Beveridge report.[26] With reservations on certain important points, both the Trades Union Congress and the Confederation of British Industry found the scheme broadly acceptable.

Consequently, it was hardly surprising that on June 26, 1973, the Select Committee adopted a report endorsing the tax-credit plan with some minor modifications.[27] What was unexpected was that the vote to do so had been along party lines and that three of the Labour Party members had even submitted minority reports. (The fourth, Douglas Houghton, still supported the plan.) When, on July 19, Barber held a press conference with the Select Committee to announce the Government's acceptance of its report and intention to introduce legislation in the next session of Parliament, a squabble broke out between the Conservative and the Labour Party members. Instead of promoting a consensus on the tax-credit plan, the appointment of a Select Committee had given time for doubts to develop within both parties on the desirability of such a radical change.

Labour's objections had, in fact, been signalled by its shadow Chancellor, Denis Healey, when the Green Paper was first published. The tax-credit plan, he claimed, was a "gigantic confidence trick" which gave as much aid to the rich as to the poor. Its vast cost, he suggested, might even have to be met through an increase in the Value-Added Tax. "There is no point in giving a family one pound a week in tax credits," Healey declared, "if at the same time the Government increases the cost of living by over one pound."[28] Moreover, if it were enacted, he pointed out the plan would eliminate only one of some forty-seven means-tested welfare programs—namely, FIS.

These arguments were made with greater detail and force in appearances before the Select Committee by two Cambridge economists, Nicholas Kaldor and A. B. Atkinson. Said Kaldor, a Labour party adviser on taxation:

> . . . [T]he introduction of the tax credit scheme would in effect be a highly regressive change which, so far from helping the lower income groups would confer a net benefit on the better-off who have nothing whatever to do with social security, while the recipients of social security, taken as a group, would bear a heavier burden than under the present system.

He had two principal objections. By establishing a single tax rate for most incomes, the tax-credit plan would set up a "firm and lasting barrier to progressive taxation." Furthermore, because much of the scheme's cost reflected the higher value of the tax credits compared to the existing personal tax deductions, only £150 million of the now-estimated £1,300 million expenditure would go to individuals and families with earnings of less than £1,000 annually.[29]

If the Heath Government's negative income tax were to be used, changing this "very wasteful method of relieving poverty . . ." would be difficult, Kaldor charged. Larger benefits for the poor required a higher rate of tax; yet a higher rate of tax meant that the net value of a larger tax credit would be reduced. The only escapes would be either to reduce other public expenditures or to rely on indirect taxes. "It is no accident," Kaldor maintained, "that the Government presented a scheme which benefits the well-to-do and the rich at the expense of the poor and did not say how it would be financed."[30]

These were familiar arguments. Indeed, they were not much more than a reworking of Conservative criticisms of universal social benefits. However, the alternative suggested first by Atkinson and endorsed by Kaldor was not more means-testing, but raising national insurance benefits and family allowances to the subsistence level intended by Beveridge, while employing clawback to confine the value of the increases to low-income families. Such a plan, they claimed could eliminate poverty for no more than the cost of the tax-credit scheme while allowing the tax system to operate as an instrument for redistributing income.

The Tax-Credit Study Group disputed the criticisms of Kaldor and Atkinson, but to little avail. Contrary to what Kaldor seemed to assume, they insisted that the tax-credit plan was not designed to eliminate poverty, only to supplement the incomes of those at work or who had retired. Nearly half of its cost would be for benefits to families whose tax credits exceeded their tax liabilities. Moreover, if year-end adjustments (in the American style) were acceptable, the Chancellor at the time the scheme was implemented could use several rates of taxation, including progressive ones. In any case, they maintained, the more progressive tax system favored by Kaldor and Atkinson—especially if it made greater use of clawback—would require the average wage-earner to pay more to the government than he now did.[31]

But the civil servants were laboring under a serious handicap in trying to rebut the two economists. Because the Green Paper was just a discussion document, the Heath Government refused to make a commitment about the actual amounts of the tax credits. Instead, it stated that they would be sufficient to replace the allowances and benefits that would be abolished, and provided a set of "illustrative" figures.[32] Though this was a proper procedure, it also invited alternative forecasts of the impact of the plan, which could, depending on a particular set of assumptions, demonstrate that the poor might suffer a terrible loss if it were adopted. (A key matter was whether the tax credits would be valued at 1973 levels or adjusted for increases in allowances and benefits that would normally occur before the scheme became operational in 1978.) In addition, by emphasizing the structural features and flexibility of the plan, rather than a specific level of benefits, the Heath Government invariably gave greater prominence to its merits as a tax reform than to its value as a welfare measure. The popular appeal of the scheme was just the reverse.

With election rumors already in the air, the Labour Party was not disposed to be more cooperative with the Conservatives than it had to be on any issue, let alone one which had the vote-gaining potential of the tax-credit plan. Early in the Select Committee's deliberations, the three members who would write minority reports had concluded that the Tory scheme sought simplicity at the expense of equity.[33] And six days after the Chancellor had accepted the majority's report, Labour's National Executive Committee adopted a statement rejecting it and labelling the tax-credit plan a "bogus scheme."[34]

The Defeat of Tax Credits

Labour's opposition alone need not have doomed the tax-credit plan. With their Parliamentary majority, the Conservatives could still have enacted the scheme and hoped that they would still be in office to implement it, or that their successors might think twice about abandoning a program for which preparations were already being made. However, in the fifteen months since the tax-credit plan had been unveiled, a political issue had arisen which caused even supporters of the Heath Government to become restive about the idea. The Conservatives' proposal, it was alleged, threatened to harm the British family.

This accusation grew out of the administrative logic of merging children's tax deductions and family allowances to create a "child tax-credit." Under the existing tax system, the family wage-earner—typically the father—benefitted from any deductions, since they reduced his taxable income. But in Britain, unlike most other countries, family allowances were paid directly to the mother in the form of order books, redeemable at the local post office. (The Churchill coalition had wanted to pay them to men, but retreated in the face of a protest from women's groups.) The Heath Government's plan to replace these two types of assistance with a single, refundable child credit raised the classic question of who should get what.

If the entire child tax-credit were paid to the mother (as a type of family allowance), the taxable income of the married factory worker with four children would be exactly the same as his benchmate with one, or none. Indeed, his tax bill could even increase, though his family's net income might not change. This was just what happened when the Labour Government introduded clawback.

On the other hand, setting the entire value of the tax credit against the husband's pay would deprive his wife of a regular income. Not a few women would be displeased and some social or financial consequences might be felt by families. Yet the logic of the tax-credit plan seemed to dictate this approach.

The Heath Government realized that the payment of child credits would be a sensitive issue and avoided a commitment in the Green Paper:

> Although . . . the description of the scheme . . . has as-
> sumed for illustrative purposes that child credits would be
> received by the father in all cases, the Government regard
> this issue as entirely open.[35]

The Select Committee was invited to air the matter and recommend a solution. Since family allowances were widely regarded as the least popular welfare program, some in the Government and civil service thought that payment to the mother might be avoided, or at worst that a split might be arranged which would preserve the simplicity of the plan. Others saw from the start that the issue of who was to get the child credit could be used not only to discredit the Government's intentions but also to alter the nature of the scheme. The latter were proved to be correct.

Between the publication of the Green Paper in October 1972 and the Select Committee report the following July, a campaign was conducted in a style inherited from the Anti-Corn Law League, and with almost as much success. All the weapons of the mass movement were employed to emphasize one point: the tax-credit plan endangered the security of the British mother. Of some 1,750 letters received by the Government about the scheme, 1,500 were concerned with that issue; the Select Committee's experience was similar.[36] Much of the newspaper coverage, nationally and especially in the local press, dealt with the plight of mothers or the activities of protest groups. A petition containing 300,000 signatures was presented to the Parliament, while individual members were lobbied by their constituents. Accounts were circulated of mothers hard-pressed to feed and clothe their children because of their husband's stinginess in providing housekeeping money, and the Gallup Poll reported that only one-third of British wives actually obtained a share of the rising wages paid to their men.[37]

In fact, good evidence about the division of money within British households was nearly impossible to obtain. Moreover, if husbands were as mean as the popular press was suggesting, statutory entitlement to family allowances or even child credits would have little real consequence. What concerned the mothers—and especially the middle and upper-middle class women who were the mainstay of the campaign—was not how much they would receive through the new arrangements or even how the money would be spent. In the generation since their establishment, family allowances had become a kind of mother's minimum wage. The campaign over child tax-credits showed that British women were not eager to accept a return to collective bargaining.

By March 1973, four months before the Select Committee would report, the Heath Government conceded defeat. At first, Anthony Barber pledged only that ". . . the Government will not adopt any arrangement which leaves mothers being paid less than they are at present."[38] In July, when he announced the Government's intention to proceed with the plan, Barber added that the entire child credit would, as recommended by the Select Committee, be paid directly to the mother.

The reasons behind this decision were not hard to understand. With the help of the Child Poverty Action Group (CPAG) and various women's organizations, the mothers' campaign had been extensive. Virtually no one presented evidence to the Select Committee in favor of paying credits to the father; even the guardians of the workingman's interest, the Trades Union Congress, hedged on this issue. The Labour Party had played a prominent part as well. Indeed, Harold Wilson marked his debut in the 1972–73 Parliamentary session by launching an attack on the Heath Government's "quite wrong proposal to withdraw family allowances from the mother," even though the matter was officially still open.[39]

More importantly, added to this was pressure coming from the Government's own supporters. For Conservative women, too, had been involved in the mothers' campaign, and lobbied directly and effectively against payment of child credits to fathers. To do this, a Tory baroness declared, would be a "retrogressive step, socially, financially, and morally. . . ."[40] If the Government had not agreed, its own majority in the Select Committee—and perhaps even in the House of Commons—would likely have compelled it to give the new benefit to the woman of the house. Its report was a "mum's charter," said a Conservative member of the Select Committee. "All the really important recommendations of the Committee," David Price added, "were designed to improve the position of mothers."[41]

Since it had left the matter to the Select Committee in the first place, the decision to pay the entire child credit to the mother was not in a sense a defeat for the Government. Yet, the months of wrangling had taken their toll on the tax-credit plan itself. A period which the Heath Government had hoped would be devoted to a discussion of a far-reaching change in taxation and social security policy turned into, for most of the public that followed it, a period of tendentious and at times acrimonious monologue on a feature of the plan that was not even at issue. Far from obtaining approval for devising a feasible negative income tax, the Conservatives were portrayed as literally wishing to take food from the mouths of babes. And in finally deciding to pay the child credit as a separate benefit, they could even be accused of abandoning their own design, as the Labour Party readily did:

> This decision of the Select Committee is a flat contradiction of the principles of the Government's tax credits [sic] scheme and shows that the problems of child poverty can, and should, be tackled separately.[42]

Rather than a single system of taxes and benefits, the Government was now proposing a non-cumulative PAYE with a refundable personal tax credit and a program of, in words attributed to Edward Heath, "family allowances writ large."[43]

This was no small accomplishment. Both Barber and Joseph had always emphasized the parity of social and tax objectives in the scheme's design. But the plan that emerged from the Select Committee was not quite the simplification that had originally been sought, and gave little hope that other welfare benefits—means-tested or not—could ultimately be incorporated in a single system of taxing and subsidizing. (Including credits for the disabled and other needy groups had been discussed.) Increasingly, the Government emphasized the social advantages of the new scheme, instead of its potential for rationalizing the network of welfare programs and tax allowances which had developed since the Second World War, and even before.

Whatever the value of this tactic for disarming the plan's critics, it also diminished the attractiveness of tax credits to many Conservatives. If the scheme was now primarily to be a step toward eliminating poverty, a comparison with other ways of spending £1,300 million was inevitable. CPAG and others on the "Left" were not the only ones able to devise a more efficient means of providing benefits; so too were those who, during the 1960s, had advocated greater selectivity.

In February 1973, George and Priscilla Polanyi, two writers for the *laissez-faire* Institute of Economic Affairs, urged the Select Committee to concentrate on:

> . . . the possibility that poverty, in the sense of incomes below a prescribed minimum, might be wholly abolished—or at least more nearly so than under the plan as at present proposed—and that this might be done at a cost well within the limits of tolerable taxation and much less than that of the present plan.[44]

After the Select Committee had reported, they concluded that the scheme had not been improved enough. Even the alternative proposed by the Labour minority (following Kaldor's design) would be

137

better, they claimed, than "the plan to give 88 percent of the proposed benefits to the non-poor."[45]

At the 1973 Conservative Party conference, a proposal to add a minimum income guarantee to the tax-credit plan was resisted by Sir Keith Joseph. He and others in the Government were wondering where the money would be found to fulfill the commitments already implied by the scheme, whose cost now seemed likely to exceed the estimate of £1,300 million.

By the standards of tax relief, this was not an unprecedentedly large sum. In the 1972 budget alone, the Conservatives had foregone £1,200 million pounds in revenue and during their first three years in office claimed to have reduced taxes by nearly £4,000 million per year.[46] But as a public expenditure, the tax-credit plan was an enormously costly item. Indeed, the supposedly drastic cuts in government spending announced by the Chancellor in December 1973 amounted to just £900 million. Moreover, by emphasizing social advantages, the Government decreased the chance that the price of the tax-credit plan would be seen to be of the same cloth as sixpence off the income tax. Instead, the scheme was more likely to be seen as another expensive welfare program, appealing more to Labour Party supporters than to Tory stalwarts.

Nonetheless, in the months after the Select Committee reported, the Heath Government continued to prepare the tax-credit plan for enactment in the Finance Act of 1974. Since the Chancellor remained in favor of it, the necessary funds would be found. In fact, the Cabinet as a whole hardly considered the plan except in a general way, as when deciding to publish a Green Paper or to include it in the legislative agenda of the Queen's speech in November. Despite its implications for social policy and public spending, the tax-credit plan was still a Treasury bill. As such, the important questions were for Barber to answer, or to seek advice from his colleagues as he saw fit.

After the Select Committee had made its views known, few unsettled issues of policy remained. Most of the unfinished work involved the dizzying number of details that seemed to crop up in trying to marry the two distinctive systems of taxation and social security. Although some members of the Heath Government thought the civil service was acting more cautiously than the complexities of the plan warranted, the budgetary advantage of postponing full implementation of tax credits until 1978 at the earliest forestalled any efforts to interfere. In any case, Barber himself was too preoccupied with a worsening economy to pay much attention to the scheme, and Cockfield had left the Treasury to become head of the Government's price control board. All that seemed to be necessary before the tax-credit plan became law were the formalities of a Parliamentary debate and a Royal Assent.

Neither occurred. A miner's strike climaxed a steadily worsening period of confrontation between the Heath Government and the trade unions. The Conservatives decided to ask the British people to decide who should really rule the country and called an election. In February 1974, just as the legislative draughtsmen were setting to work on the tax-credit plan, Parliament was dissolved. The Finance Act that would be introduced later that year was presented not by a Conservative but by a Labour Chancellor, and it did not contain the Heath Government's negative income tax.

Conclusion

Like FAP, the tax-credit plan was partly a casualty of its own ambitiousness. In fashioning a remedy for the problems surrounding FIS and other means-tested programs, the Heath Government created a measure so comprehensive that it was difficult to understand and hard to support. Only those who had followed the long debate over the negative income tax could really appreciate what the British and American policy-makers had accomplished. And even those experts often had questions about some of the details, which further contributed to the sense among politicians and the interested public that the revised versions of FAP and the tax-credit plan were unformed and sought to do too much too quickly. Not surprisingly, trial runs or partial steps (like enacting only the child tax-credits) began to have a growing appeal.

However, the political problems encountered by the two measures were caused not just by the ambiguity of key provisions. The scope of the plans held out the prospect of substantial changes in the existing welfare programs, provoking concern and eventually opposition among those who would be affected. In some cases, as in the states of the American South and among British social workers and tax assessors, the proposals were really threatening. In others, the losses were more procedural than substantive. Neither British mothers receiving family allowances nor American women heading families supported by AFDC would have been victimized financially by the adoption of the tax-credit plan and FAP. But the new programs would have altered significantly the manner in which they had been getting help, and this was sufficient ground for opposition.

According to one model of the development of welfare policy, programs once adopted are gradually improved through a process akin to learning.[47] Under the guidance of bureaucrats and professionals, existing measures are modified to solve problems revealed by experience or to achieve unfinished tasks. As a result, the growth of the "welfare state" tends to follow a pattern of steady expansion, rather than of growth alternating with contraction.

The history of FAP and the tax-credit plan suggests another reason behind this pattern. David B. Truman once noted:

> Whether one looks at efforts to redistribute the tax load, to alter market practices, to restrict the exploration of natural resources, to equalize opportunities for public education, or to accomplish any of hundreds of other objectives, one will find a large share of group activity dedicated to preventing any change in the existing order of things.[48]

To judge from the debate over the negative income tax, this observation seems applicable to efforts at welfare reform as well, and as much to the more tightly controlled British political system as to the open system of the United States. Once given, social benefits seem unable to be taken away, even to be replaced by a program at least as generous. Moreover, efforts to correct problems uncovered in existing programs may only engender more opposition to any change at all.

In the case of FAP and the tax-credit plan, British and American policy-makers were in fact able to learn from experience. But once they thought they understood the problem, the difficulty arose of persuading others to try a new approach. The stability and steady expansion of the "welfare state" may have less to do with planned development than with the defense (and aggrandizement) of the status quo.

Notes

1. S. G. and E. O. A. Checkland, eds., *The Poor Law Report of 1834* (Penguin ed.; 1974), pp. 376–77.

2. U.S., Senate, Committee on Finance, *Hearings: Family Assistance Act of 1970* (1970), p. 606.

3. Ibid., p. 510.

4. U.S., Senate, Committee on Finance, *Material Related to Administration Revision of H.R. 16311* (1970), pp. 51–53.

5. U.S., Senate, Committee on Finance, *Family Assistance Act of 1970*, pp. 905–75.

6. "Welfare Reform is Again Rejected by Senate Panel," *The New York Times*, November 21, 1970, p. 1.

7. Quoted in Daniel Patrick Moynihan, *The Politics of a Guaranteed Income* (1973), p. 522.

8. Testimony of James D. Hodgson in U.S., Senate, Committee on Finance, *Family Assistance Act of 1970*, p. 890.

9. U.S., Senate, Committee on Finance, *H.R. 16311 The Family Assistance Act of 1970: June Revision Revised and Resubmitted* (1970), p. A4.

10. Moynihan, *The Politics of a Guaranteed Income,* pp. 532–33; Vincent J. and Vee Burke, *Nixon's Good Deed: Welfare Reform* (1974), pp. 161–63.

11. "Welfare Plan Rejected by Senate Unit," *The Washington Post,* November 21, 1970, p. 1.

12. Quoted in *The New York Times,* November 21, 1970, p. 1.

13. "Panel Rejects Welfare Bill, 10–6," *The Washington Star,* November 20, 1970, p. 1.

14. U.S., *Congressional Record,* vol. 116, part 32 (December 19, 1970), 42752.

15. U.S., *Congressional Record,* vol. 116, no. 208 (December 18, 1970), S21238.

16. U.S., *Congressional Record,* vol. 116, no. 208 (December 28, 1970), S21238.

17. F. A. Cockfield, "Report of the Royal Commission on the Taxation of Profits and Income: A Commentary," *National Provident Bank Review* (November 1977), p. 17.

18. F. A. Cockfield, "Central Government Taxation," *Public Sector Economics,* ed. A. R. Prest (1968), p. 27.

19. This is the British equivalent of the American withholding tax.

20. The best discussion of how the tax-credit plan would have worked is contained in Institute for Fiscal Studies, *Conference on Proposals for a Tax-Credit System,* Publication No. 5 (March 1973), pp. 53–63 *et passim.*

21. Personal interview with the author.

22. Great Britain, *Hansard's Parliamentary Debates* (Commons), 833 (March 21, 1972), col. 1385.

23. Ibid., col. 1383.

24. *Hansard,* 834 (March 27, 1972), col. 159.

25. Great Britain, Chancellor of the Exchequer and the Secretary of State for Social Services, *Proposals for a Tax-Credit System,* Cmnd. 5116 (1972), p. iii.

26. Great Britain, Select Committee on Tax-Credit, *Evidence* (1973), p. 358.

27. Great Britain, Select Committee on Tax-Credit, *Report and Proceedings* (1973), pp. 5–7.

28. "Healey Condemns Plan," *The Financial Times,* October 11, 1972, p. 5.

29. *Evidence,* pp. 212 and 217.

30. Ibid., pp. 227 and 268.

31. Ibid., pp. 237–44.

32. *Proposals for a Tax-Credit System,* p. 23.

33. Cf. Barbara Castle's comments of February 15, 1973, in *Evidence,* p. 84.

34. Labour Party, *Report of the 72d Annual Conference* (1973), pp. 357–78.

35. *Proposals for a Tax-Credit System,* p. 20.

36. *Report and Proceedings,* p. 20.

37. The Gallup Poll (London), "Family Allowances," Private survey, January 1973, Table 2.

38. *Hansard,* 852 (March 6, 1973) col. 241.

39. Cited by *The Economist,* December 2, 1972, p. 15.

40. Great Britain, *Hansard's Parliamentary Debates* (Lords), 338 (January 24, 1973), col. 169.

141

41. Quoted in *Hampshire Chronicle* (England), August 10, 1973, p. 3.

42. Labour Party, *Report of the 72d Annual Conference,* p. 357.

43. Personal interview with the author.

44. George and Priscilla Polanyi, "Tax Credits: A Reverse Income Tax," *National Westminster Bank Quarterly Review* (February 1973), p. 34.

45. George and Priscilla Polanyi, "Tax Credits: A Missed Opportunity," *National Westminster Bank Quarterly Review* (February 1974), p. 56.

46. Conservative Research Department, "Three Years' Work," *Notes on Current Politics,* No. 16 (September 24, 1973), 260.

47. Hugh Heclo, *Modern Social Politics in Britain and Sweden* (1974), pp. 304–22.

48. David B. Truman, *The Governmental Process: Political Interests and Public Opinion* (2d ed.; 1971), p. 353.

7

Aftermath of an Idea

The end of the 91st Congress and of the Heath Government did not conclude the debate over the negative income tax. The Nixon Administration, still in office, apparently remained committed to FAP. Even before the Senate adjourned without acting on welfare reform, plans were being made to try again in the 92d Congress. Indeed, some thought the experience gained in the preceding session, along with the retirement of the leading foe of FAP, Senator John J. Williams, had increased the prospects of enactment.[1]

In Britain, Labour had come to power with its traditional commitment to aiding the poor, but with no better idea of how to do so than when it left office in 1970. Although alternatives to the tax-credit plan had been offered by Labour members of the Select Committee and by advisers like Nicholas Kaldor, important support for it could also be found within the party. Since the British economy was again teetering on the brink of collapse, the new Wilson Government had little leeway for simply expanding the existing welfare programs. Endorsing a plan devised by the Tories and backed by the civil service offered perhaps the only chance for a major accomplishment in social policy that would not set off another financial crisis.

Nonetheless, this was not the course Labour chose. Nor did the Nixon Administration (or its successors) manage to enact FAP, despite numerous revisions. At the end of the 1970s, FIS was still operating in Britain; and, ironically, at the instigation of the Senate Finance Committee, a small negative income tax for the working poor had been established in the United States. Otherwise, nearly two decades of discussion about changing welfare policy had resulted in the continuation and expansion of existing programs. How this disappointing aftermath came about is the subject of this chapter.

The Passage of H.R. 1

In the United States, despite the retirement of Senator Williams, the sequence of events in the 92d Congress proved to be similar to that in the 91st. If anything, the previous experience led to a hardening of positions rather than to compromises. Thus, Wilbur Mills and John Byrnes sought to make their handiwork impervious to the sort of assault that had been launched in the Finance Committee. On the assumption that their votes would again hold the balance, liberals became more insistent on obtaining changes in the benefits and other details of the program in return for their support. Meanwhile, conservatives of both parties were more determined to fashion an alternative of their own. At the same time, the White House grew increasingly less willing to make any modifications at all.

To the welfare reform planners in the Nixon Administration, the setback in the 91st Congress was blamed on a lack of time, coupled with misinformation about the proposal. Since the increase in old-age insurance benefits had also failed to be enacted, it was expected that another Social Security bill would be the first order of business when the legislators returned to Washington, and Mills and Byrnes were willing to attach FAP to it. In a meeting with the President, Senators Russell B. Long and Wallace F. Bennett (who had become the senior Republican on the Finance Committee) promised that FAP would be acted upon in the new Congress, although each asked for some changes. In his State of the Union message delivered in January, Nixon listed welfare reform as one of the Administration's six "great goals" for 1971, and White House aides were privately forecasting a bill-signing ceremony in September.

The supporters of FAP seemed determined to meet this schedule. On January 22, the opening day of the 92d Congress, Mills and Byrnes introduced a Social Security bill that included the Administration's welfare reform in the version approved by the House of Representatives nine months earlier. As the first item in the docket, it received the prestigious number, H.R. 1, and was referred to the Ways and Means Committee which decided that further public hearings were unnecessary. Executive sessions commenced on February 2 with Elliot Richardson, the Secretary of Health, Education, and Welfare (HEW), testifying:

> The Administration expected welfare reform to be law by now. We had hoped that it would have been approved as expeditiously by the Senate as it was by this Committee and the House during the last session of Congress. But the time and effort already invested in prior hearings by the Committee and its staff, as well as by the Administration, provide a solid foundation for speedy, definitive action. I believe we can achieve enactment of H.R. 1 by working together, and look forward to this opportunity to eliminate the current wel-

fare mess with you. Only one element has changed significantly in the past twelve-months—the urgency of the
situation.[2]

As if to emphasize the need to act quickly, all three national news-
weeklies appeared on February 8 with cover stories about the problem
of dependency.

Even so, nearly four months elapsed before H.R. 1 was put before
the House of Representatives. This time, not the principles of the incentive theory but rather its details preoccupied the committee. With
one eye on his fellow Representatives and another on the Senate,
Mills directed the Administration to compile a list of all the questions
that had been raised about the measure and to provide answers. Almost as if too little attention had been given the plan during the 91st
Congress, Ways and Means now undertook a section-by-section examination of it. Despite the ominous stories about the growing welfare "crisis," matters like the treatment of alimony payments and the
frequency of reassessing earnings commanded the interest of the
Congressmen. The Administration's officials did not really object;
they too had been embarrassed in the Senate and wanted to avoid a
repeat performance. But instead of gathering momentum at the start
of the new Congress, FAP was once again mired in a committee.

There was more to this delay than legislative caution. Both the
Administration and the committee's leadership believed that the
events of the 91st Congress had cost FAP some support and made a
closer vote likely in the House. During the executive sessions, they
were also looking for ways to enhance the political appeal of H.R. 1.
By "cashing out" food stamps, the basic benefit level was increased to
$2,400 for a family of four. At the same time, the penalty for refusing
to register for work or training was raised to $800. In response to
liberal concerns, 200,000 public service jobs were to be created; to satisfy conservatives, employable recipients were to be treated separately
and come under the auspices of the Department of Labor, instead of
the supposedly more lenient HEW. This latter change also had the
effect of distinguishing the working poor from AFDC families in an
effort to avoid the charge that FAP was simply creating additional welfare cases.

Much of this was costly. In order to restrain the expense and
coverage of the plan, the benefit-reduction rate was raised to 67 percent. After an initial disregard of work expenses, two dollars in assistance would now be deducted for every three dollars in earnings.
Partly by design, partly as a consequence of other decisions, H.R. 1

would place less emphasis on financial incentives, and more on administrative devices to prevent dependency.

In addition to modifying the proposal significantly, Mills, in particular, sought to strengthen support among the nation's governors for FAP. Both he and Byrnes were adamantly opposed to the Nixon Administration's companion measure, revenue-sharing, which they felt would be an abdication of Congressional responsibility for Federal spending. In February, seemingly as part of an effort to defeat this giveaway, Mills began to hint that his committee might consider substituting for FAP a measure that would provide fiscal relief by federalizing the existing welfare programs. Although the governors favored the idea, it had a serious flaw as an alternative to revenue-sharing. If Washington assumed all the costs of public assistance, two states—New York and California—would have obtained 40 percent of the new grants-in-aid and most cities would have received no money at all. FAP spread the new Federal funds more widely. In the context of fiscal relief, most governors would have preferred the Administration's version of welfare reform, not least since enacting it would not preclude seeking revenue-sharing as well. As a result of Mills' threat, state and local officials were added to Social Security recipients and other groups with a substantive interest in the passage of H.R. 1 as originally introduced—and that might well have been the committee chairman's aim all along.

As in the 91st Congress, however, this maneuvering took time, during which backing for the bill began to erode. The first to go were the pensioners, who could be put off no longer. On March 16, the Senate unanimously adopted an amendment to a debt-ceiling measure that increased Social Security benefits by 10 percent. With no real choice, it was accepted by Mills and signed into law by the President the next day.

Later in the month, a coalition of liberal groups—the Campaign for Adequate Welfare Reform Now—unveiled its alternative to H.R. 1, a program with a basic benefit level of $3,600 for a family of four. On April 7, Representative Don Fraser of Minnesota, a past chairman of the Democratic Study Group, introduced a bill embodying this measure in the House. Liberals also began to criticize changes made in the executive sessions of Ways and Means, most notably the decision again not to require the more generous states to supplement the FAP grant.

Conservatives were just as dismayed by some of the modifications, as well as the total cost of the welfare titles, $5.5 billion, an increase of $1 billion over the 1970 version.[3] Nor did they find the new administrative controls reassuring. To the contrary, alternative pro-

146

posals emphasizing job training and social services, and not including the working poor, were put forth on March 3 by Governor Ronald Reagan of California, and on March 11 by Representative Al Ullman of Oregon, the third-ranking Democrat on Ways and Means.

House opposition to FAP, mostly polemical and uninspired during the 91st Congress, had become sufficiently formidable in the 92d for Mills and Byrnes to agree to a "modified closed rule" for the floor debate, which permitted a separate vote on the welfare reform portion of H.R. 1. Nonetheless, FAP survived, albeit by a smaller margin.

Ways and Means completed its work on May 12. Five days later, it voted to report H.R. 1, as amended, to the House. Although the tallies on some of the individual provisions had been close, only three of the twenty-three members—Ullman and two Southerners—dissented. (Four other Democrats, representing California, New York, Ohio, and Pennsylvania, filed "additional views" in support of raising the benefit level and giving more fiscal relief to the states.)[4] A month later, the 687-page bill reached the full chamber, where debate went on for two days. Finally, on June 22, by a vote of 234 to 187, the House rejected a motion to delete FAP and, shortly afterwards, approved H.R. 1, with 288 Congressmen in favor, only 132 against.[5]

Although the margin on the first and most crucial vote was reduced to half of what it had been in the 91st Congress, the coalition behind the Nixon Administration's welfare reform was still sufficient to assure passage. The Democratic Study Group again managed to sway liberals toward FAP, although its "fact sheet" was not as laudatory as it had been. Its chairman, Representative Philip Burton, took a more active role, obtaining supportive letters from groups like the AFL-CIO and seven former HEW Secretaries.

Likewise, the White House was successful in its appeal for Republican backing. In a series of speeches throughout the spring, the President conveyed the unmistakable impression that FAP was not only his most important legislative proposal, but also one designed to encourage people to take work, no matter how menial. To a degree, even Governor Reagan's opposition was softened by his need to obtain Federal approval for changes he wanted to make in California's welfare programs.

Also effective was Mills. Just beginning the strange path that would lead him from campaigning for the Presidency to personal disgrace, the Ways and Means Committee chairman was increasingly eager to be seen as a national figure. Time and again, he lobbied his fellow Southerners and portrayed FAP as the only alternative to the discredited AFDC. For good measure, he engineered a last-minute amendment to H.R. 1 that gave another 5 percent raise in benefits to pensioners. Since the welfare provisions would face a separate vote, this addition was superfluous in the House. More likely, Mills was thinking ahead to the Senate, where the bill with which he was now closely associated would face a sterner test and such "sweeteners" might really be necessary.

The Dismantling of H.R. 1

The ploy backfired. Although FAP did encounter serious opposition in the Senate, which the actions of the Nixon Administration again managed to abet, the provisions attached to H.R. 1 to make it more appealing could not dislodge the measure from the Finance Committee. Instead, with another long delay in prospect, several Senators tried to enact the most widely supported parts separately, thereby worsening FAP's chances for eventual passage.

Indeed, by the time the Finance Committee began work on H.R. 1, it was already the end of June. With a summer recess likely in August, a September bill-signing ceremony appeared impossible. Moreover, the members of the committee did not seem eager to expedite matters. Speaking for the liberals, Senator Abraham A. Ribicoff called for a number of changes, including an increase in the benefit level. Chairman Long, although his antipathy to FAP was apparent, indicated his willingness to support a version modified to give more emphasis to employment. After the House had acted, Long commended its work and promised that his committee would report a bill to the Senate. But even if no slippage were to occur, the schedule he outlined would not have produced a vote by the full chamber until November or December, uncomfortably close to the start of the 1972 presidential election campaign.

Public hearings began on July 27. They were, an Administration observer noted privately, like a "re-run of last year."[6] The committee chairman opened by declaring that H.R. 1 "like its predecessor . . . does not provide economic incentives to work." Long then went on to warn, "Either with or without the help of the Department of Health, Education, and Welfare we shall explore the myth that H.R. 1 will reduce the welfare rolls."[7] After Richardson had presented the Administration's case, Senator Carl T. Curtis, a Republican from Nebraska, inquired:

> Mr. Secretary, last year, there were some charts prepared at the request of the Committee. I believe Senator Williams requested them. And this Committee has asked that they be updated to show the same factors in reference to H.R. 1 that is now before us. Do you have those here?[8]

The HEW Secretary did, along with a more adroit account of why they "distort the nature of the work decision."[9] This time, however, the committee staff had also prepared charts, and theirs demonstrated that an extra dollar earned would still cost some families more than one dollar in higher taxes and lower benefits.[10]

In short order, Ribicoff objected to eliminating the requirement for state supplements to the FAP grant:

> SENATOR RIBICOFF: In other words, you are assuring that millions of Americans will receive less under the administration proposal than they now will receive. . . .

> SECRETARY RICHARDSON: You have put that point with a very straight face, Senator.[11]

And in this fashion, the hearings continued for three more days, with Cabinet or sub-Cabinet witnesses parrying thrusts aimed not just at H.R. 1 but also at earlier versions of FAP, as when Senator Harry F. Byrd, the Virginia independent, reminded Richardson that in 1970, he had testified that $1,600 was an adequate benefit level. They concluded in stalemate, a majority of Senators apparently unconverted, but this time the Nixon Administration also seemed unwilling to yield.

That changed during the summer recess. On August 15, the President announced a "new economic policy" whose central feature was to be a freeze, followed by some form of control, of prices and wages. He also proposed a series of reductions in taxation and public spending, one of which concerned H.R. 1:

> . . . [S]ince the Congress has already delayed action on two of the great initiatives of the administration, I will ask Congress to amend my proposals to postpone the implementation of Revenue Sharing for three months and Welfare Reform for one year.[12]

With a Senate vote not likely before the end of 1971 (if then), it was doubtful FAP could have paid benefits by the planned starting-date of July 1972 anyway. A further twelve-month delay to obtain legislation and implement the program was easily justified.

Even so, just as its willingness to redraft FAP in May 1970 raised questions about the Administration's commitment to the measure, so this "new economic policy" created the impression that its support was again wavering. Three days after the President's speech, Senator Long, citing the postponement and the extra work for his committee as a result of the proposed tax changes, forecast a delay in the consideration of welfare reform until 1972. Meanwhile, more liberal Democrats, as well as several of the interest groups that had been actively lobbying for the measure, complained that the Administration was abandoning FAP. At the end of August, after talking with the President in San Clemente, Richardson emphatically denied this allegation, and on September 9, in an address to a joint session of Congress, Nixon himself urged the enactment of welfare reform before the end of the year.

These efforts to recover were only partly successful. Instead of providing the steadfast backing that was needed, the President had again shown he was willing to make some concessions on welfare reform in order to secure conservative support for other major proposals, in this case a controversial economic program. In light of the Senate hearings, Nixon might well have had the better of the deal. In any event, the August speech left Long and his allies in a commanding position on welfare reform, and greatly diminished the prospect of enacting FAP.

As a result of this development, efforts to bypass the Finance Committee intensified. Criticizing the President's economic program for providing more for the wealthy than for the poor, Senate liberals threatened to attach FAP to the forthcoming tax bill. Whether they could have done so was questionable. Both the Nixon Administration and the Ways and Means Committee were likely to oppose any amendment that might delay the vital revenue measure. More importantly, no version of FAP could command the support of a substantial number of Senators. Among the fifty civic and labor organizations which participated in the drafting, the major point of agreement was that the welfare title of H.R. 1 was unacceptable, but there was no consensus on what should replace it. Nearly two months elapsed before Ribicoff, on October 29, was able to introduce a compromise amendment setting the benefit level at $3,000 for 1973 and at the poverty-line in 1976. Even this lacked the backing of Senator Fred R. Harris and the National Welfare Rights Organization (NWRO). When apprised that it would cost at least half again as much as H.R. 1, Ribicoff himself professed to be astounded and briefly threatened to withdraw his support from *any* version of FAP.[13]

In the meantime, under pressure from the Senate leadership and the Administration, Long agreed to resume hearings in January 1972 and to try to report a bill by March 1. With this commitment, Ribicoff decided to forego an attempt to add the liberals' version of FAP to the pending tax legislation.

Other Senators were not so patient. Instead of trying to fashion their own welfare proposals, however, they looked to attach to other bills those features of H.R. 1 which were not thought to be controversial. One such effort, led by Senator Charles H. Percy, a Republican from Illinois, sought to relieve state governments of the increase in public assistance costs since July 1971, a provision approved by Ways and Means to guard against extra expenses incident to the transition to FAP. With the backing of 21 governors, it was introduced on November 15 as an amendment to the tax-reduction act. If it were to pass, the Administration feared that support for FAP would be diminished and a precedent would be created for similar actions. After another pledge from Long to expedite welfare reform and a commitment from John D. Ehrlichman, the President's chief domestic policy adviser, to accept his amendment later, Percy agreed to withdraw it.[14]

The same tactic could also be used by those who did not wish to see FAP pass. In responding to the President's August speech, Long observed that postponing hearings on H.R. 1 would also delay enactment of changes in the old-age insurance program. Although throughout the session he warned he might introduce these provisions separately, he remained satisfied with blaming the Administration's welfare reform proposal for Congressional failure to raise pensions again.

Senator Herman Talmadge, Long's Democratic colleague from Georgia, did succeed in amending a routine death-benefits bill to include the major changes in the work and training programs contained in H.R. 1.[15] Considered under a suspension of the normal rules by a nearly deserted Senate on the first Saturday in December, the measures went unopposed, catching the Administration's lobbyists as well as the interest groups by surprise. As a result, FAP's supporters faced a serious dilemma. Accepting the Talmadge amendments risked the loss of some conservative support for H.R. 1; yet neither the leadership of the Ways and Means Committee nor the Nixon Administration wished to object strenuously to speeding up efforts to put welfare recipients to work. Although an effort was made to delete it in the House-Senate conference committee and a presidential veto was considered, "workfare" was signed into law after further assurance from Long that what was left of the welfare reform plan would be taken up in the new year.

The Finance Committee Bill

The Finance Committee chairman was true to his word. On January 20, 1972, the first day of second session of the 92d Congress, consideration of H.R. 1 resumed. However, little seemed to have changed.

Once again, the comments of the Senators about FAP ranged from unenthusiastic to hostile. So too, with the occasional exception of governors like New York's Nelson A. Rockefeller, did the testimony of the public witnesses. Particularly revealing was the presentation by Alice M. Rivlin, who, as an HEW assistant secretary, had presided over the planning of the negative income tax in the last years of the Johnson Administration. Now in 1972, she (along with her Brookings Institution colleague, Joseph A. Pechman) concluded that because of the persisting notches, H.R. 1 "does not make it worthwhile for people receiving welfare payments to hold jobs." She went on to tell the Finance Committee:

> It is outrageous to give lipservice to work incentives, indeed to require welfare recipients to register for work and training, while at the same time making it virtually impossible for them to improve their families' well-being by taking a job.[16]

With liberal economists echoing former Senator Williams, FAP was indeed in dire straits.

This kind of criticism no longer held much interest for Long and other members of the committee. Even before hearings resumed, they had begun to think of writing their own welfare reform bill, and the witnesses were selected as much to present a case for expanding "workfare" as to discredit FAP further. By February 9, testimony was finished. Shortly afterward, the committee started a heavy schedule of executive sessions to fashion an alternative.

What emerged during the next three months fit the worst stereotypes of collective decision-making. The Finance Committee's bill was a massive proposal incorporating the favorite schemes of the group's leaders with the barest effort at coordination. Moreover, by the Nixon Administration's reckoning, it was at least twice as expensive as FAP (although the Senators who authored it disagreed). The bill's centerpiece was a "guaranteed job opportunity program" that abolished AFDC eligibility for employable recipients—families headed by an able-bodied man or a woman with no children under the age of six, approximately 40 percent of the entire caseload—and subsidized or created jobs for them, including tasks such as "beautifying their apartments" or "providing a pleasing home atmosphere."[17] Nothing would be paid to any in this group who did not work. "Slavefare," Ribicoff called the plan; "a $9 billion step backward, backward into the leaf-raking schemes of the 1930s," declared Richardson and Labor Secretary, James D. Hodgson.[18] Nevertheless, on April 28, by a vote of ten to four, with Ribicoff, Harris, and two other Democrats in the minority, the Finance Committee adopted the program as a substitute for FAP.[19]

This outcome came as no surprise to the Nixon Administration. Its officials had been barred from the committee's executive sessions whenever welfare reform was being discussed, lest they delay the proceedings by debating principles instead of furnishing technical advice, and in mid-April, Ehrlichman had predicted publicly that the Senators' work would bear a "very remote resemblance" to the President's proposal.[20] Although some effort was made to reach agreement on a limited test of FAP prior to national implementation, the Administration's lobbyists concentrated on minimizing the amount of time H.R. 1 spent in the committee. But by writing a 1,000-page bill and an even lengthier report, Long and his allies could keep busy throughout the summer. ("Tentative" final approval of their measure was announced on June 13; drafting, other business, and the summer recess kept it from the Senate floor until September 26.)

Yet even if H.R. 1 had been extricated from the Finance Committee sooner, it was becoming less likely that the Senate would prefer the Administration's version of FAP to no welfare reform at all. One reason was that the "sweeteners" added in the House of Representatives had been gradually digested by the Senate. With an election approaching, a 20 percent increase in old-age insurance benefits was attached to a debt-ceiling bill, quickly approved by the Congress, and on July 1 signed by the President, even though he believed it was fiscally irresponsible. Similarly, spurred by Mills' candidacy for the Presidency, revenue-sharing had moved through the legislative process, reaching the Finance Committee in June and arriving on the Senate floor two months later (with H.R.1 having been set aside). Its enactment in the autumn not only provided most of the financial aid sought by state and local officials, but also gave the Nixon Administration a major triumph in domestic policy.

In addition, the support of liberal Democrats and Republicans for FAP was becoming increasingly uncertain. With White House backing, Richardson and his aides had negotiated with Ribicoff and several allied groups throughout the spring to determine areas of agreement. In exchange for a slight relaxation of the work-registration requirement and promises that no AFDC recipient would suffer a loss in aid, the liberals were willing to accept a benefit level of $2,600. Despite the endorsement of his HEW Secretary, Nixon rejected this package. Part of the reason was its cost, an additional $1 billion plus the potentially expensive precedent of bargaining over the amount of assistance. More importantly, with his own re-election campaign underway and with many of his supporters unhappy about FAP, Nixon wanted to avoid the appearance of a shift to the "Left," which he judged to be unnecessary anyway. "My own present intention . . . is to stay by our middle position," he told a press conference in June. "I think it is the right position and I believe that it is a position that can get through this Congress."[21]

However, the liberals needed some concession. They had too often criticized the provisions of H.R. 1 and pledged to amend it for them to accept the bill unaltered. Many were also being assailed by groups on their "Left." Three months earlier, for example, a NWRO-organized "children's march" had linked Ribicoff with Nixon, Mills and Long in a "D.C. Four Against the Poor."[22] If the President could not yield, neither could they.

While this Congressional maneuvering was going on, a more significant development was occurring outside Washington. On November 12, 1971, HEW officials reported a decline of 84,000 people in the welfare rolls during July, the third consecutive month in which a reduction had taken place.[23] Although growth would resume in August, the rate had been slowed, and within a year, would virtually cease altogether. The welfare crisis was waning.

This, in part, was a natural consequence of the program's earlier expansion. By the end of 1971, most of those who were eligible for AFDC were obtaining benefits.[24] At the same time, with welfare reform apparently stalled in the Congress, state and city officials had begun to find their own ways to curtail expenditures. Several announced reductions in payments or eligibility standards; New York as well as California established "workfare" programs; and New York City's liberal mayor, John V. Lindsay, having failed to obtain a court order making public assistance solely a federal and state charge, prepared to introduce a "zero-growth" policy.

None of these changes meant that FAP was no longer necessary. To the contrary, some Administration officials, such as Richard P. Nathan, who was now a deputy undersecretary at HEW in charge of welfare reform planning, maintained that enacting H.R. 1 would permit still greater efficiencies. However, with state and local actions apparently having some effect, FAP could not be portrayed as the only way to avoid a social disaster.

The White House and Welfare Reform

At any rate, this was becoming the view from the White House. Far from being a problem that was out of control and endangering national stability, dependency appeared to be manageable by the sort of measures advocated by Arthur Burns and his allies in the Cabinet debate of 1969. This lesson was drawn for the President not just by the actions of governors and mayors, but also in discussions with conservative Senators opposed to FAP. The departure of Moynihan, Nathan, and other proponents of the incentive theory left no one close to Nixon who could effectively present a countervailing argument. Worse yet, the lengthy process of redrafting and lobbying had given FAP the stamp of an HEW product, and White House attitudes toward the measure could not help being affected by ambivalent feelings about the department and its leadership. Nonetheless, Nixon remained publicly committed to his version of welfare reform. Even if the growth of AFDC had slowed, he had reason to think that a welfare system relying more on financial incentives to work would be an improvement.

What had changed, though, were the President's own stakes in FAP's passage. Even if it became law, he was unlikely to reap much partisan advantage nor, perhaps, much credit for dealing with the national crisis in welfare. In any case, by this time, Nixon knew that his Administration would be judged more by its record in foreign than in domestic policy. As the 92d Congress began its second session, his main incentive for urging the enactment of H.R. 1 was simply that it was his program; failure to obtain some part of it would be construed as a presidential defeat. Once, when proposing it, Nixon had equated FAP to the Apollo moon-landing as a test of national resolve. By 1972, in the State of the Union and other messages, the President mainly referred to welfare reform as an "item of unfinished business."[25]

The final blow to FAP, when it came, offered dramatic evidence that supporting a guaranteed income was still a high political risk. In an effort to enlist aid for his bid to win the Democratic Party's presidential nomination, Senator George S. McGovern of South Dakota had endorsed several alternatives to FAP, including the NWRO's version (now with a benefit level of $6,500) and a plan advocated by a wealthy New York industrialist to provide a refundable tax credit of $1,000 to every man, woman, and child. Little notice was paid to these commitments until, during the California primary campaign, his main challenger, Senator Hubert H. Humphrey of Minnesota, charged that they would add millions of people to the welfare rolls and be so expensive that the average family would pay much higher taxes. Since both these claims contained more than a bit of truth, McGovern was unable to furnish an effective reply.

Although he won the primary and eventually the nomination, McGovern's "income redistribution" proposal was thought to have cost him votes. Within hours after the polls in California closed, the candidate backed away from it. However, it haunted him throughout the rest of his campaign, despite a major address renouncing any immediate intent to aid the working poor. In hindsight, judged public opinion specialist, Louis Harris, the exposure of McGovern's alternative to FAP in the first week of June might well have started him toward his landslide defeat in November.[26]

McGovern's predicament also had an effect on the fate of welfare reform. Instead of making an issue of Congressional failure to act on FAP, as some Republican strategists desired, the Administration was again compelled to defend its program as one to restore the work ethic and reduce public spending. Although more in keeping with other campaign themes, these were no longer the most persuasive arguments for the plan, nor did they allow much flexibility for compromise with Ribicoff and his allies. If anything, the White House was more wary than ever of moving to the "Left," lest the Democratic candidate be given an opportunity to escape further damage by simply endorsing a revised version of H.R. 1. "President Nixon himself has proposed a guaranteed annual income," McGovern had already observed. "We do not disagree on that principle."[27] FAP's last asset had thus become a liability. Rather than having it identified as *his* program, the President was likely to be better served if this version of the negative income tax seemed a creation of his opponent.

The Senate Acts

Although during the summer Nixon and other members of his Administration reaffirmed their desire for the passage of H.R. 1, neither they nor Congressional leaders seemed anxious to hasten it to a vote. Not until the last week of September did the bill, as amended by the Finance Committee, reach the full Senate. As in the 91st Congress, FAP's prospects depended on end-of-session maneuvering, and once again its conservative opponents, ready to filibuster if necessary, proved more proficient.

The floor debate lasted over a week and was climaxed by a seventeen-hour session going into the early hours of October 6, during which forty separate amendments were considered. Two versions of FAP, offered without the Administration's backing by Ribicoff and Senator Adlai E. Stevenson III, Democrat of Illinois, were defeated by convincing margins of eighteen and sixteen votes.[28] On a close tally of forty-four to forty-one, the Finance Committee's welfare reform was approved.[29] However, Long had agreed to an amendment from Senator William V. Roth, Jr., the Republican who had succeeded John J. Williams, which authorized tests of both the President's and the liberals' proposals for public assistance, as well as of the "guaranteed job opportunity program." Although the Administration objected that this would delay welfare reform for several years, Roth's substitute for the measures approved by the Finance Committee was carried by six votes.[30] It, together with the rest of H.R. 1, was finally passed on a vote of sixty-eight to five.[31]

A week remained before the agreed date for adjournment and a month before Election Day. Since H.R. 1 contained several popular provisions for the elderly, neither Mills nor the Administration was disposed to impede it by trying to resurrect FAP in the conference committee. In return, Long and his colleagues agreed to withdraw the proposed changes in AFDC adopted by the Senate. Thus, when H.R. 1 became law on October 30, it contained virtually no alterations in the provisions concerning public assistance for families. Though AFDC was a program which pleased no one, though it needed a major overhaul and seemed for a time even to threaten the nation's stability, it had successfully withstood four years of intensive efforts at reform.

Even so, Public Law 92-603, the Social Security Amendments of 1972, was not a minor measure. It contained nearly one hundred changes in the old-age and medical insurance programs, including the replacement of the state-run public assistance programs for the elderly, blind, and disabled with a national one: the Supplemental Security Income program (SSI). Beginning with the pre-inaugural task force, the Nixon Administration's planners regarded a Federal floor and standards for aid in these "adult" categories as a politically necessary counterpart to the main effort of reforming the manner of helping mothers and children. With each setback to the latter, the former gathered more support. A key factor was the willingness of the highly regarded Social Security Administration to operate the new scheme. In addition, more generous treatment of the aged, blind, and disabled, whose votes counted and whose dependency was presumably not due to personal fault, was characteristic of American welfare policy. (After the enactment of SSI and the establishment of national— i.e., more liberal—standards, disability claims began to soar.) Not least among its liabilities, FAP had sought to create parity for families.

The working poor did have something to show for the debate over welfare policy: an expanded food stamp program. Since its creation in 1964, any household which met the program's income requirements had been entitled to obtain special coupons which were redeemable for most types of food at participating stores. However, by the end of the Johnson Administration, fewer than half of the nation's counties were operating the program; most of the rest relied on the distribution of surplus commodities to supplement the diets of the poor. Moreover, out of three million users of food stamps at the end of 1968, nearly two-thirds were public assistance recipients.[32]

At the instigation of a coalition of Washington pressure groups and the Congressional agriculture committees, which had jurisdiction over the program, the Nixon Administration took a series of steps to increase the use of food stamps. The amount budgeted was doubled in two years; the coupons were made easier to obtain, especially by families with very low incomes; an "out-reach" campaign to raise the number of participants was begun. By the middle of 1974, more than fourteen million people were receiving this form of assistance. Nearly half were in households headed by a full-time worker.[33]

Although FAP had not been enacted, a major, federally-financed income support program for the working poor had come into being. Significantly, while it guaranteed a "nutritionally adequate diet," it did not provide cash. To Southerners and Midwesterners, giving coupons for food was not the same as giving relief.

Alongside these accomplishments in social policy, welfare dependency persisted. During the Nixon Administration's first term, the number of families receiving AFDC doubled, reaching more than three million (and including nearly eleven million children and adults) by early 1972. Thereafter, growth stopped, but the size of the welfare rolls diminished only marginally. Although differences among the states remained in benefit levels, eligibility conditions, and the like, public assistance was no longer the small, uncertain source of aid it had been in most parts of the country a decade earlier. This change, Gilbert Y. Steiner has argued, was the real welfare reform of the 1960s and 1970s.[34] If so, it was not what was intended, and with the defeat of FAP in the 92d Congress, it was not likely to go unchallenged.

Even before the Senate acted, some Administration officials had turned their attention to improving the management of the existing public assistance programs. In October 1970, all of the states had been required to undertake "quality control" surveys. The first results, released at the beginning of 1972, showed that errors occurred in nearly 30 percent of all AFDC cases; 5.6 percent of the current recipients were judged ineligible for any payment whatsoever.[35] By the end of the year, HEW had established targets for improvement and threatened to withhold Federal welfare grants from states which did not attain them.

This was more than just a new step in intergovernmental relations. Together with the appointment of California's welfare commissioner to an equivalent national post, it underscored the

Administration's intent to put the burden of reforming welfare outside Washington. But more importantly, it signified that the conventional view, held initially by Nixon and defended unsuccessfully by Arthur Burns—namely, that high rates of dependency reflected individual failings, lax management, or both—was again governing official decisions. Among the consequences of the Senate debate was a setback to the idea that financial incentives were what really mattered.

The Abandonment of the Incentive Theory

Not all the supporters of the incentive theory were ready to concede defeat. After the second rejection of FAP, policy planners within the Nixon Administration persisted in trying to make the scheme viable. Joining them was a subcommittee of the Congressional Joint Economic Committee, which was chaired by Representative Martha Griffiths. Its two-and-one-half year program of studies and hearings—purportedly the first such examination of welfare and related programs to be done by a Congressional body—presented much the same case for major reform as was being made within the Administration. Scholars at universities and think-tanks added more research and ideas.

Within little more than a year after the end of the 92d Congress, third-generation versions of FAP, more carefully fashioned and based on more extensive information, were ready or nearly so. A coalition of interest groups, including some which had come to regret their failure to support FAP originally, had formed to promote such proposals. Yet none of them received serious consideration.

The main reason was that another bout with the Congress over welfare reform held little appeal for the President or his Cabinet. At a press conference two months into his second term, Nixon acknowledged as much:

> . . . With regard to family assistance, I thought at the time that I approved it—and this view has not changed—that it was the best solution to what I have termed, and many others have termed before me, the welfare mess. . . .
>
> Now, there are many who object to it and because of those objections there is no chance . . . we can get it through the Senate. . . .

However, his remarks contained a strong hint that his views *had* changed:

> I have told Secretary [of Health, Education, and Welfare, Caspar W.] Weinberger . . . to go back to the drawing board

and also to go to the members of the Senate on both sides and to bring me back a program which will stop this unconscionable situation where people who go on welfare find it more profitable to go on welfare than to go to work, and I think we will find an answer.

"The family assistance plan may be part of that answer," Nixon concluded, "but I know we are going to have to change it in order to get a vote. . . ."[36]

Whatever Nixon really thought, a satisfactory solution seemed to elude his Administration. In September 1973, a plan to include a version of FAP as part of a message setting forth a new program of rent subsidies was rejected at the last moment. Likewise, a welfare reform message promised in the 1974 State of the Union address never appeared. By then, the program's legislative prospects were not the most important consideration. If he had again submitted FAP, or something like it, Nixon would have risked antagonizing those conservative Congressmen and Senators whose support he needed to stay in office.

His successor, Gerald R. Ford, had a similar problem. Although both Secretary Weinberger and a White House policy group recommended proposal of a comprehensive "income security program," the new President, facing a primary election challenge from Republican conservatives in 1976, avoided a decision. Instead, his welfare officials continued to emphasize administrative actions aimed at simplifying public assistance programs and saving money.

Presidential unwillingness to take on Congress again was not the only cause of inaction on welfare reform. The events of the 92d Congress had established the dominance of the Senate Finance Committee over welfare legislation, and both the White House and the Ways and Means Committee waited for Long and his colleagues to take the initiative. In the 93d Congress, they did. Their major contribution was to be a Federal child-support program, designed to track down the absent father of the AFDC family and obtain a financial contribution from him. In addition, the social services offered to welfare recipients were reorganized to tighten Federal control and encourage state and local planning of programs to reduce or prevent dependency. As in the bureaucracy, so in the Congress, the problems of public assistance were attributed to individual failings and lax management.

Not even the election of a progressive Democrat as President was able to revive the incentive theory. In Jimmy Carter's Administration, welfare reform was given a high priority. Following a series of public hearings and Cabinet-level discussions, Carter did present, in a nationally televised address, a comprehensive proposal for replacing AFDC with an income support plan that was unmistakably descended from FAP. (Indeed, previous liberal objections notwithstanding, its benefits as a proportion of the poverty-line were nearly identical.) However, accompanying it was a massive program of public service jobs. Those who received aid under the plan were not just to be given a financial incentive to work or even just to be required to register or look for employment. If employable and unable or unwilling to find a job, they were to be given one, or face a substantial reduction in benefits. In effect, the Carter Administration had merged FAP with the Finance Committee's favored alternative, the "guaranteed job opportunity program."

The new measure, the Program for Better Jobs and Incomes, fared worse than either of its predecessors. Criticized by liberals for being insufficiently generous and by conservatives for being too costly and complex, the plan never came to a vote in the House of Representatives. On June 22, 1978, less than a year after it had been proposed, Speaker of the House Thomas P. O'Neill announced that due to lack of time in the 95th Congress, further consideration of welfare reform would have to be postponed. The following year, the Carter Administration returned with a simpler bill that called for increased Federal funds and standards for AFDC, but it too went nowhere.

All but lost amid these efforts to revive FAP was the fact that a small income supplement for the working poor had been enacted. Contained in the mammoth alternative to H.R. 1 devised by the Finance Committee was a provision creating a "work bonus." Any family with earnings below $4,000 was to be given a grant equal to 10 percent of its income; above $4,000, the amount of the benefit would gradually decline, reaching zero at $5,600.[37] Some members of the committee felt this would be a way to reduce the burden of social insurance taxes on the low-wage workers. Others, including Long, saw it as a means of rewarding families who were not on welfare. Yet, unlike FAP, which gave the highest benefit to those with the least income, this scheme would provide the poorest recipients with more money as they earned more. Nonetheless, along with the proposed modifications of AFDC, the "work bonus" was dropped from H.R. 1 in the conference committee at the end of the 92d Congress.

Twice during the 93d Congress, the Finance Committee attached it to pending amendments to the Social Security Act. Each time, the Ways and Means Committee, which had not held hearings on the measure, refused to concur. At last, in the 94th Congress, over the objections of the Ford Administration, the House added it to a temporary tax-reduction bill in order to give some aid to families which paid little or no income taxes. Renamed the Earned Income Tax Credit (EITC), it was passed after refinements in the Senate and signed into law on March 29, 1975.

Except for some financial journalists, few people appreciated what had been done. For the first time, the United States had a program which gave cash assistance to the able-bodied worker and relied on financial incentives to keep him employed. Payable through the tax system, it was nothing less than a miniature negative income tax. If neither as generous nor as comprehensive as FAP, the EITC was a direct outgrowth of the Nixon Administration's proposal.

Labour and the Negative Income Tax

In Britain, determining the fate of the negative income tax was not as time-consuming nor as complicated as in the United States. Almost as soon as it returned to office, Labour's intention of standing by its opposition to the tax-credit plan became evident. However, devising an alternative proved difficult.

One clue to what Labour would do was given during the election campaign of February 1974. In their manifesto, the Conservatives promised to introduce legislation for the tax-credit plan in the next Parliament, but to implement it only "as soon as the economic situation allows."[38] Its value as a tax reform was noted, but so were its social objectives. Indeed, paying child credits to mothers in an amount higher than the existing family allowances was set forth as a priority.

Labour's platform dealt only with this latter aspect. Under the heading of "social justice," the party vowed to create a new system of "child cash allowances," which were essentially child credits by another name.[39] Its tax program made no mention of the remainder of the Tory plan, but did pledge to create a wealth tax and other revenue measures to redistribute income. In effect, Labour had accepted the Select Committee minority's alternative of universal benefits and more progressive taxes.

With the formation of the new Wilson Government, the destiny of the tax-credit plan was sealed. Not only did Denis Healey become Chancellor of the Exchequer, but Nicholas Kaldor joined the Treasury as his tax adviser. All three members of the Select Committee who had submitted minority reports were given important appointments, with the most ardent dissenter, Barbara Castle, replacing Sir Keith Joseph as Secretary of State for Social Services. Douglas Houghton, the sole Labour supporter of the plan, retired from Commons and entered the House of Lords.

Although some Labour backbenchers still favored the scheme, the Wilson Government had other business to attend to before it could reconsider the party's opposition to tax credits. The same civil servants who had devoted so much effort to working out the details of Cockfield's ideas were now assigned, in Inland Revenue, to designing wealth and other taxes, and in Health and Social Security to replacing the Conservatives' pension program with one closer in principle to the superannuation plan that had been on Labour's agenda since 1957. (Brian Abel-Smith, the one member of the Titmuss group to have supported tax credits, other than the now-deceased Richard Titmuss himself, entered the Government as an adviser to Mrs. Castle on pensions.) In any case, Labour's razor-thin edge in Parliament meant that another election could occur at any time. Highest priority had to be given to those steps, like raising social insurance benefits, that were easy to accomplish and certain to be popular.

Not until it had improved its position in the October 1974 elections did the Wilson Government's plans for dealing with family poverty become clearer. One aspect entailed a revival of an extensive system of food subsidies, one of the few parts of the Beveridge design that had been eliminated when the Conservatives returned to power in 1951. Through grants to food producers, the price of basic commodities was to be controlled, thus helping not only low-income families but also the households of better-paid workers who might otherwise insist on inflationary wage increases. Additionally, in a November budget message, the Chancellor announced a hike in family allowances. However, it was not to be effective until the following April and would only restore the benefit to its 1968 level.

Another five months elapsed before, in April 1975, Labour finally unveiled its "child benefits" scheme. With all-party support, the proposal to combine family allowances with children's tax deductions and pay the new grant to mothers sailed through the House of Commons. The Chancellor did not specify the amount of the benefit, noting that it would depend on the budget situation at the time the program was to be implemented in April 1977. Ironically, had the Conservatives remained in office, this would also have been the date for their child tax-credits to commence.

No sooner had the Royal Assent been given on August 7 than the Wilson Government apparently began having second thoughts. Its child benefits proposal had never been a politically popular idea; to the contrary, a private poll done during the February campaign showed it to be among the least favored of the Labour Party's pledges.[40] Moreover, with the Government still committed to a policy of voluntary wage restraint to reduce inflation, a program that would have lowered the take-home pay of most workingmen (while raising aid to their wives) seemed likely to roil already troubled waters. As Britain slipped into virtual bankruptcy, the £200 million cost of a child benefits plan that left no family worse off increasingly appeared politically and financially unaffordable.[41]

Shortly after James Callaghan succeeded Harold Wilson as Prime Minister in April 1976, the Government tried to escape from this commitment. On May 25, citing its possibly harmful effect on wage negotiations, the new Secretary of State for Social Services, David Ennals, announced the postponement of the child benefits program until funds were available to implement it properly. In its place, he offered changes in family allowances that cost half as much.[42]

An angry reaction ensued. Faced with a possible rebellion of backbenchers and the loss of support outside Parliament, the Government met with representatives of the Trades Union Congress and produced a compromise. Child benefits were to be phased in gradually over a three-year period. They would now not become fully operational until 1980.

Although the Callaghan Government kept to this schedule and appropriated sizable amounts for child benefits, it did so reluctantly. In Britain, the last half of the 1970s was a period of recurrent economic crisis, reaching a nadir with the acceptance of an austerity plan in exchange for an International Monetary Fund loan at the end of 1976. When Labour returned to office in 1974, a Royal Commission had been appointed to study and "to help secure a fairer distribution of income and wealth in the community. . . ."[43] Although it continued throughout the party's term and produced an impressive series of studies and reports, nothing substantive was accomplished. Even without restrictions imposed from outside, the leeway for new social policies was small.

Under the circumstances, Labour again turned to selectivity. In July 1978, the Department of Health and Social Security published a report on the operation of the Supplementary Benefits program.[44] It called for a number of changes aimed at establishing clearer standards of entitlement and reducing administrative discretion. (Also recommended was disregarding a portion of any earnings by eligible claimants or their spouses; this was done partly to encourage self-support and partly to induce more accurate reporting of available resources.) When implemented two years later, they marked another step away from the view that public assistance was to be just a small measure of help for people with special needs. As in 1966, one of Labour's contributions to reducing poverty would be to increase the availability of relief.

In addition, the Labour Government continued the practice of increasing FIS along with other social benefits. At the end of March 1974, Mrs. Castle told the House of Commons:

> We remain as always opposed to the principle of means testing underlying this scheme. We do not like it and intend to replace it with something better in the lifetime of a normal parliament. In the meantime we cannot allow the poorest in the land to be left worse off.[45]

Almost immediately, the new Government came under criticism for this decision. Because it had agreed to maintenance of the "poverty trap," the director of the Child Poverty Action Group wondered whether Labour—or any party—was really interested in eliminating poverty.[46] Nonetheless, Labour stood fast. Lacking any better alternative, it had finally accepted a small version of the negative income tax.

Conclusion

At the beginning of the 1980s, Conservatives had returned to office in Britain and Republicans in the United States. Yet neither displayed any further interest in the negative income tax. In fact, even though the new leaders of each party were committed to increasing the financial rewards for working and saving, they opposed use of the incentive theory as the basis of welfare policy.

In Britain, Margaret Thatcher drew the core of her support from among those Tories who had thought the tax-credit plan was too costly and inefficient. For budgetary reasons, her Government continued to rely on FIS, but appeared unconcerned about the criticisms of it that were still being made. Welfare strategy consisted largely of a crackdown on "scroungers." Except in an occasional paper from the Bow Group, the tax-credit plan had virtually dropped from sight.

Likewise, the new American President, Ronald Reagan, had been one of the major opponents of FAP within Republican ranks. As Governor of California, he had taken a different approach to welfare reform, relying chiefly on tighter administration and work requirements. Once in the White House, he began to introduce a similar program nationwide. (He also suggested the rather opposite idea of ending Federal funding and standards for AFDC entirely.) Although welfare experts claimed these steps would eliminate incentives to work, little influential support developed for preserving incentives and none for reviving one or another version of FAP.

Thus, the hope that a program could be created which would reduce poverty without increasing dependency had been all but abandoned. The incentive theory had left traces, but almost no one now believed that simply the prospect of a higher income would encourage welfare recipients to seek work. Moreover, even politicians of the "Right" seemed resigned to extensive dependency as the price of assisting the "truly needy." Even if their own welfare reforms were to be as successful as predicted, both the Thatcher and Reagan Governments would have been left with caseloads that only one decade earlier were considered of crisis proportions.

Because of inherent limitations and the opposition of those who favored the existing arrangements, two decades of effort to adopt a negative income tax had ended up with additional growth and complexity in British and American welfare programs. If anything, the rise of the incentive theory may have actually contributed to this result by suggesting that dependency could be prevented with the right formula. Eventually, this argument failed to convince those most concerned with encouraging self-sufficiency, but did embolden those most interested in increasing the amount of help given the needy. While the negative income tax may have been discarded, the effects of the debate over it remained, creating a new set of problems with which future policy-makers would have to cope.

Notes

1. Abe Ribicoff, "He Left at Half Time," *The New Republic* (February 17, 1973), p. 22.

2. Elliot L. Richardson, Statement before the House Committee on Ways and Means (February 2, 1971), pp. 1–2.

3. U.S., House of Representatives, Committee on Ways and Means, *Social Security Amendments of 1971*, 92d Cong., 1st Sess., 1971, H. Rept. No. 92-231 to accompany H.R. 1, p. 207.

4. Ibid., pp. 378–84.

5. U.S., *Congressional Record*, vol. 117, no. 96 (June 22, 1971), H5716–7.

6. Letter from Paul Barton, Chief, Division of Special Projects, Office of Policy Development, Department of Labor, Washington, D.C., to Dr. Daniel P. Moynihan, July 30, 1971 (in the author's files).

7. U.S., Senate, Committee on Finance, *Hearings: Social Security Amendments of 1971* (1971–72), p. 2.

8. Ibid., pp. 50–51.

9. Ibid., pp. 72–74.

10. Ibid., pp. 366–71.

11. Ibid., p. 105.

12. Richard M. Nixon, Remarks of the President on Nationwide Radio and Television (August 15, 1971), p. 3.

13. U.S., Senate, Committee on Finance, Social Security Amendments of 1971, pp. 968–87.

14. U.S., Congressional Record, vol. 117, no. 176 (November 17, 1971), S18854–74.

15. U.S., Congressional Record, vol. 117, no. 188 (December 4, 1971), S20567–70.

16. U.S., Senate, Committee on Finance, Social Security Amendments of 1971, pp. 802–805.

17. U.S., Senate, Committee on Finance, Social Security Amendments of 1972, 92d Cong., 2d Sess., 1972, S. Rept. No. 92-1230 to accompany H.R. 1, pp. 405–582.

18. "Senate Panel Votes for Tough 'Workfare' Plan," The Boston Globe, April 29, 1972, p. 1.

19. Ibid.

20. "Senate Panel Acts to Curb Welfare Costs and Suits Against U.S.," The New York Times, April 20, 1972, p. 14.

21. "News Conference Text," Congressional Quarterly (July 1, 1972), p. 1, 583. The press conference was on June 22.

22. "Children March on White House," Boston Sunday Globe, March 26, 1972, p. 41; "Welfare Reformers Disagree," ibid., p. 53.

23. "Total on Welfare Drops Across U.S.," The New York Times, November 13, 1971, p. 23.

24. Barbara Boland, "Participation in the Aid to Families with Dependent Children Program (AFDC)," in the U.S., Congress, Joint Economic Committee, Subcommittee on Fiscal Policy, The Family, Poverty, and Welfare Programs: Factors Influencing Family Stability, "Studies in Public Welfare," Paper no. 12, part I (November 4, 1973), pp. 139–79.

25. Richard M. Nixon, Text of State of the Union Message to be Presented to the Members of the Second Session of the 92d Congress (January 20, 1972), p. 13.

26. Louis Harris, Speech to the National Press Club (November 10, 1972), pp. 8–9.

27. "McGovern Address Excerpts," The New York Times, August 6, 1972, p. 36.

28. For Ribicoff measure, see, U.S., Congressional Record, vol. 118, no. 157 (October 3, 1972), S16696; for Stevenson measure, see, U.S., Congressional Record, vol. 118, no. 158 (October 4, 1972), S16834.

29. Ibid., S16818.

30. Ibid., S16819.

31. U.S., Congressional Record, vol. 118, no. 159 (October 5, 1972), S17052.

32. Kenneth W. Clarkson, Food Stamps and Nutrition (1975), pp. 28–29.

33. U.S., Congress, Joint Economic Committee, Subcommittee on Fiscal Policy, Handbook of Public Income Transfer Programs: 1975, "Studies in Public Welfare," Paper no. 20 (December 31, 1974), p. 290.

34. Gilbert Y. Steiner, "Reform Follows Reality: The Growth of Welfare," *The Public Interest* (Winter 1974), pp. 64–65.

35. "25% of Relief Payments Erroneous, U.S. Says," *The Boston Globe*, January 4, 1972, p. 2.

36. "Transcript of President's News Conference on Foreign and Domestic Issues," *The New York Times*, March 3, 1973, p. 12.

37. U.S., Senate, Committee on Finance, *Social Security Amendments of 1972*, pp. 93–94.

38. *Firm Action for a Fair Britain: The Conservative Manifesto* (1974), p. 14.

39. *Let Us Work Together—Labour's Way Out of the Crisis* (1974), p. 8.

40. Personal interview with the author.

41. "Killing a Commitment: The Cabinet v the Children," *New Society* (June 17, 1976), p. 632.

42. Nick Bosanquet and Peter Townsend, eds., *Labour and Equality* (1980), p. 191.

43. Great Britain, Royal Commission on the Distribution of Income and Wealth, *Initial Report on the Standing Reference*, Report no. 1, Cmnd. 6171 (July 1975), p. v.

44. Great Britain, Department of Health and Social Security, *Social Assistance: A Review of the Supplementary Benefits Scheme in Great Britain* (July 1978), *passim*.

45. Great Britain, *Hansard's Parliamentary Debates* (Commons), 871 (March 27, 1974), col. 456.

46. Frank Field, "No Party for the Poor," *The Guardian* (London), April 2, 1974, p. 16.

8

The Politics of Convergence

If, instead of being an eighteenth century farmer, Rip Van Winkle had been a modern policy analyst and had gone to sleep after visiting Britain and the United States in 1960, he would have found upon awakening twenty years later that their welfare programs had expanded enormously. From little more than 5 percent of Gross Domestic Product, the two countries were now spending around 11 percent on income transfers.[1] To help the poor, both still relied on a mixture of social insurance and means-tested programs, but although the former had grown substantially in the two decades, the latter, far from being made unnecessary, had become more important. As the 1970s ended, three and one-half million American families were enrolled in AFDC, four times the number when the Kennedy Administration took office, and another four million people received SSI.[2] The number of British families supported by Supplementary Benefits had also quadrupled, reaching more than three hundred thousand as the 1980s began, out of nearly three million households dependent on this program (more than half of which were headed by pensioners).[3] Despite sporadic attempts to "tighten up" or get rid of "scroungers," government officials on both sides of the Atlantic had learned to live with large portions of their populations on relief.

Even families headed by able-bodied workers had benefitted from this largess. In Britain, they could now obtain support through FIS as well as through the new child benefit program. In the United States, they could get cash from the EITC and aid in-kind from food stamps, medicaid, and other measures. Although the terms were sometimes restrictive and the amounts sometimes small, two decades of social legislation had resulted in granting eligibility for some form of assistance to virtually everyone in need.

Nonetheless, in one crucial respect, little had changed: large numbers of Britons and Americans remained poor. In the United States at the end of the 1970s, nearly fourteen million people—6.4 percent of the population—lived in households with incomes below the official poverty-line.[4] In Britain, the comparable figure was more than three million, or 5.4 percent of the population.[5] Welfare programs did provide considerable help; without them, the amount of poverty would have been at least twice as great in the United States and three times more extensive in Britain. However, even after taking these programs into account, one out of every twenty citizens in each country apparently lived on sub-minimal incomes. Despite two decades of often intensive debates and full-scale efforts by several governments to revise them, the measures used by Britain and the United States to provide support to the needy were still insufficient.

Moreover, those who had been most involved in these efforts now saw little prospect for further improvements. "The assumptions of the Butskellite years have been washed away," wrote David Donnison, a member of the Titmuss group and former chairman of the Supplementary Benefits Commission. He continued:

> The assumption that the growth of the economy will continue, generating resources which governments can use to create a more equal society without anyone suffering a real fall in their living standards; the assumption that equalising policies and the steadily rising tax rates required to sustain them will be accepted by the mass of voters; the assumption that government and the public service professions are the natural instruments of social progress—all have been abandoned.[6]

In the United States, one of the designers of the Family Assistance Plan, Daniel Patrick Moynihan, now a Senator from New York State, worried about preserving existing programs. In connection with the Reagan Administration's 1982 proposal to give authority over AFDC to the states, he observed:

> One would have thought that a program firmly in place for nearly half a century would have acquired a certain acceptance, even an aura of necessity, and that the governors would not be so casual in offering to swap it for this or that program. But no. The life of the AFDC program remains as chancy and skimpy as the lives of the children it supports.[7]

The expansion of welfare programs during the 1960s and 1970s had been fueled by the belief that improving the lot of the poor was not just an urgent necessity, but also a test of the decency of each society. By the 1980s, this feeling had receded and both Britain and the United States were embarked on other tasks that seemed more compelling and worthwhile.

What had happened? Why had two of the world's wealthiest countries been unable to do better? Why could they not assure a minimum income for all their citizens? The preceding chapters have told the story of attempts to do so in both the United States and Britain. This chapter will try to draw some lessons about what they did and why they failed.

The Spread of Ideas

That the efforts of the United States and Britain were similar in the first place would seem to be remarkable. Most descriptions of welfare policy in the two countries have emphasized their differences. British programs have usually been portrayed as comprehensive and generous, American ones as patchy and mean. In the United States, individualism is supposedly the dominant value, whereas in Britain, collective security is more important.

Although not without merit, these characterizations overlook a strong family resemblance between the two countries that helped interest each in the negative income tax. Both nations share a tradition that has generally frowned on providing income to people who could be expected to aid themselves. In each, the first line of welfare policy has consisted of social insurance programs, whose benefits are nominally earned. Means-tested help has normally been given only to certain groups, such as mothers with young children, who are assumed to be incapable of self-support. (Even in Britain, where public assistance was available to the unemployed, rules were established to prevent those who were merely out-of-work from drawing more from relief than from their usual wages.) Other aid is given in-kind or for the purpose of subsidizing particular expenditures, such as for food, housing, and medical care. The main exception is the British program of family allowances, but it is mostly a subsidy for the expenses of raising children; to underscore that point, benefits are paid directly to mothers.

To be sure, the details of these measures sometimes differ in major ways. For example, Britain provides medical care through a public health service that can be used by anyone, while the United States pays the medical bills only of the needy and leaves others to make their own arrangements. American welfare programs are more often run by state and local governments, in contrast to the British preference for centralization.

But the practical significance of such differences has proved to be elusive. Americans do not seem to spend less money on health care than Britons, nor, except for some conspicuous out-riders, has decentralization impeded the progress of national standards in the administration (and to some degree, the benefits) of public assistance. Despite its greater scope and generosity, there is no reason to think that the British "welfare state" should have had more success in eliminating poverty than its American counterpart.

Nor is it valid to assume that Britain would have been more concerned than the United States about helping the needy. To the contrary, much recent evidence suggests that values in the two nations have been converging. At least since the mid-1950s, the individualistic heritage of Britain has been resurgent, touching even the Labour Party and its supposedly "embourgeoised" supporters and eventually leading to the election of Margaret Thatcher in 1979 on a platform placing greater stress on freedom than on security. In the United States, the same period has seen an enormous surge of popular support for social programs, which not even the election of Ronald Reagan seems likely to quell. Differences undoubtedly persist, but on a matter of the utmost importance for welfare policy, Britons now sound more like Americans than Europeans in blaming poverty chiefly on personal failings, not social injustices.[8]

Yet, if anything, these similarities would seem to imply that neither the United States nor Britain would be inclined to guarantee a minimum income to all its citizens. The reason each tried to do so has less to do with the characteristics of either country than with the nature of the negative income tax: it offered the possibility of radically changing welfare policy without violating traditional commitments. The convergence seen in the proposal of FAP, FIS, and the tax-credit plan primarily testifies to the power of an attractive idea to spread and influence decisions in countries that would not appear to be receptive to it.

As the 1960s began, both Britain and the United States were eager to apply intellectual analysis to a host of public issues. Just as the Kennedy Administration gave new prominence to its economic advisers, Harold Wilson relied conspicuously on consultants like Nicholas Kaldor and Thomas Balogh. In each country, social scientists were brought into the bureaucracy to examine major issues and propose solutions. In the White House and Whitehall, central staffs were created to do likewise for the chief executives. The purpose of this was not just to economize, but to rationalize. Through analytic methods, government could accomplish more and work better.

This modernized version of reform had an understandable fascination for politicians, regardless of ideological bent. (Out-of-office conservatives in both the United States and Britain set up think-tanks or study groups in the 1960s to develop their own ideas for improving public policy.) Even more did it appeal to the growing class of professionals who stood to gain access and influence as a result. Before long, no less venerable an institution than the British civil service was being urged to replace its Oxbridge generalists with more scientists and other specialists.[9]

FAP, FIS, and the tax-credit plan were products of this approach applied to the "welfare state." In the United States, the route was direct. Social scientists obtained key positions in government and, together with allies in the universities and elsewhere, managed to persuade political leaders that the incentive theory offered a way of reducing poverty without increasing dependency. In Britain, because professionalization had not progressed as far, the path was more roundabout. Working through the political parties and in advisory roles, British specialists first documented the persistence of poverty, developed the idea of merging benefit and tax systems, and led politicians toward further reforms by identifying continuing problems. Although the negative income tax was not a totally new notion in either country, only after experts had become more important in policymaking did it move from the pages of economics journals to the agenda of government. Social policy has historically been open to this sort of influence and the efforts to guarantee a minimum income in Britain and the United States show that it still is.[10]

Since they came out of essentially the same intellectual tradition, social scientists in the two countries moved along parallel paths. Indeed, the degree of familiarity that experts in one nation had with the debates over poverty and welfare programs in the other was truly extraordinary. The writings of Richard Titmuss, Peter Townsend, and other British specialists were known and read by their counterparts in the United States, just as Milton Friedman, Daniel Patrick Moynihan, and the University of Wisconsin group were recognizable to interested Britons. Major newspapers and professional journals, such as *New Society*, reported regularly on developments in both countries; occasionally, more direct exchanges occurred. (In April 1970, Richard Crossman, then Secretary of State for Social Services, recorded in his diary that "a member of Nixon's Cabinet, a Professor Moynihan from Harvard, was passing through London and wanted to lunch with me"; after drink and food, they discussed FAP, among other items.)[11] At least in this case, Britons and Americans were not "two peoples separated by a common language."

The fact that the United States relied more extensively on experts, and that it enjoyed pre-eminence in economics and other relevant disciplines, also explains why it was in the unusual position of leading the world in welfare policy. As part of its anti-poverty program, the Wilson Government adopted measures modelled on American efforts in compensatory education and community organization. In opposition, British Conservatives visited the United States to learn about the

173

negative income tax, as well as the latest techniques in program analysis and planning. (Ironically, one of the obstacles to implementing the tax-credit plan was the inadequacy of British computers and the reluctance of the Inland Revenue to buy American ones.) The income maintenance experiments were a source of great curiosity in Britain; in another country (Canada), one such experiment was even tried.[12] Just as Bismarck's Germany had been the place to go to find out about the invention of social insurance, the United States, after declaring its "war on poverty," became the country to visit to discover new ways to aid the poor.

The professionalizing of policy-making was supposed to bring not only sounder ideas but also politically more acceptable ones. On the surface, this seemed true of the negative income tax. It proposed to redistribute income without greatly impairing work incentives. It claimed the ability to concentrate limited resources on the most needy, while avoiding the stigma and administrative headaches of a separate means-test. It sought to expand the role of government, but also to make it less intrusive. The negative income tax was an idea that could appeal to liberals and to conservatives, to those who liked the "welfare state" and to those who valued individualism. Whether by design or out of ambiguity, it seemed to transcend ideological differences, and this was no small advantage in its travels from country to country.

The novelty of the negative income tax also helped. No country had tried anything like it, and to introduce it required skill and daring. The disastrous history of Speenhamland served as a constant reminder of what could go wrong. But applying rationalism to policy-making not infrequently produces such unconventional proposals—and, as Michael Oakeshott has written, there is a political profit as well.[13] To the Republicans and Tories who took office in the United States and Britain at the end of the 1960s, the negative income tax provided a way of putting their stamp on an area of policy that had long been the territory of their opponents. Far from being a deterrent, the challenge of making the idea work proved to be a considerable part of its attraction.

Ideas do not take root just anywhere. Despite the growing influence of experts in policy-making, many issues remain where Britain and the United States take different paths. For example, in race relations, the American preference for litigation has not displaced the British insistence on conciliation, even though professionals played prominent roles in both countries and communicated with one another extensively.[14] A common disposition must exist before the same solution will seem promising in disparate places. It was the underlying likenesses in their welfare policies, their shared problems of poverty and dependency, and their broadly similar social values that led Britain and the United States toward the negative income tax. (But not, it is worth recalling, without some important differences.) In this respect, the convergence of policy seen in the proposal of FAP, FIS, and the tax-credit plan is an example of the diffusion of innovations among countries resembling each other.

Nonetheless, the most important similarity was not one of conditions but in the nature of policy-making. The greatest influence in the development of the negative income tax in Britain and the United States was the presence of experts at every step in the process. They identified what was wrong with the existing programs, devised solutions for the problems of poverty and dependency, and molded them to fit each nation's political and cultural circumstances. Although they were primarily attuned to events at home, they also lived in an international community and not only knew about but also learned from what was going on elsewhere. The spread of the negative income tax from the United States to Britain and on to other countries did not just happen, but was stimulated and hastened by exchanges among experts.

There are other examples of similar ideas taking hold in dissimilar places. In economic policy, nations have repeatedly tried on each other's favorite fiscal and monetary nostrums. In housing and town planning, borders have been no obstacle to the passage of new designs. Recently, the notion of tax-free "enterprise zones" has travelled from Britain to the United States and then to other countries. In each case, home-grown sources of inspiration and encouragement also existed and adaptation more than imitation was the rule. However, especially among nations with common intellectual traditions and facing broadly comparable problems, the adoption of similar ideas may have more to do with transference than with diffusion. What the proposal of FAP, FIS, and the tax-credit plan shows is that the advent of professionalization in government has made ideas more contagious.

The Limits of Expertise

At the same time, the history of the negative income tax also demonstrates that even in an age when experts influence policy-making, their most accomplished creations may still fail. Despite the immensely sophisticated effort that went into designing and defending FAP, FIS, and the tax-credit plan, the results did not satisfy many of their principal proponents. Furthermore, this was as true in the

175

United States, where professionalization was well-advanced, as in Britain, where it was not, but where the political system presumably made changes of direction easier.[15] In neither country did an overhaul of the "welfare state" prove possible even with the growth of rationalism in policy-making.

Not that nothing was accomplished. To the contrary, in both countries, elements of the negative income tax were added to welfare policy during the 1960s and 1970s. In Britain, of course, FIS was enacted and Supplementary Benefits recipients were given a financial incentive to earn income. Similar provisions to encourage work found their way into AFDC and the expanded food stamp program in the United States. Both nations also took modest steps toward integrating income support with taxation: the British through the child benefit scheme, and the Americans through the refundable Earned Income Tax Credit (EITC).

But these changes paled next to what was left undone. Neither country managed to simplify its ways of providing money to the needy; in fact, the British and American "welfare states" became more complex and costly than they had been two decades earlier. Even so, gaps in coverage persisted, as did dependency. Despite greater generosity, the problems besetting welfare policy in Britain and the United States remained much like those of the 1960s. As for the negative income tax, which had once given hope of a solution, as the 1980s began it looked like an idea whose time had come—and passed.

Ironically, a major reason for these disappointing results may have been that the idea was too sophisticated. Far from being an elegant device for streamlining a set of uncoordinated programs, the negative income tax turned out to be inordinately complicated and hard to understand. Moreover, the longer it was under consideration, the greater the difficulties became. Only those schooled in the intricacies of disregards, notches, take-up, multiple tracks, and similar concepts seemed to comprehend fully what was going on, and even these experts took to arguing among themselves about the significance of various features or the desirability of proposed refinements. Politicians and the public seemed increasingly confused and disaffected from an idea that promised much travail for uncertain gains.

Moreover, in moving from textbook to political agenda, the negative income tax entered a world replete with other welfare programs. FAP affected the concerns of no fewer than five Cabinet departments, as well as several White House staffs. The tax-credit plan would have merged some of the newest undertakings in British government with one of the oldest and most hoary (Inland Revenue). Each also would have changed the rules for groups dependent upon the existing set of programs, from mothers receiving AFDC or family allowances to state or local officials who administered (and sometimes had to pay for) them. Accommodating to differences not just in programmatic details, but, more importantly, in traditions and patterns of influence meant adding layers of political and technical complexity to what might otherwise have been a simpler design.

If the proposal of FAP, FIS, and the tax-credit scheme revealed the new power of rationalism in policy-making, what happened afterward displayed its customary weakness. Sooner or later, even the most erudite notions run into the most recalcitrant interests and are either altered or demolished entirely. The more comprehensive the idea, the more obstacles it is apt to encounter, including many that cannot be anticipated at the outset. Applying greater expertise is rarely the answer, and may even become the source of more trouble, as comprehensibility fades. The only versions of the negative income tax to succeed were the simplest, FIS and the EITC, each of which affected only one department and replaced no other program. Conversely, FAP and the tax-credit scheme proved impossible to defend and easy to misrepresent. Even in an age of professionalization, politics has a rationale of its own, distinct from that of the planners. Government remains much more than a mechanism for solving problems as defined by policy experts.

In the United States, the difficulties encountered by the negative income tax were predictable, but in Britain they came as more of a surprise.[16] Although experts were not as influential there, the British political system afforded fewer opportunities for competing interests. Once endorsed by the Heath Government, the tax-credit plan, like FIS, should have been approved by Parliament and have gained the Royal Assent. That this did not happen suggests that Britain can be just as indecisive about major matters as other countries in the world.

One reason has to do with the often unrecognized restraints of Parliamentary government. Despite his status as leader in the House of Commons and head of his political party, a British Prime Minister is far from unchecked in his power. In the first instance, he needs the continued backing of his ministers and backbenchers, or else risks losing office. In addition, he needs cooperation from the civil service if he is to develop and implement a program. Beyond that, he must have at least the tacit agreement of the opposition party (and often the relevant interest groups) if he is to leave a record that will last. One of the oldest doctrines in Britain's political self-understanding is that the sovereign can do no wrong, even when reversing actions taken by the preceding government. With divisions between the British parties becoming ever sharper (especially over social policy), it has seemed increasingly advisable to obtain a consensus before making substantial changes.

This was particularly so for the tax-credit plan, since at least five years would have been needed to implement it. Accordingly, to secure approval by key members of the Labour Party, the Heath Government decided to submit it to an all-party Select Committee, rather than go directly to Parliament. (A number of loose threads still had to be tied up as well.) In the end, that proved to be a mistake. Despite the initially favorable reaction of Titmuss and others to tax credits, a majority of the Labour Party members wound up opposing it. Perhaps more importantly, the committee's deliberations led to numerous questions about the scheme, embarrassing the Government and forcing it back to the drawing board. As with FAP, the result was a proposal that was more complicated, costlier, and less appealing. Compared to FIS, which was adopted and administered in a spirit of "rough justice," the extensive airing given the tax-credit plan sensitized both officials and the public to its supposed inequities and compromised its carefully designed virtues.

In any case, the tax-credit scheme suffered because of an important difference between prime ministerial and presidential government. Even on a major issue like this, policy-making in Britain is apt to occur mostly at the departmental level. For tax credits, political appointees and civil servants in the relevant bureaucracies worked out the details, while the rest of the Cabinet essentially minded its own business. In the United States, by contrast, the White House is likely to be the focal point for proposals such as FAP, and senior presidential aides as well as departmental aides will be involved. Winning the President's support was crucial in American government, while in Britain avoiding the Prime Minister's opposition was sufficient. For all the difficulties attending its birth, FAP possessed an unquestionably powerful pedigree, unlike the tax-credit plan, whose political backing was more ambiguous and consequently less effective.

Party loyalty did not prove to be an advantage in Britain, either. As with the Republicans, Tory commitment to the negative income tax did not run deep. The debates and planning of the 1960s involved relatively few members, and while many more shared a general disposition in favor of the new idea, no one really knew what it would look like (or cost). British parties, despite their greater ideological consistency, despite their research departments, and despite the duties of opposition, seem no better than American parties at preparing programs for governing; out of office, information is inevitably less complete, bargaining less realistic, and the future less predictable. To Conservative stalwarts, the proposal of the tax-credit plan was almost as much of a surprise as it was to the rest of the nation. Although Heath might have been able to rally his troops around it (as Nixon had done for FAP), not long after his fall from power the Tories (like their American counterparts) abandoned the negative income tax too.

As the history of FIS shows, British government can act quickly and decisively, but apparently on relatively simple issues, not relatively complex ones. For the latter, building a winning coalition out of a variety of interests seems just as necessary as in the United States. Although certain customs and powers of the British political system, like party discipline, make this task somewhat easier, the fate of the tax-credit plan (and numerous other major proposals) cautions against expecting too much from Parliamentary government. Indeed, the measures apt to be most troublesome may be those like the negative income tax, which are more the product of expert ideas applied to policy than extensions of long-held views.[17] If rationalism inclines governments toward the new and the bold, democratic politics may serve to anchor them in the traditional, contrary to what many have feared.

Nowhere was the radicalizing effect of expertise more evident than in the extraordinary response of the "Left" to proposals from the "Right" to guarantee a minimum income to the needy. In the United States and Britain, innovations in welfare policy had normally come from the Democrats and Labour, while Republicans and Conservatives served a reactive function. FAP, FIS, and the tax-credit plan followed the reverse path; in both countries, the "Left" denounced the measures despite its presumably greater affinity for generous social programs. "Bogus," "counter-revolution," and "repressive" were just some of the ways in which they characterized what were, in reality, unprecedented efforts to help the poor.

Part of this was no more than the customary behavior of politicians in opposition, but also involved was a more fundamental change in how the "Left" viewed the "welfare state." To neither Labour nor the Democrats was the negative income tax a stranger. During the 1960s, the two parties had opportunities to endorse it, but chose to remain with the conventional approaches to relieving poverty. Over the years, they had come to believe in them and, perhaps as important, derived much support from their constituencies. These were reasons enough to object to replacing them when the notion of doing so was broached by Republicans and Conservatives.

At the same time, the proposal of FAP, FIS, and the tax-credit plan had a disconcerting effect on the "Left." For years, the Democrats and Labour had made eliminating poverty a central objective of domestic policy, but had not put forth anything so daring and well-ac-

179

claimed as their opponents had almost as soon as they returned to office. Worse, it was these particular Republicans and Tories, who were thought to draw some of their advice and much of their support from those who stood *against* the most progressive features of the British and American "welfare states." Now, Richard Nixon and Edward Heath appeared to be in the vanguard of social policy, while politicians of the "Left" seemed to be clinging to outmoded ideas.

Before long, Labour and the Democrats caught up. If the "Right" could support a plan for redistributing income, so could they. Moreover, theirs would provide *real* help to the poor. So began a bidding war that contributed greatly to the derogation of FIS and the defeat of FAP and the tax-credit plan. Using its own experts, the "Left" challenged both the level and the breadth of the income guarantees and offered its own, more generous versions. If rationalism could make Tories and Republicans bold, it could turn Labour and Democratic politicians positively adventuresome. Instead of thinking of welfare policy as a means of preventing hardship, the "Left" came to view it as a way of promoting a more radical egalitarianism.

The extent of the miscalculation became apparent when Labour and the Democrats returned to office. After much internal debate, the Carter Administration managed to produce a minimum income proposal no more generous than what Nixon had put forth. Even that, coupled with a guaranteed jobs program, proved too expensive and had smaller legislative success than FAP. Similarly, the Wilson-Callaghan Government, although it did enact Labour's child benefit plan, tried to postpone its implementation and reduce its costs. The broader "social compact," which was to be a device for moderating wage demands by providing more generous social benefits, eventually collapsed in a torrent of labor disputes that led to the election of the Thatcher Government. In neither Britain nor the United States did the plans for greater income redistribution prove financially or politically feasible.

The advice of experts, though not the only factor, played no small part in leading the "Left" on this odyssey. Far from replacing ideology, or even tempering it, rationalism in politics helped develop and sustain a more radical ideology. Professionalization has not resulted in the demise of doctrinaire ideas about welfare policy; if anything, it has provided a new and more compelling set of arguments for them (as well as, of course, for opponents of them). If part of the attraction of the negative income tax lay in its compatibility with quite different objectives, it could and did just as easily become the vehicle for serving competing goals. The debate over FAP, FIS, and the tax-credit plan shows that growing reliance upon experts in policy-making probably assures activism more than consensus.

180

Poverty and the Incentive Theory

In the case of the negative income tax, the growth of knowledge eventually led to greater uncertainty about the wisdom of the idea as well. To both the "Right" and the "Left," the appeal of the negative income tax lay in its apparent ability to transfer income (either for the relief of poverty or for more radical purposes) without inducing dependency. The elderly and others outside the labor force would be given money as needed to supplement social insurance, pensions, and savings; those still able to work would be given aid plus a strong financial incentive to earn more. Simply and efficiently, the negative income tax would assure a decent standard of living, without removing the poor from the economic mainstream.

Doubts about this wondrous device were expressed from the start. In theory, there was no reason to expect that the able-bodied poor would be more responsive to the financial incentive to work than to the *dis*incentive of having a minimum income without working. Some—exactly how many could not be known in advance—might prefer to get by on less money in order to avoid the arduousness of a low-paying job; others might simply desire leisure over labor. Withdrawal from the work force could be as rational a response to the negative income tax (depending on its provisions) as staying in, although proponents argued the numbers so withdrawing would be small.

Moreover, the factors keeping at least a portion of the poor out of the economic mainstream seemed unlikely to be affected by a change in incentives. For some, the problem was location; even full-time employment in traditionally low-wage regions—the South in the United States, Wales and Northern Ireland in Britain—might not be enough to bring some up to a poverty-level income. For others, the problem was family composition: too few earners (as in households headed by women who could work only part-time or not at all) and too many children. Nor did all the poor possess values concerning work and savings that disposed them to respond to the new incentives in the way the planners hoped.[18] In each case, the negative income tax would provide additional support, but whether it would also help reduce dependency was open to question.

In a sense, it still is. In both the United States and Britain, designing (let alone adopting and implementing) a negative income tax that combined "adequate" benefits with a strong incentive to work proved impossible at an acceptable cost. Unless considerably more money had been spent than the politicians of either nation were prepared to do, to raise the minimum level of aid meant to reduce more sharply (i.e., to tax) the assistance given those with earnings, while to lower it meant to leave in place the network of existing programs, many of which contained disincentives of their own. Although the incentive theory had made inroads on these measures, the results bore little resemblance to a properly designed negative income tax. In Britain, according to Jonathan Bradshaw, the typical family now encounters a "poverty plateau" over the £40 to £80 range, where earning more nets virtually no additional income.[19] Similar situations abound in the American system.[20] Despite more generous support, in neither country do welfare recipients face the kinds of conditions that would give the incentive theory a fair test.

Nonetheless, something close to such a test was provided by the American income maintenance experiments. Carried out over a decade in several cities at a cost exceeding $100 million, this was perhaps the most ambitious social scientific research ever undertaken. The nearly nine thousand families involved were divided into two groups: one which was given money (varied according to amount and the rate at which it was reduced as earnings rose) and another which was not. Although each group could also benefit from existing welfare programs, any differences between them should have been due to differences in incentives or income. Designed at a time when serious consideration of the negative income tax seemed a distant prospect, the experiments yielded final results just as such consideration was ending. Fittingly, these results were not encouraging.

Far from providing an incentive to work, the negative income tax, as some had always feared, seemed to have just the opposite effect. In the largest experiment, conducted over a five-year period in Seattle, Washington, and Denver, Colorado, the hours worked by male heads of households eligible for special support were 11.4 percent fewer than those of their counterparts in the control group. Their wives devoted 25.3 percent fewer hours to employment; female heads of households, 15 percent fewer. Similar results, though somewhat smaller in magnitude, came out of the other experiments.[21]

Just as vexing was the finding that making all needy families eligible for support (not just single-parent ones, as AFDC primarily did) failed to have a consistently salutary effect upon their stability. To the contrary, at benefit levels approximating those of FAP, the prospect of assured income may *increase* the likelihood that intact families will break up.[22] According to the most widely accepted explanation, the certainty of such publicly financed alimony makes a person less dependent upon his or her spouse, and thus provides the financial ability to end an unsatisfactory marriage. In hindsight, this is not a particularly surprising result, but it is also not particularly encouraging to those who thought that changing incentives would produce happier homes, stronger families, and consequently less poverty.

182

Neither these findings nor their implications escaped challenge. Some critics charged that the income maintenance experiments were too brief, too artificial, and too contaminated by exogenous factors (like changes in the economy or existing welfare programs) to say anything meaningful about what a permanent support plan might achieve. Others pointed out that for the most part, the reductions in working hours were relative, not absolute. Even those who received cash payments generally increased their own efforts, though not as much as those who were unaided. With regard to family stability, the Seattle-Denver results also suggested that exceptionally generous benefits—well above the poverty-line—might actually enhance home life, presumably by easing the financial strain that had made it quarrelsome. In short, according to these critics, the problems of the incentive theory either were not excessive or else were matters of design rather than conception.

At best, this was an extraordinarily rosy interpretation. Together with other research on welfare programs, the income maintenance experiments revealed a major flaw in the incentive approach.[23] The trouble was not that the theory failed; recipients did respond to financial rewards in reasonably rational ways. Rather, the problem was that the result was not a reduction in dependency, but an increase. Extending assistance to those who were able to support themselves expanded substantially the number eligible. With the negative income tax, increasing incentives for those on relief meant diminishing them for the greater number who were not. Some people might indeed work more, but more people could work relatively less and still have as much income. Moreover, even small reductions in individual earnings could add up to a large amount for the population as a whole. Extrapolating the Seattle-Denver results suggested that as much as half the additional cost of a program like FAP might have gone to replace money that would otherwise have been earned.[24]

Nearly two decades of analysis, experiments, and policy-making showed that the poor, like most other people, were primarily concerned about reaching a satisfactory level of income. Whether the money came from work or public assistance or a combination of both was increasingly less important than what the total was. The incentive system, although it did enable the poor to increase their incomes by earning more, also gave them the opportunity to maintain their present living standards with governmental support. Which impulse would win out hinged not just on the generosity of available benefits and the rate at which they were reduced but also on innumerable other factors, such as employment opportunities, the acceptability of welfare, and so on. The explosion in AFDC caseloads at the same time that incentives were being added and grant levels raised should have been a warning. The growth of FIS, food stamps, and similar programs, together with the income maintenance experiments, provided further confirmation. In practice, the incentive theory turned out to be more a means of replacing the earnings of the able-bodied than of encouraging them toward self-support.

If this was a strange way of reducing dependency, it was also questionable as a strategy for relieving poverty. To be sure, in Britain and the United States, the expansion of income transfer programs during the 1960s and 1970s markedly diminished the number of people officially counted as poor. Yet, in both countries, the proportion of households whose *earnings* were sufficient to lift them above the poverty-line stayed the same, or even rose (depending upon the method of accounting for inflation), during the period.[25] Especially in Britain, a large cause of this was an increase in the number of elderly in the population but in each nation the number of impoverished families headed by someone below retirement age also grew. In 1976, a person at least potentially in the labor force presided over one-third of the British households in poverty and one-half of the American ones. Of those families still poor after calculating the effects of cash and in-kind assistance, one-quarter in Britain (including one-half of all individuals) and more than 80 percent in the United States were headed by someone younger than 65.[26]

To some observers, the generosity of these benefits seemed to be a principal reason for the persistence of poverty among people presumably capable of working. As evidence, they cited the startling increase—permitted, if not encouraged, by public assistance—in the number of female-headed families, which from 1971 to 1976 rose by 32 percent in Britain and 25 percent in the United States.[27] In both countries, close to half were poor.[28] The easier availability of governmental support, it was argued, also fostered other income-reducing trends, such as longer spells of unemployment, shorter working hours, and more numerous claims for disability. In addition, particularly prevalent in the United States but not absent in Britain were fears that the expansion of welfare had helped create an underground culture, which thrived on unreported earnings and public assistance and which was being passed along to succeeding generations.[29] Echoing Malthus, critics of income transfer programs argued that poverty was rising in direct relation to the growth of efforts to eliminate it.

Others denied that public assistance was at fault and found the causes of continued poverty elsewhere. In both countries, they maintained, the trend towards family dissolution was found at all income levels and had only a small effect on changes in the number of poor.[30] In any case, a link between welfare programs and separation or illegitimacy remained difficult to prove.[31] On the other hand, it was not hard to see that joblessness was increasing in both Britain and the United States. In every year but two since 1966, the British unemployment rate had risen, reaching postwar highs in the late 1970s. Though not quite so dismal, the American record was also one of steady growth in the underlying jobless rate. The persistence of poverty owed more to this economic slackening, along with other conditions like low wages and the relocation of industries, than to the debilitating influence of public assistance, some observers claimed; therefore, contracting income transfer programs would only worsen the lot of the poor, not improve it.[32]

This argument was not likely to be resolved, since it was fundamentally about values more than facts. If poverty could most easily be ended by redistributing money, then advocates of expanding public assistance were prepared to tolerate some increases in the number of broken homes or some decline in the number of hours worked. Since such changes would only make poverty worse, others opposed widening eligibility for welfare to anyone who could be expected to support himself. To each according to his needs, or to each according to his deserts? That was really the issue.

After two decades of examination and trial, the once bright hope that the negative income tax could provide a programmatic resolution to this conflict of principles has all but disappeared. The bi-partisan agreement and admiration it used to command both in Britain and the United States has been replaced by controversy and vilification. Even its supporters have become reluctant to claim too much for it. (Testifying on behalf of the Carter Administration's version, HEW Assistant Secretary Henry J. Aaron stressed primarily that it was a "patently sensible change" and that the burden of proof should be placed on those who disagree.)[33] Once the idea had seemed likely to sweep the industrialized world; it seemed an invention that would reduce poverty while encouraging self-help. Now it seemed more likely to accomplish neither.

In Place of the Incentive Theory

In fact, in both Britain and the United States, the view that over-reliance on the incentive theory was a source of the probems of welfare policy was now gaining acceptance on the "Right" as well as the "Left." As the 1980s began, a search was under way for new approaches to helping the poor that would avoid expanding (and perhaps even curtail) means-tested, income transfer programs. Although no consensus had emerged, a number of similar ideas were being tried or discussed in each country.

The most ambitious was the notion of providing jobs instead of income to the needy. This was the centerpiece of the Carter Administration's welfare reform proposal and could also be seen in the Thatcher Government's plans for reducing unemployment among teenagers. By paying a poverty-level wage, such publicly-financed jobs would presumably raise the living standards of the poor, without destroying their incentive to work. (Since families headed by an employed person tend to be stabler ones, it was suggested that this strategy would also slow down the creation of single-parent families.) If it were done on a sufficiently large scale, this program would also affect the supply of cheap labor, leading to a general increase in wage-rates. Recipients of public jobs could then find private employment without the risk of slipping back into poverty.

Whether this would actually happen was doubtful. Rather than paying more for low-skilled labor that was in short supply, employers might be more inclined to look for ways of doing without it, or so experience with minimum wage laws suggested. Similarly, the history of earlier public jobs programs offered little hope that participants would enter the private sector in great numbers. In any case, the cost of creating so many positions paying poverty-level wages would be great—supervisory expenses would mean that the cost would be higher than an equivalent amount of public assistance—and the difficulties formidable. Even so, such a program would still require extensive income support for those deemed unable to work, while for those who could work it would amount to little more than dependency in a different form.

At the opposite extreme were proposals to give more money to everyone (or to selected groups) regardless of need. In the United States, this took the form of calls for refundable income tax credits or family allowances.[34] In Britain, more generous child benefits were suggested, along with similar allowances for single-parent families, pensioners, and the disabled. The idea was that such "universal" benefits would not decline as earnings rose. They could thus increase the total income of the poor, without affecting incentives to work.

Unless set at a high level, however, these benefits would not replace the aid given by the existing welfare programs and would leave all their disincentives in place. Yet if they were set too high, the cost of paying money to everyone or even just to families or pensioners would be prohibitive. Increasing taxes for those above the poverty-line could recover some or all of this assistance from those who did not need it, but at the price of adding a penalty for higher earnings. (Moreover, the overlap had become sizable between being poor, and close to it, and being taxable; as the 1980s began, nearly three-quarters of those who received FIS also helped pay for it, and analogous situations obtained in the United States.)[36] Even without this, the claim that universal benefits would not alter incentives was incorrect. Regardless of their level, refundable tax credits, family allowances, or other income supplements could not help influencing decisions about how much to work or whether to preserve a family. Providing money to everyone had all the problems of the negative income tax without any of its efficiency.

Perhaps the most widespread idea was that the best way to correct welfare policy was to move back toward its original design. This meant trying to restore and, as necessary, improve the strategies laid out by the Beveridge report in Britain and the Social Security Act in the United States. Social insurance was to be reformed so as to provide a more adequate income for those outside the labor force. Means-tested assistance would be confined only to the "truly needy." For the able-bodied, any financial help would be small and subject to work requirements or penalties. (Even unemployment insurance benefits would be taxed.) Although quite substantial differences existed among advocates of this approach, all agreed that income support should not be given solely on the basis of need.

Such proposals assured a complicated welfare system, not a smaller one. With an increasing proportion of mothers (not to mention the disabled) in the labor force, simple distinctions could no longer be made between those presumably able to support themselves and those not. At the same time, lessened reliance on financial incentives required the making of many more distinctions of precisely that sort. Raising benefits for those who qualified only added to the problem, and because of their unpopularity and administrative difficulty, work tests or penalties would be little more than a mild deterrent. Both the Carter and Reagan Administrations sought to tighten the rules affecting public assistance, as did the Callaghan and Thatcher Governments in Britain. Despite their efforts, the number of AFDC and Supplementary Benefits recipients hardly fluctuated in the latter half of the 1970s; even if completely successful, the supposedly severe restrictions proposed by President Reagan would bring caseloads down only to about what they were at the end of President Nixon's term.[37] (To be sure, higher unemployment and rising benefits offset some of the administrative savings.) Although changing eligibility conditions could always alter the scope of income support programs, plans to restore the integrity of their original design seemed as likely to be a way of accepting permanently increased dependency as a way of reducing it.

Indeed, this was precisely what some proponents of the idea had in mind. For them, the real welfare reform of the last two decades consisted in the expansion of the existing programs. Instead of a set of under-financed, badly utilized, and sometimes disreputable measures, income transfer programs had become the first line of help for the poor, and acceptable to if not beloved by the public. The unfinished business was not to limit their size, but to equip them to serve better what one British publication called a "mass role."[38] This required doing something about the confusing mix of benefits and rules, conflicting incentives and disincentives, inequities among equally needy recipients, cost-increasing inefficiencies, and similar anomalies. In other words, it meant rationalizing welfare policy. Although most thought this could more easily be done piecemeal, considering the alternatives, the negative income tax might yet acquire a new life.[39]

The Future of Welfare Reform

The story of FAP, FIS, and the tax-credit plan suggests that whatever the future brings in Britain and the United States will emerge from the interplay of historical, political, economic, and cultural factors in each nation. Public policies are often examined in isolation; precisely for that reason it is worth remembering that they are developed and debated within a particular context. While similar ideas can be borne from one country to another, their reception—their very meaning— depends crucially on the soil in which they take root.

But it remains the case as well that certain features of "welfare states" like Britain and the United States seem relatively general. One such feature is the influence of experts in identifying problems and devising potential solutions. This lends a perpetual sense of experiment, if not instability, to societies that once were expected to be smothered in security. A counterweight of sorts comes as a result of the maturing of existing programs. Once in being, no kind of benefit is easy to remove, even if no real loss is incurred. The resulting constant tug-of-war between the innovative and the obsolete helps explain why efforts at welfare reform are so spasmodic and frustrating.

In addition, the story of FAP, FIS, and the tax-credit plan offers a cautionary lesson about the limits of welfare reform. Despite two decades of trying, neither Britain nor the United States ever found an income support scheme that seemed likely to reduce poverty without increasing dependency. Perhaps that was too much to ask of any such program. Although the poor indisputably need money, many of them also lack the habits and skills, as well as the less tangible characteristics—like stable communities, supportive religious or kinship ties, and "middle-class" values—which traditionally have been essential for upward mobility. The debate over the negative income tax shows that a better-designed welfare system cannot replace these; some may be beyond the reach of public policy entirely.

The undeniably more important task is to find ways to prevent welfare programs from being as destructive of the traits necessary for self-sufficiency as they have historically been. In his "Memoir on Pauperism" presented to the Royal Academic Society of Cherbourg in 1835, Tocqueville described the way in which the generosity of the more advanced nations of Europe seemed to worsen the lot of their poor as compared with those in less munificent countries. At the conclusion of his talk, he announced he would deliver another paper the following year explaining what could be done to remedy the situation. According to Seymour Drescher, "the promised sequel never appeared and was apparently never written."[40] Nearly one and a half centuries later, the debate over FAP, FIS, and the tax-credit plan in Britain and the United States demonstrates that the problem remains unresolved.

Notes

1. "Schools Brief," *New Society* (January 29, 1981), p. 4. The figures were compiled by the O.E.C.D.

2. U.S., Senate, Committee on Finance, *Statistical Data Related to Public Assistance Programs* (February 1980), table 8, pp. 24–26.

3. Frank Field, *Inequality in Britain: Freedom, Welfare and the State* (1981), p. 48.

4. U.S., Department of Commerce, Bureau of the Census, *Alternative Methods for Valuing Selected In-Kind Transfer Benefits and Measuring their Effect on Poverty*, Technical Paper 50 (March 1982), p. ix. This estimate takes into account the impact of in-kind, as well as cash assistance programs.

5. Wilfred Beckerman and Stephen Clark, *Poverty and Social Security in Britain Since 1961* (1982), table 5.1, p. 33. Data are for 1976.

6. David Donnison, "New Times, New Politics," *New Society* (October 2, 1980), pp. 25–26.

7. Daniel P. Moynihan, "One Third of a Nation," *The New Republic* (June 9, 1982), p. 18.

8. Commission of the European Communities, *The Perception of Poverty in Europe* (1977), table 29, p. 72.

9. This was one of the themes of the Fulton Committee. See, Great Britain, Committee on the Civil Service, *Report*, vol. 1 (1968), par. 17.

10. Hugh Heclo, *Modern Social Politics in Britain and Sweden* (1974), pp. 304–22.

11. Richard Crossman, *The Diaries of a Cabinet Minister,* vol. 3 (1977), pp. 891–92.

12. On Canada's negative income tax experiment, see, Christopher Leman, *The Collapse of Welfare Reform: Political Institutions, Policy, and the Poor in Canada and the United States* (1980), pp. 57 and 68.

13. Michael Oakeshott, *Rationalism in Politics* (1962), pp. 1–36.

14. On the development and nature of Britain's Race Relations Acts, see, Anthony Lester and Geoffrey Bindman, *Race and Law* (1972), pp. 107–149 *et passim.*

15. Cf., James Q. Wilson, "What Can Be Done?," *AEI Public Policy Papers,* ed. American Enterprise Institute (1981), pp. 27–28.

16. For a prediction that a guaranteed income would not be enacted in the United States, see, Bill Cavala and Aaron Wildavsky, "The Political Feasibility of Income by Right," *Public Policy* (Spring 1970), pp. 321–54.

17. Prime Minister Thatcher's difficulties in applying a "monetarist" approach to economic policy offer a parallel example.

18. Edward C. Banfield, *The Unheavenly City: The Nature and Future of Our Urban Crisis* (1970), chap. x.

19. Jonathan Bradshaw, "An End to Differentials," *New Society* (October 9, 1980), pp. 64–65.

20. Martin Anderson, "The Roller-Coaster Income Tax," *The Public Interest* (Winter 1978), pp. 17–28.

21. Statement of Jodie Allen in U.S., Senate, Committee on Finance, Subcommittee on Public Assistance, *Hearings: Welfare Research and Experimentation* (1978), p. 31.

22. Statement of Robert Spiegelman, ibid., pp. 89–92.

23. Statement of Henry Aaron, ibid., pp. 314–323.

24. Statement of Robert Spiegelman, ibid., p. 84.

25. For Britain, see, Beckerman and Clark, table 5.4, p. 38; for the United States, see, Sheldon Danziger and Robert Plotnick, "Has the War on Poverty Been Won?" (unpublished paper, Institute for Research on Poverty, University of Wisconsin-Madison, March 1980), table 2, p. 14, and Peter T. Gottschalk, "Have We Lost the War on Poverty?" *Challenge* (May/June 1982), p. 57.

26. Beckerman and Clark, tables 5.1, 5.2, and 5.3, pp. 33, 36, and 37; U.S., Congress, Congressional Budget Office, *Poverty Status of Families under Alternative Definitions of Income* (January 13, 1977), table 6, p. 14; U.S., Department of Commerce, Bureau of the Census, tables A and B, pp. ix–x.

27. Nick Bosanquet and Peter Townsend, eds., *Labour and Equality* (1980), p. 188; U.S., Senate, Committee on Finance, Subcommittee on Public Assistance, *Hearings: Welfare Reform Proposals* (1978), table 2, p. 84.

28. Bosanquet and Townsend, p. 183; U.S., Senate, Committee on Finance, *Welfare Reform Proposals,* loc. cit.

29. For the United States, see, George Gilder, *Visible Man* (1978), pp. ix–xi *et passim,* and Susan Sheehan, *A Welfare Mother* (1975), pp. 87–88 *et passim;* for Britain, see David Piachaud's criticism of "scroungermania" in Bosanquet and Townsend, p. 181.

30. Danziger and Plotnick, pp. 18–19; U.S., Senate, Committee on Finance, *Welfare Reform Proposals*, table A, p. 76; Beckerman and Clark, pp. 39–43.

31. Danziger and Plotnick, p. 23; U.S., Senate, Committee on Finance, *Welfare Research and Experimentation*, pp. 410–11.

32. Gottschalk, p. 58.

33. U.S., Senate, Committee on Finance, *Welfare Reform Proposals*, p. 27.

34. Statement of Irwin Garfinkel in U.S., Senate, Committee on Finance, *Welfare Research and Experimentation*, pp. 71–72.

35. Field, pp. 180–99.

36. "Taxing Family Life," *New Society* (March 26, 1981) p. 546.

37. U.S., Congress, Congressional Budget Office, *An Analysis of the President's Budgetary Proposals for Fiscal Year 1983* (February 1982), pp. 126–27.

38. "The New SB Scheme: I," *New Society* (November 20, 1980), p. 375; for a similar view from the United States, see, Frederick Doolittle et al., "The Mirage of Welfare Reform," *The Public Interest* (Spring 1977), pp. 62–87.

39. One recent call for a "unified income maintenance scheme" can be found in Nick Morris, "How to Sustain Incentives to Work," *New Society* (November 27, 1980), pp. 411–12. See also, Leslie Lenkowsky, "Great Britain: The Negative Income Tax Rediscovered," *The Public Interest* (Summer 1985), pp. 121–26.

40. Seymour Drescher, ed., *Tocqueville and Beaumont on Social Reform* (1968), p. 27.

Appendix
List of People Interviewed*

Britain

Brian Abel-Smith
London School of Economics

Paul Barker
New Society

Lord Balniel
Minister
Department of Health and
Social Security (DHSS), 1970–1972

H. M. Barclay
House of Commons
Staff

John Biffen
Member of Parliament
Conservative

G. Bish
Labour Party
Research Department

J. M. Bolitho
DHSS

David Caldwell
DHSS

David Donnison
Centre for Environmental Studies,
London

Kay Carmichael
University of Glasgow

Barbara Castle
Member of Parliament
Labour

William Clark
Member of Parliament
Conservative

Sir Arthur Cockfield
Adviser
Treasury Department

Richard H. S. Crossman
Secretary of State for Social Services,
1968–1970

Paul Dean
Minister
DHSS

James Douglas
Director, Conservative Party
Research Department

Charles Dumas
The Economist, London

B. J. Ellis
DHSS

Frank Field
Executive Director, Child Poverty
Action Group

Patrick Gordon Walker
Secretary of State for Education and
Science, 1967–1968

J. S. Gummer
Member of Parliament
Conservative

Caroline Harvey
Conservative Party
Research Department

Barney Hayhoe
Member of Parliament
Conservative

Margaret Herbison
Minister of State for Social Security,
1964–1967

Douglas Houghton
Member of Parliament
Labour

*Titles or affiliations are as of the time of interview, 1972–1974, unless otherwise indicated.

Sir Geoffrey Howe
  Member of Parliament
  Conservative

David Howell
  Member of Parliament
  Conservative

A. R. Isserlis
  Director, Centre for Studies in Social
  Policy, London

Peter Jacques
  Trades Union Congress

Patrick Jenkin
  Member of Parliament
  Conservative

Nicholas Kaldor
  Cambridge University

Norman Kiernan
  DHSS

D. S. Lees
  University of Nottingham

Dick Leonard
  Member of Parliament
  Labour

F. E. Lording
  DHSS

Tony Lynes
  Child Poverty Action Group

Norman Macrae
  The Economist, London

J. Monaghan
  Treasury Department

Della Nevitt
  London School of Economics

John Nott
  Member of Parliament
  Conservative

T. J. Painter
  Treasury Department

William Plowden
  Central Policy Review Staff

Timothy Raison
  Member of Parliament
  Conservative

D. M. Rea
  Confederation of British Industry

Brian Reading
  The Economist, London

Sir Brandon Rhys Williams
  Member of Parliament
  Conservative

Barbara Rodgers
  Centre for Studies in Social Policy,
  London

Mark Schreiber
  Civil Service Department

Arthur Seldon
  Institute of Economic Affairs, London

Brendon Sewill
  Adviser
  Treasury Department

J. W. Stacpoole
  DHSS

T. C. Stephens
  DHSS

Dick Taverne
  Member of Parliament
  Labour

Peter Townsend
  University of Essex

Sir John Walley
  DHSS, retired

Sir Marcus Worsley
  Member of Parliament
  Conservative

United States

Josephine (Jodie) Allen
  The Urban Institute, Washington

Charles Armentrout
  U.S. Chamber of Commerce

Frederick B. Arner
  Congressional Research Service
  Library of Congress

J. Patrick Baker
  Committee on Ways and Means
  Staff

Paul Barton
  Department of Labor

Wallace F. Bennett
  United States Senate
  Republican

APPENDIX

Hyman Bookbinder
American Jewish Committee
Washington

Philip Burton
U.S. House of Representatives
Democrat

John W. Byrnes
U.S. House of Representatives
Republican

Barber B. Conable, Jr.
U.S. House of Representatives
Republican

Eugene S. Cowen
White House Staff

Loren C. Cox
Aide to Congressman Al Ullman
Democrat

Carl T. Curtis
United States Senate
Republican

Fred Davis
National Association of Manufacturers

James O. Edwards
Office of Management and Budget

Clint Fair
AFL-CIO

Leonard Garment
White House Staff

Mitchell Ginsberg
Columbia University School of Social
Work

William J. Green
U.S. House of Representatives
Democrat

Charles Hawkins
Committee on Ways and Means
Staff

Nathan Hayward
Aide to Senator William V. Roth
Republican

Allen C. Jensen
U.S. Governors' Conference

Carol Kocheisin
League of Cities-Conference of Mayors

Stephen Kurzman
Assistant Secretary
Department of Health, Education and
Welfare (HEW)

Leonard Lesser
Center for Community Change,
Washington

Russell B. Long
United States Senate
Democrat

William McHenry
U.S. Chamber of Commerce

Jonathan Moore
Assistant to the Secretary
HEW

Richard P. Nathan
The Brookings Institution
Washington

Richard Neustadt
1972 Platform Committee
Democratic Party

Lee R. Nunn
White House Staff

Paul H. O'Neill
Office of Management and Budget

Jeff Peterson
Aide to Senator Abraham A. Ribicoff
Democrat

Hal Rosenthal
Aide to Congressman Hugh L. Carey
Democrat

Michael Stern
Committee on Finance
Staff

Ralph L. Tabor
National Association of Counties

Herman E. Talmadge
United States Senate
Democrat

John G. Veneman
Undersecretary
HEW

Peter Wheeler
Executive Secretariat
HEW

Bibliography

Public Documents

Commission of the European Communities. *The Perception of Poverty in Europe.* Brussels, Belgium: By the Commission of the European Communities, March 1977.

Great Britain. Central Statistical Office. *Social Trends.* No. 4, 1973. London: HMSO, 1973.

Great Britain. Chancellor of the Exchequer and the Secretary of State for Social Services. *Proposals for a Tax-Credit System.* Cmnd. 5116. October 1972.

Great Britain. Committee on the Civil Service. *Report.* Vol. 1. Cmnd. 3638. 1968.

Great Britain. Department of Health and Social Security. *Social Assistance: A Review of the Supplementary Benefits Scheme.* London: HMSO, 1978.

Great Britain. *Hansard's Parliamentary Debates* (5th series). (Commons.) Vols. 723–871.

Great Britain. *Hansard's Parliamentary Debates* (5th series). (Lords.) Vol. 308.

Great Britain. Ministry of Social Security. *Circumstances of Families.* London: HMSO, 1967.

Great Britain. Royal Commission on the Distribution of Income and Wealth. *Initial Report on the Standing Reference.* Report No. 1. Cmnd. 6171. July 1975.

Great Britain. Royal Commission on the Taxation of Profits and Income. *Second Report.* Cmnd. 9105. April 1954.

Great Britain. Select Committee on Tax-Credit. *Report and Procedings.* Vol. 1. London: HMSO, 1973.

———. *Evidence.* Vol. 2. London: HMSO, 1973.

Great Britain. *Social Insurance and Allied Services.* A Report to Parliament by Sir William Beveridge, 1942. Cmnd. 6404. London: HMSO, 1968.

U.S. Bureau of the Census. *Statistical Abstract of the United States: 1972.* 93d ed. Washington, D.C.: Government Printing Office, 1972.

U.S. Congress, Congressional Budget Office. *Poverty Status of Families under Alternative Definitions of Income.* Background Paper No. 17. January 13, 1977.

U.S. Congress, Congressional Budget Office. *An Analysis of the President's Budgetary Proposals for Fiscal Year 1983.* February, 1982.

195

U.S. *Congressional Record.* Vol. 116. 91st Cong., 2d Sess., 1970.

U.S. *Congressional Record.* Vol. 117. 92d Cong., 1st Sess., 1971.

U.S. *Congressional Record.* Vol. 118. 92d Cong., 2d Sess., 1972.

U.S. Congress, Joint Economic Committee. *Hearings: Income Maintenance Programs.* Vols 1 and 2. 90th Cong., 2d Sess., 1968.

U.S. Congress, Joint Economic Committee, Subcommittee on Fiscal Policy. *The Family, Poverty, and Welfare Programs: Factors Influencing Family Stability.* "Studies in Public Welfare," Paper No. 12, part 1. 93d Cong., 1st Sess., 1973.

———. *Handbook of Public Income Transfer Programs: 1975.* "Studies in Public Welfare," Paper No. 20. 93d Cong., 2d Sess., 1974.

U.S. Department of Commerce, Bureau of the Census. *Alternative Methods for Valuing Selected In-Kind Transfer Benefits and Measuring Their Effect on Poverty.* Technical Paper 50. March 1982.

U.S. Department of Health, Education, and Welfare. *Equality of Educational Opportunity.* A Report Prepared by James S. Coleman et al. Washington, D.C.: Government Printing Office, 1966.

U.S. Department of Health, Education, and Welfare, Social Security Administration *Public Attitudes Toward Social Security 1935–65.* Research Report No. 33 by Michael E. Schiltz. Washington, D.C.: Government Printing Office, 1970.

U.S. Department of Labor. *The Negro Family: The Case for National Action.* Washington, D.C.: Office of Policy Planning and Research, 1965.

U.S. House of Representatives, Committee on Ways and Means. *Hearings: Social Security and Welfare Proposals.* 91st Cong., 1st Sess., 1969.

———. *Family Assistance Act of 1970.* Report No. 91-904. 91st Cong., 2d Sess., March 11, 1970.

———. *Social Security Amendments of 1971.* Report No. 92-231. 92d Cong., 1st Sess., May 26, 1971.

U.S. Office of Economic Opportunity. *The Poor in 1970: A Chartbook.* Washington, D.C.: Government Printing Office, 1972.

U.S. President, 1969–74 (Nixon). *Weekly Compilation of Presidential Documents.* Vol. 5, no. 16. April 21, 1969.

U.S. Senate, Committee on Finance. *Hearings: Family Assistance Act of 1970 (H.R. 16311).* 91st Cong., 2d Sess., 1970.

———. *Material Related to Administration Revision of H.R. 16311.* 91st Cong., 2d Sess., July 1970.

———. *H.R. 16311 The Family Assistance Act of 1970: June Revision Revised and Resubmitted.* 91st Cong., 2d Sess., November 5, 1970.

———. *Hearings: Social Security Amendments of 1971 (H.R. 1).* 92d Cong., 1st–2d Sess., 1971–72.

————. *Social Security Amendments of 1972*. Report No. 92-1230. 92d Cong., 2d Sess., September 26, 1972.

————. *Statistical Data Related to Public Assistance Programs*. 96th Cong., 2d Sess., February 1980.

U.S. Senate, Committee on Finance, Subcommittee on Public Assistance. *Hearings: Welfare Reform Proposals*. 95th Cong., 2d Sess., 1978.

————. *Hearings: Welfare Research and Experimentation*. 95th Cong., 2d Sess., 1978.

Books

Abel-Smith, Brian and Townsend, Peter. *The Poor and the Poorest*. "Occasional Papers on Social Administration," no. 17. London: G. Bell and Sons Ltd., 1965.

Altmeyer, Arthur J. *The Formative Years of Social Security*. Madison, Wisconsin: The University of Wisconsin Press, 1966.

Anderson, Odin W. *Health Care: Can There Be Equity?* New York: John Wiley, 1972.

Atkinson, A.B. *Poverty in Britain and the Reform of Social Security*. "Occasional Papers," University of Cambridge, Department of Applied Economics, no. 18. Cambridge, England: Cambridge University Press, 1969.

Bailey, Stephen Kemp. *Congress Makes a Law*. New York: Columbia University Press, 1950.

Banfield, Edward C. *The Unheavenly City: The Nature and Future of our Urban Crisis*. Boston: Little, Brown and Co., 1968.

Beckerman, Wilfred, ed. *The Labour Government's Economic Record: 1964–1970*. London: Duckworth, 1972.

Beckerman, Wilfred, and Clark, Stephen. *Poverty and Social Security in Britain since 1961*. Institute for Fiscal Studies, no. 3. Oxford, England: Oxford University Press, 1982.

Beer, Samuel H. *British Politics in the Collectivist Age*. New York: Random House, 1969.

Beer, Samuel H., et al. *Patterns of Government: The Major Political Systems of Europe*. 3d ed. revised. New York: Random House, 1973.

Bosanquet, Nick, and Townsend, Peter, eds. *Labour and Equality*. London: Heinemann Educational Books, 1980.

Bremner, Robert H. *From the Depths: The Discovery of Poverty in the United States*. New York: New York University Press, 1956.

Brittan, Samuel. *Steering the Economy*. Revised ed. Harmondsworth, Middlesex, England: Penguin Books, 1971.

Bruce, Maurice. *The Coming of the Welfare State*. London: B. T. Batsford, 1961.

Bull, David, ed. *Family Poverty: Programme for the Seventies.* London: Gerald Duckworth and Co., 1971.

Burke, Vincent J., and Burke, Vee. *Nixon's Good Deed: Welfare Reform.* New York: Columbia University Press, 1974.

Butler, David, and King, Anthony. *The British General Election of 1966.* London: Macmillan, 1966.

Butler, David, and Pinto-Duschinsky, Michael. *The British General Election of 1970.* London: Macmillan, 1971.

Butler, David, and Stokes, Donald. *Political Change in Britain: Forces Shaping Electoral Choice.* New York: St. Martin's Press, 1969.

Caves, Richard E., et al. *Britain's Economic Prospects.* Washington, D.C.: Brookings Institution, 1968.

Checkland, S. G., and E. O. A., eds. *The Poor Law Report of 1834.* Hardmondsworth, Middlesex, England: Penguin Books, 1974.

Congressional Quarterly Almanac. Vol. 24, 1968. Washington, D.C.: Congressional Quarterly Inc., 1969.

Craig, F. W. S., ed. *British Election Manifestos, 1918–66.* London: Political Reference Publications, 1970.

Crosland, C. A. R. *The Future of Socialism.* 2d ed. London: Jonathan Cape, 1964.

Crossman, Richard. *The Diaries of a Cabinet Minister.* Vol. 3. New York: Holt, Rinehart, and Winston, 1977.

deCrèvecoeur, J. Hector St. John. *Letters from an American Farmer.* New York: E. P. Dutton and Co., 1957.

Derthick, Martha. *Policymaking for Social Security.* Washington, D.C.: Brookings Institution, 1979.

Drescher, Seymour, ed. *Tocqueville and Beaumont on Social Reform.* New York: Harper Torchbooks, 1968.

Eckstein, Otto, ed. *Studies in the Economics of Income Maintenance.* Washington, D.C.: Brookings Institution, 1967.

Field, Frank. *Inequality in Britain: Freedom, Welfare and the State.* Glasgow: Fontana Paperbacks, 1981.

Fisher, Nigel. *Iain Macleod.* London: Andre Deutsch, 1973.

Fishman, Leo, ed. *Poverty amid Affluence.* New Haven and London: Yale University Press, 1966.

Friedman, Milton. *Capitalism and Freedom.* Chicago: University of Chicago Press, 1962.

Galbraith, John Kenneth. *The Affluent Society.* New York: The New American Library, 1958.

Gilbert, Bentley B. *The Evolution of National Insurance in Great Britain: The Origins of the Welfare State.* London: Michael Joseph, 1966.

Gilder, George. *Visible Man.* New York: Basic Books, 1978.

Goodman, Leonard H., ed. *Economic Progress and Social Welfare*. New York and London: Columbia University Press, 1966.

Green, Christopher. *Negative Taxes and the Poverty Problem*. Washington, D.C.: Brookings Institution, 1967.

Heclo, Hugh. *Modern Social Politics in Britain and Sweden*. New Haven: Yale University Press, 1974.

Hirschman, Albert O. *Journeys Toward Progress*. New York: Doubleday Anchor, 1965.

Kershaw, Joseph A. *Government Against Poverty*. Chicago: Markham Publishing Co., 1970.

Lampman, Robert J. *Ends and Means of Reducing Income Poverty*. "Institute for Research on Poverty Monograph Series." Chicago: Markham Publishing Co., 1971.

Leman, Christopher. *The Collapse of Welfare Reform: Political Institutions, Policy, and the Poor in Canada and the United States*. Cambridge, Massachusetts: The MIT Press, 1980.

Lester, Anthony, and Bindman, Geoffrey. *Race and Law*. Harmondsworth, Middlesex, England: Penguin Books, 1972.

Levine, Robert A. *The Poor Ye Need Not Have with You: Lessons from the War on Poverty*. Cambridge, Massachusetts: The MIT Press, 1970.

Manley, John F. *The Politics of Finance: The House Committee on Ways and Means*. Boston: Little, Brown and Co., 1970.

Marshall, T. H. *Class, Citizenship, and Social Development*. New York: Doubleday and Co., 1965.

———. *Social Policy in the Twentieth Century*. 3d ed. revised. London: Hutchinson University Library, 1970.

Moynihan, Daniel P. *Maximum Feasible Misunderstanding: Community Action in the War on Poverty*. New York: The Free Press, 1969.

———. *The Politics of a Guaranteed Income*. New York: Random House, 1973.

Oakeshott, Michael. *Rationalism in Politics*. New York: Basic Books, 1962.

Paglin, Morton. *Poverty and Transfers In-Kind*. Stanford University, Stanford, California: Hoover Institution Press, 1980.

Parsons, Talcott, and Clark, Kenneth B., eds. *The Negro American*. Boston: Beacon Press, 1967.

Prest, A. R., ed. *Public Sector Economics*. Manchester, England: Manchester University Press, 1968.

Rainwater, Lee, and Yancey, William L. *The Moynihan Report and the Politics of Controversy*. Cambridge, Massachusetts: The MIT Press, 1967.

Rhys Williams, Lady Juliet. *Something to Look Forward To*. London: MacDonald and Co., 1943.

Rowntree, B. S., and Lavers, G. R. *Poverty and the Welfare State: A Third Social Survey of York Dealing Only with the Economic Questions.* London: Longmans, Green, 1951.

Runciman, W. G. *Relative Deprivation and Social Justice.* Harmondsworth, Middlesex, England: Penguin Books, 1972.

Schultze, Charles L., et al. *Setting National Priorities: The 1972 Budget.* Washington, D.C.: Brookings Institution, 1971.

Sheehan, Susan. *A Welfare Mother.* New York: The New American Library, 1975.

Steiner, Gilbert Y. *Social Insecurity: The Politics of Welfare.* Chicago: Rand McNally and Co., 1966.

———. *The State of Welfare.* Washington, D.C.: Brookings Institution, 1971.

Sundquist, James L., ed. *On Fighting Poverty.* New York: Basic Books, 1969.

Titmuss, Richard M. *Income Distribution and Social Change.* London: George Allen and Unwin, 1962.

———. *Commitment to Welfare.* London: George Allen and Unwin, 1968.

———. *Essays on the Welfare State.* 2d ed. revised. Boston: Beacon Press, 1969.

Truman, David B. *The Governmental Process: Political Interests and Public Opinion.* 2d ed. New York: Alfred A. Knopf, 1971.

Walley, Sir John. *Social Security: Another British Failure?* London: Charles Knight and Co., 1972.

Wilensky, Harold L. *The Welfare State and Equality.* Berkeley, California: University of California Press, 1975.

Wilson, Harold. *A Personal Record: The Labour Government, 1964–1970.* Boston: Little, Brown and Co., 1971.

Wynn, Margaret. *Family Policy.* 2d ed. revised. Harmondsworth, Middlesex, England: Penguin Books, 1972.

Articles and Pamphlets

Abel-Smith, Brian, et al. *Socialism in Affluence: Four Fabian Essays.* London: The Fabian Society, 1970.

A Better Tomorrow: The Conservative Programme for the Next 5 Years. London: Conservative Central Office, 1970.

American Enterprise Institute, ed. *AEI Public Policy Papers.* Washington, D.C.: American Enterprise Institute for Public Policy Research, 1981.

Anderson, Martin. "The Roller-Coaster Income Tax." *The Public Interest,* no. 50 (Winter 1978), pp. 17–28.

Armstrong, Richard. "The Looming Money Revolution Down South." *Fortune*, June 1970, pp. 66ff.

Beer, Samuel H. "The Comparative Method and the Study of British Politics." *Comparative Politics* 1 (October 1968):19–36.

Blaug, Mark. "The Poor Law Reexamined." *Journal of Economic History* 14 (June 1964):229–45.

Bradshaw, Jonathan. "An End to Differentials." *New Society*, vol. 54, no. 934 (October 9, 1980), pp. 64–65.

Brittan, Samuel. "Economic Viewpoint: The Tax-Credit Scheme." *The Financial Times* (London), October 11, 1972, p. 18.

Cavala, Bill, and Wildavsky, Aaron. "The Political Feasibility of Income by Right." *Public Policy*, vol. 18, no. 3 (Spring 1970), pp. 321–54.

Child Poverty Action Group. *Poverty and the Labour Government.* "Poverty Pamphlet," no. 3. London: Child Poverty Action Group, 1970.

Christopher, Anthony, et al. *Policy for Poverty.* "Research Monograph" no. 20. London: Institute of Economic Affairs, 1970.

Clarkson, Kenneth W. *Food Stamps and Nutrition.* "Evaluative Studies," no. 18. Washington, D.C.: American Enterprise Institute for Public Policy Research, 1975.

Cockfield, F. A. "Report of the Royal Commission on the Taxation of Profits and Income: A Commentary." *National Provident Bank Review* (London), November 1955, pp. 10–17.

Conservative Political Centre, ed. *Future of the Welfare State.* London: Conservative Political Centre, 1958.

Conservative Research Department. "Three Years' Work." *Notes on Current Politics,* no. 16 (Conservative Central Office, September 24, 1973), pp. 258–88.

"Correspondence with the Prime Minister." *Poverty: Journal of the Child Poverty Action Group,* no. 16/17 (n.d.), p. 30.

Crossman, Rt. Hon. Richard. *The Politics of Pensions.* "Eleanor Rathbone Memorial Lecture." Liverpool, England: Liverpool University Press, 1972.

Donnison, David. "New Times, New Politics." *New Society*, vol. 54, no. 933 (October 2, 1980), pp. 25–26.

Doolittle, Frederick, Levy, Frank, and Wiseman, Michael. "The Mirage of Welfare Reform." *The Public Interest,* no. 47 (Spring 1977), pp. 62–87.

Erskine, Hazel. "The Polls: Government Role in Welfare." *Public Opinion Quarterly* 39 (Summer 1975):257–74.

Field, Frank. "Poor People and the Conservative Government." *Poverty: Journal of the Child Poverty Action Group,* no. 16/17 (n.d.), pp. 3–17.

———. *One Nation: The Conservatives' Record since June 1970*. "Poverty Pamphlet," no. 12. London: Child Poverty Action Group, 1972.

———. "No Party for the Poor." *The Guardian* (London), April 2, 1974, p. 16.

Firm Action for a Fair Britain: The Conservative Manifesto. London: Conservative Central Office, 1974.

Gallup, George. "Public Opposes Guaranteed Minimum Income, Supports Guaranteed Work Plan." *The Gallup Report*. Princeton, N.J.: American Institute of Public Opinion, June 15, 1968.

Glazer, Nathan. "The Limits of Social Policy." *Commentary*, 52 (September 1971):51–58.

Gottschalk, Peter T. "Have We Lost the War on Poverty?" *Challenge*, vol. 25, no. 2 (May–June 1982), pp. 57–58.

Gummer, John Selwyn. "The Social Services." *The Political Quarterly*, vol. 44, no. 4 (October–December 1973), pp. 425–34.

Harris, Ralph, and Seldon, Arthur. *Choice in Welfare 1970*. "An IEA Research Report." London: Institute of Economic Affairs, 1971.

Hayhoe, Barney. *Must the Children Suffer? A New Family Benefit Scheme*. London: Conservative Political Centre, 1968.

Heidenheimer, Arnold. "The Politics of Public Education, Health and Welfare in the USA and Western Europe: How Growth and Reform Potentials Have Differed." *British Journal of Political Science* 3 (July 1973):315–40.

Houghton, Douglas. *Paying for Social Services*. "Occasional Papers," no. 16. London: Institute of Economic Affairs, 1967.

Howe, Geoffrey. *In Place of Beveridge?* London: Conservative Political Centre, 1965.

Howell, David, and Raison, Timothy, eds. *Principles in Practice: A Series of Bow Group Essays for the 1960's*. London: Conservative Political Centre, 1961.

Institute for Fiscal Studies. *Conference on Proposals for a Tax-Credit System*. Publication No. 5. London: Institute for Fiscal Studies, 1973.

Jones, Jack. "Wages and Social Security." *New Statesman*, vol. 83, no. 2129 (January 7, 1972), p. 7.

Joseph, Sir Keith. *Social Security: The New Priorities*. London: Conservative Political Centre, 1966.

"Killing a Commitment: The Cabinet v the Children." *New Society*, vol. 36, no. 715 (June 17, 1976), pp. 630–32.

Labour Party. *Report of the 72d Annual Conference* (Blackpool, 1973). London: The Labour Party, 1973.

Lees, D. S. "Poor Families and Fiscal Reform." *Lloyds Bank Review*, no. 86 (October 1967), pp. 1–15.

Lenkowsky, Leslie. "Great Britain: The Negative Income Tax Rediscovered." *The Public Interest*, no. 80 (Summer 1985), pp. 121–26.

Let Us Work Together—Labour's Way Out of the Crisis. London: The Labour Party, 1974.

Macleod, Iain, and Powell, J. Enoch. *The Social Services: Needs and Means.* 2d ed. revised. London: Conservative Political Centre, 1954.

Martin, Andrew. *The Politics of Economic Policy in the United States: A Tentative View from a Comparative Perspective.* "A Sage Professional Paper: Comparative Politics Series," no. 4. Beverly Hills, California: Sage Publications, 1973.

Mishra, Ramesh. "Convergence in Welfare Programs." *Sociological Review* 21 (November 1973):535–60.

Morris, Nick. "How to Sustain Incentives to Work." *New Society,* vol. 54, no. 941 (November 27, 1980), pp. 411–12.

Moynihan, Daniel P. "The Crises in Welfare." *The Public Interest,* no. 10 (Winter 1968), pp. 3–29.

————. "One-Third of a Nation." *The New Republic,* vol. 186, no. 23 (June 9, 1982), pp. 18–21.

National Union of Conservative and Unionist Associations. *Verbatim Report of 83d Annual Conference* (Brighton, 1965). London: Conservative Central Office, 1965.

————. *Verbatim Report of 86th Annual Conference* (Blackpool, 1968). London: Conservative Central Office, 1968.

"The Negative Income Tax: A Ripon Research Paper." *The Ripon Forum,* April 1967, p. 1.

"The New SB Scheme: I." *New Society,* vol. 54, no. 940 (November 20, 1980), p. 375.

"News Conference Text." *Congressional Quarterly,* vol. 30, no. 27 (July 1, 1972), pp. 1582–85.

Now Britain's Strong—Let's Make It Great to Live In. London: The Labour Party, 1970.

Patterson, Ben. *The Character of Conservatism.* London: Conservative Political Centre, 1973.

Peacock, Alan. *The Welfare Society.* "Unservile State Papers," no. 2. London: The Liberal Publication Department, 1961.

Piachaud, David. "Poverty and Taxation." *The Political Quarterly,* vol. 41, no. 1 (January–March 1971), pp. 31–44.

Polanyi, George and Priscilla. "Tax-Credits: A Reverse Income Tax." *National Westminster Bank Quarterly Review* (London), February 1973, pp. 20–34.

————. "Tax-Credits: A Missed Opportunity." *National Westminster Bank Quarterly Review* (London), February 1974, pp. 44–56.

Poverty: Journal of the Child Poverty Action Group, no. 4 (Autumn 1967), p. 1.

Prest, A. R. *Social Benefits and Tax Rates.* "Research Monograph," no. 22. London: Institute of Economic Affairs, 1970.

Ribicoff, Abe. "He Left at Half Time." *The New Republic,* vol. 168, no. 7 (February 17, 1973), pp. 22–26.

Schlotterbeck, Karl T. "Jobs for Welfare Clients Seen as Alternative to Guaranteed Income." Chamber of Commerce of the United States. *Washington Report,* vol. 8, no. 23 (June 23, 1969), pp. 3–5.

"Schools Brief." *New Society,* vol. 55, no. 950 (January 29, 1981), insert.

Sewill, Hilary. *AUNTIE.* London: Conservative Political Centre, 1966.

Steiner, Gilbert Y. "Reform Follows Reality: The Growth of Welfare." *The Public Interest,* no. 34 (Winter 1974), pp. 47–65.

Stigler, George. "The Economics of Minimum Wage Legislation." *American Economic Review* 36 (June 1946):358–65.

"Taxing Family Life." *New Society,* vol. 55, no. 958 (March 26, 1981), p. 546.

Titmuss, Richard M. Letter to the Editor. *The Times* (London), October 14, 1972, p. 17.

Townsend, Peter, and Atkinson, Tony. "The Advantages of Universal Family Allowances." *Poverty: Journal of the Child Poverty Action Group,* no. 16/17 (n.d.), pp. 18–22.

Townsend, Peter, and Bosanquet, Nicholas, eds. *Labour and Inequality: Sixteen Fabian Essays.* London: The Fabian Society, 1972.

Townsend, Peter, Reddin, Mike, and Kaim-Caudle, Peter. *Social Services for All? Part One.* "Fabian Tract 382." London: The Fabian Society, 1968.

Trades Union Congress. *Report of 103d Annual Congress* (Blackpool, 1971). London: The Trades Union Congress, 1971.

———. *Report of 104th Annual Congress* (Brighton, 1972). London: The Trades Union Congress, 1972.

Williams, Walter. *The Struggle for a Negative Income Tax.* "Institute of Governmental Research Public Policy Monograph," no. 1. Seattle, Washington: University of Washington Press, 1972.

Newspapers

The Boston Globe. 1972.

Daily Telegraph (London). 1971.

The Economist (London). 1972.

The Financial Times (London). 1972.

Hampshire Chronicle (England). 1973.

The New York Times. 1970–1973.

Sunday Times (London). 1966.

The Times (London). 1966–1974.

The Washington Post. 1969–1970.

Unpublished Material

AFL-CIO. Transcript of Interview with George Meany. Washington, D.C.: August 28, 1969. (Mimeographed.)

Agnew, Spiro T. "Welfare Reform." Memorandum for the President. Office of the Vice President, August 4, 1969.

Barton, Paul. Letter to Dr. Daniel P. Moynihan. Office of the Assistant Secretary, U.S. Department of Labor: July 30, 1971. (Author's files.)

Collier, David, and Messick, Richard E. "Functional Prerequisites *Versus* Diffusion: Testing Alternative Explanations of Social Security Adoption." Unpublished paper delivered at the Annual Meeting of the Midwest Political Science Association, Chicago, Illinois, 1973.

Danziger, Sheldon, and Plotnick, Robert. "Has the War on Poverty Been Won?" Unpublished paper, Institute for Research on Poverty, University of Wisconsin-Madison, March 1980.

Davis, Otto A., and Jackson, John E. "Representative Assemblies and Demands for Redistribution: The Case of Senate Voting on the Family Assistance Plan." Unpublished paper, The Urban Institute, Washington, D.C., October 1972.

The Gallup Poll (London). "Family Allowances." Private survey for the Child Poverty Action Group, January 1973.

Harris, Louis. Speech to the National Press Club. Washington, D.C.: November 10, 1972. (Mimeographed.)

Heath, Edward. Speech at the Free Trade Hall, Manchester. London: Conservative Central Office, February 20, 1974. (Mimeographed.)

Kain, John F., and Schafer, Robert. "Regional Impacts of the Family Assistance Plan." Unpublished paper, Program on Regional and Urban Economics, Harvard University, Cambridge, Massachusetts, June 1971.

Nixon, Richard M. Audio Transcript of Remarks to Meeting of the American Association of Editorial Cartoonists. Washington, D.C.: May 17, 1968. (Typescript.)

————. Text of the President's Domestic Speech. Washington, D.C.: Office of the White House Press Secretary, August 8, 1969. (Mimeographed.)

————. Remarks of the President on Nationwide Radio and Television. Washington, D.C.: Office of the White House Press Secretary, August 15, 1971. (Mimeographed.)

————. Text of State of the Union Message to be Presented to the Members of the Second Session of the 92d Congress. Washington, D.C.: Office of the White House Press Secretary, January 20, 1972. (Mimeographed.)

Raines, Franklin D. "Presidential Policy Development: The Genesis of the Family Assistance Plan." Unpublished senior honors thesis, Harvard College, Cambridge, Massachusetts, 1971.

Richardson, Elliot L. Statement before the House Committee on Ways and Means. Department of Health, Education, and Welfare, February 2, 1971. (Typescript.)

Shultz, George P. Memorandum to the President. Department of Labor, June 10, 1969.

Shultz, George P., et al. Transcript of Press Conference. Washington, D.C.: Office of the White House Press Secretary, March 5, 1970. (Mimeographed.)

Task Force on Public Welfare. "Programs to Assist the Poor." Report to President-Elect Richard M. Nixon. December 28, 1968.

Tillmon, Johnnie, and Wiley, George A. Letter to President Richard M. Nixon. Washington, D.C.: National Welfare Rights Organization, August 6, 1969. (Author's files.)

U.S. Department of Health, Education, and Welfare. "Analysis of Initial Editorial, Columnist, Magazine and Public Opinion Reaction to the President's Welfare Message." Washington, D.C.: Office of the Secretary, October 21, 1969. (Typescript.)

About the Author

Leslie Lenkowsky is president of the Institute for Educational Affairs, a non-profit organization in Washington, D.C., devoted to enhancing innovative thinking in higher education and philanthropy. He is also an adjunct professor of public policy at Georgetown University and on leave from the American Enterprise Institute for Public Policy Research, where he was concentrating on social policy issues such as the importance of mediating structures, non-governmental institutions that help define the relationship between the individual and society. He has also served as Deputy Director of the United States Information Agency and a member of the National Voluntary Service Advisory Council.

From 1976 to 1983, he was Director of Research at the Smith Richardson Foundation in New York. He has also been a consultant to Senator Daniel P. Moynihan (D.-N.Y.) and an assistant to the secretary of the Pennsylvania State Department of Public Welfare. He is a graduate of Franklin and Marshall College, Lancaster, Pennsylvania, and earned his Ph.D. from Harvard University.

He is the author of numerous articles in such journals as *Commentary*, *The Public Interest*, *The Wall Street Journal*, *This World*, *Fortune*, *The American Spectator*, and *Public Opinion*.